Understanding International Bank Risk

Wiley Finance Series

Understanding International Bank Risk

Andrew Fight

John Wiley & Sons, Ltd

Published by   John Wiley & Sons Ltd, The Atrium, Southern Gate, Chichester,
                      West Sussex PO19 8SQ, England

                      Telephone   (+44) 1243 779777

Email (for orders and customer service enquiries): cs-books@wiley.co.uk
Visit our Home Page on www.wileyeurope.com or www.wiley.com

Other Wiley Editorial Offices

John Wiley & Sons Inc., 111 River Street, Hoboken, NJ 07030, USA

Jossey-Bass, 989 Market Street, San Francisco, CA 94103-1741, USA

Wiley-VCH Verlag GmbH, Boschstr. 12, D-69469 Weinheim, Germany

John Wiley & Sons Australia Ltd, 33 Park Road, Milton, Queensland 4064, Australia

John Wiley & Sons (Asia) Pte Ltd, 2 Clementi Loop #02-01, Jin Xing Distripark, Singapore 129809

John Wiley & Sons Canada Ltd, 22 Worcester Road, Etobicoke, Ontario, Canada M9W 1L1

Wiley also publishes its books in a variety of electronic formats. Some content that appears
in print may not be available in electronic books.

Library of Congress Cataloging-in-Publication Data

Fight, Andrew.
    Understanding international bank risk / Andrew Fight.
        p.   cm.
    Includes bibliographical references and index.
    ISBN 0-470-84768-9 (cloth : alk. paper)
    1. Banks and banking, International—Management.   2. Risk management.   3. Country risk.
    I. Title
HG3881 .F514 2003
332.1′068′1—dc22   2003021829

British Library Cataloguing in Publication Data

A catalogue record for this book is available from the British Library

ISBN 0-470-84768-9

Typeset in 10/12pt Times by TechBooks, New Delhi, India
Printed and bound in Great Britain by TJ International Ltd, Padstow, Cornwall, UK
This book is printed on acid-free paper responsibly manufactured from sustainable forestry
in which at least two trees are planted for each one used for paper production.

Contents

Foreword

Having worked as a financial analyst for 10 years, specialising in bank analysis at Chase Manhattan and later at one of the credit rating agencies, and as a financial consultant with a variety of clients in Eastern Europe, the ex-USSR, the Middle East, Asia and Africa, it seemed to me that there was a need to write a book on "understanding international bank risk".

It seemed to me that the theory of financial analysis which I had been taught at Chase came up against difficulties in emerging market economies. The nature of the banks' regulatory regime, and indeed banks themselves, was different to those operating in the mature markets of the EU. In many cases, I saw the phenomenon of importing western quantitative techniques without looking at the local context and considering some very basic issues. Moreover, the wave of banking failures and international banking crises, and their ability to propagate their effects internationally with extreme rapidity, rendered this an important and topical subject.

Bank financial analysis has the reputation of being a dull subject – to the general public it is, at least until a major bank goes bust, in which case panic ensues. Even in banks, corporate analysts tend to look at bank analysis as a dull subject. But far from dull it is! Once involved, bank analysis reveals itself to be an endlessly fascinating topic that assumes international scope. Understanding the different types of banks, the different cultures of various banks, their international differences, the national and international regulatory environment, the similarity of causes leading to bank failure all render the subject fascinating. Once you get past the word bank, what you are dealing with are entities with their own histories and specialisations which are effectively unique.

The bulk of the literature on international bank risk has hitherto been prepared by the big three credit rating agencies, and it is unfortunate to say that this literature is more marketing driven (rationalising shortcomings in the ratings process which failed to anticipate bank failure), than information driven (enabling the investor–creditor community to understand how to analyse international bank risk). This is most likely because the common sense "street cred" signals of bank failure are reveal too many unpleasant realities to address head on.

Moreover, the big three credit rating agencies all tend to look at risk in the same way, since they are all US-oriented companies using US-oriented methodologies on countries which have differing characteristics. Not only do they exercise a monopoly, they tend to use perspectives and methodologies which lend themselves to the accusation of being ethnocentric, not to mention ineffective. To those who find this excessively critical, consider that if the rating agencies' methodologies are so excellent, why is their track record in predicting bank failure and crises so much less than excellent, and why do they spend so much time rationalising their performance with verbal gymnastics? And why is such performance failure nevertheless enshrined in law and banking regulation?

This book therefore aims to consider some of the analytical techniques of bank financial analysis, bank failure, risk management, understanding the control mechanisms and regulatory framework, and explains how and why and when these fail. As such, we will consider the mechanisms of financial analysis in order to understand their methodologies and shortcomings.

The tools are well known and are presented. Despite the existence of these predictive tools, failure occurs, often amidst feigned surprise, officially unexpected by auditors and credit rating agencies. It is with this process that we shall primarily be concerned. We will consider financial analysis and consider why the effectiveness of those techniques is not translated into effective prediction of failure. Cases of bank failure and industry developments in regulation and disciplinary measures will also feature to place these abstract tools in the proper context. Either the tools are ineffective or there are other forces at work.

The book looks at some of the main elements of analysing bank and country risk, examining specialised sectors such as bank risk, bank financial analysis, bank qualitative analysis, bank ratings criteria and country risk analysis, and considers their advantages and shortcomings.

Bank mergers, resulting in larger banks (and thus increased risk concentration and volatility) further stimulates the need to understand the risks inherent in these entities, their operating environment and management culture, and the risks involved in dealing with them as trading counterparties.

With the financial services industry characterised by increasing international homogenisation, consolidation, concentration of risk, and volatility, it is important that bank managers, creditors, investors, and financial analysts keep abreast of these trends and developments.

Moreover, the impact of new technologies such as the internet and online banking offers new areas of activity and analysis to cover. Investment in information technology, or IT, is rapidly becoming the means to achieving competitive advantage in mature markets. It is fine to look at a bank's ALM policy in classic financial analysis terms, for example, but IT can be instrumental in strengthening a bank's retail depositor base. A chapter on some of the major categories of IT and e-finance is therefore also included.

The current environment underscores the increased need to know. It is hoped that this book goes some way to shedding light on the matter for bank analysts and managers.

Finally, I would like to express my thanks to Mr Kenneth I'Anson, Training Director at Euromoney Training and to Mr F X Noir, Directeur International of the Centre de Formation de la Profession Bancaire for the valuable material support and comments for this book. I would also like to thank Mr Tony Pringle, Managing Director of BVD Electronic Publishing in London, for kind permission to feature "Bankscope" in this book. I would also like to express my gratitude to various professionals at a number of firms in the City of London who provided valuable thoughts and insight; though many prefer to remain anonymous, their contributions are recognised and appreciated. Last but not least, I would like to thank Chris Swain, Sam Hartley, Rachael Wilkie, and Sally Smith at John Wiley & Sons for their support of this project and invaluable comments, thoughtful guidance and suggestions. Any errors or omissions, of course, are my own.

Andrew Fight
www.andrewfight.com

About the Author

Andrew Fight provides financial consulting and training services in the areas of Financial Analysis, Commercial, Syndicated, and Project Finance Lending, Asset Liability Management, Credit Risk Management, and Problem Loan Management.

He has over 15 years of experience in international banking and financial analysis gained in Paris and London with Chase Manhattan Bank, IBCA Rating Agency, Euromoney Training, the French and German Bank Training Institutes.

He is a consultant and financial trainer to the European Commission, USAID, several banks, central banks, and IT companies, and a successful author, having written over 15 books on financial analysis, banking risk analysis, credit risk management, credit rating agencies, and information technology in financial services.

A full description of his activities can be accessed on his website at www.andrewfight.com.

He divides his time between London, where he works, and his home in the South of France.

1
The Banking Background

When equipped with trustworthy, up-to-date, and independent information on a company and its competitors, investors, whether professional or amateur, can choose stocks wisely. But without sound information or, even worse, with misleading information, they may as well go gambling.[1]

The regulatory and banking environment as seen in *Newsweek*, August 2002

1.1 DIFFERENT TYPES OF BANKS AND THEIR RISK PROFILE

1.1.1 Bank failure and the financial services community

Bank of Credit and Commerce International, Continental Illinois, Crédit Lyonnais, RUMASA, Barings. Major bank failures years in the making. Yet all were surprises when they occurred. Why?

The list of banking collapses and losses seems to be endless, and endlessly entertaining. How is it that the most heavily regulated of industries seems to provide us with a steady stream

---

[1] Sen. Joe Lieberman, The Watchdogs Didn't Bark: Enron and the Wall Street Analysts, United States Senate Hearing Before the Committee on Governmental Affairs, 27 February 2002.

of highly entertaining and edifying stories in which record amounts of monies are lost and bankruptcies occur?

How is it that a galaxy of economic gurus from academia and business, CEOs with their legions of disciples, accountants, bankers, and consultants, regulated by governments and transnational entities, seem not only to get it wrong, but massively wrong, and so often?

Can this be attributed simply to the fact that the business environment is ridden by incompetence and greed? Or is the state of the industry more complex than these mere generalisations?

The fact is, that individually, all experts and parties agree on the risks and pitfalls which characterise the liberal economic model (which resides on apparently ineffective structures attempting to regulate the twin pillars of human nature and greed), which presents itself as the universal panacea and most perfect system of allocating resources ever devised by mankind.

Individually. All the players, of course, are in on the secret.

The secret is that these "failures" are indeed not "failures" but rather the manifestation of various players interacting on a tableau of greed and chaos, and that when the balloon bursts, scandal and outrage ensue. Fall guys are left holding the bag. Mea culpas are made. A few sacrificial lambs are thrown in the fire to give the illusion that the system is self-cleansing. At the end of the day, however, the exercise is highly profitable for the few that have the intuition or connections to pull their chestnuts out of the fire before it is too late. Consider the quote in Box 1.1.

Box 1.1

Moody and other bankers seem to have believed that Wall Street analysts could use non-public information concerning the railroad industry to earn superior profits from bond trading. When Moody was considering his rating idea, one "old Wall Street buccaneer" advised him:

"You young pipe dreamer, why throw away your ten years' experience of learning the rules of the game? Why give the public all the facts regarding the corporations for the price of a book? You will be showing them how to play safe and get rich, while you will make nothing yourself. Anyway, if you begin to flaunt too many facts, there won't be much inside knowledge left to work on; you will be spoiling our game. Use your information yourself; don't be a philanthropist. There's no money in it!"

John Moody, *The Long Road Home*, 91 (1933)

Moreover, Moody's rationale for marketing bond ratings was that he did not have sufficient capital to benefit from using inside information directly to earn profits from trading. According to Moody, although a person with capital could take advantage of inside information in the short-run, a person without capital (such as Moody) could earn greater long-run returns by selling the information "wholesale in a book".

Collectively, things assume a momentum of their own, as varying individuals and parties, with interests and agendas of their own, collide in the wonderfully speculative, volatile, and chaotic free for all game which is our economic system. In order to protect oneself in a zero sum game, whose short-term focus means that resources are merely reallocated rather than created, parties will act to further their own interests at the expense of overall economic performance and rationality.

Banks of course are the indispensable intermediaries in the game and their role and the risks attending them will form the focus of this book.

This book will endeavour to explore the underlying nature of the industry, regulatory environment, and analytical techniques in vogue to try to answer some of the questions underlying the basic question of bank and country risk. For the truth of the matter is that the industry is comprised of several players with differing agendas and the occasional hiccups manifested by the industry are merely the logical outcome of their interactions.

In other words, the problems are not due to the specific personal characteristics, honesty or competence of individuals, they are the manifestation of those most basic of human characteristics – greed and fear – and how individuals with those characteristics interact within their structures as well as with the regulatory system.

The problems are also the manifestation of another human characteristic – creativity. Creativity at the service of the incessant and ongoing quest to circumvent rules (created by compromise, allegedly designed to minimise the volatile excesses and risks inherent in the financial services arena), and generate quick profits.

1.1.2 What do banks do? How do they earn their money?

Let us begin with basic questions. What are banks? What do banks do? How do they earn their money?

Banks, as with all business enterprises, establish goals and make the decisions necessary to achieve those goals. Banks, however, have specificity in that they do not actually manufacture tangible goods but rather are in the role of intermediaries and manage abstract resources (more commonly known as "money"). The management and processing of these abstract resources moreover bears some resemblance to the processing and transferring of information. This has important implications in an era in which information technology not only accelerates transaction cycles but also enables the processing of information crucial to the ongoing management of a bank's operations (e.g. asset liability management, capitalisation, and customer centric database systems).

Implementation of the Basle capitalisation directives means that the unspoken goal of banks (those that can, that is) is to make money by collecting fees as deal originators as well as operating as intermediaries in the money markets (arrangers as well as lenders of monies).

The ability to integrate information systems in order to provide a seamless one-stop shop to major corporate clients is increasingly becoming the key differentiator in building market positioning. Hence, the issues of economies of scale and the wave of mergers witnessed. To illustrate, the present day JP Morgan Chase is the amalgam of four venerable New York banks – Manufacturer's Hanover, which was taken over by Chemical Bank, which in turn took over Chase Manhattan (and adopted the more upmarket name in the process), which in turn merged with JP Morgan). This quest to increase economies of scale, however, has other negative ramifications which we shall cover later.

Despite the high school soporifics of Economics 101 and buzzwords referring to "multiple providers" and "perfect competition", the industry, at least in European countries where the major retail banks are rarely more than a half-dozen, is basically exhibiting some of the characteristics of an oligopoly, and has witnessed increasing consolidation and elimination of marginal players.

This trend has been welcomed and fostered by governments and their regulatory bodies, as part of the current ideological movement which originated during the Reagan–Thatcher era as an antidote designed to dismantle the Keynesian economic model which came into existence during the administration of Franklin Roosevelt. The heart of the current "Globalisation" agenda, which is the dismantling of the "New Deal", the exorcising of Woodrow Wilson, and the building of a New World Order akin to the mercantile model pre 1914, except it's wired and interconnected.

This poses two dilemmas.

* The first is ideological: the increasing concentration and oligopolisation of the business is a very negation of the basic principles of capitalism and competition, where buyers ostensibly enforce discipline on the market by selecting the most efficient or best product and eschewing the uncompetitive one. It is the erection of an oligopoly or monopoly structure designed to ensure that the providers can dictate their own prices and conditions, and stamp out any potential entrants or competitors threatening not their *existence*, but their ability to *dictate the terms of the market*. In the words of investment banker Felix Rohatyn, it is a "betrayal of capitalism".
* The second is a practical one: with the weeding out of several players, risk becomes increasingly concentrated and the economic system increasingly vulnerable and volatile. To take an example, consider the syndicated loan. This has traditionally been a vehicle to raise large amounts of funds to lend to major corporates. A large loan will be underwritten by one or two banks and parcelled out to some say 20 banks, which results in reducing the loan into digestible chunks, as well as in dissipating the risk among the participating institutions. In the New York example, however, where in the past you had four banks able to assume the risk (or provide varying services and lending policies to the corporate borrower), you now have only one. Moreover, due to the onset of capitalisation ratios limiting a bank's level of exposures, the larger entity does not necessarily take a proportionally larger commitment. This means that risk becomes more concentrated and the number of players reduced, thereby increasing the possibility of volatility and confidence sensitivity in the markets.

This reduction in the number of players in the market and increasing concentration of risk mean that the market increasingly assumes the characteristics of an oligopoly.

The New York example is similarly paralleled by Citicorp merging with Travellers Corp., Bank of America merging with NCNB, HSBC taking over Midland Bank, BNP merging with Paribas, Crédit Agricole merging with Banque Indosuez, the spate of bank mergers in Scandinavia, the merging of three Japanese banks into the Mizuho leviathan, etc.

The industry is increasingly assuming the attributes of a one entity state monopoly provider (a criticism oft levelled at the defunct Soviet Union by disciples of "free trade") except that they are not accountable to any government or indeed effective regulation as the spate of financial scandals witnessed in 2002 testifies. They are increasingly becoming de facto if not de jure arbiters of the system, in no small part due to their ability to channel funds into the political process. And they are fostering the increasing concentration of risk.

Rather than have some 50 banks, of which say 10 may lend to an entity such as Enron, you now have three leviathans, all queuing up to fill up at the Enron trough (with resultant concentration of risk), and the economic system collectively getting a massive case of indigestion when the house of cards collapses (except for the loan officers who cashed in their bonuses for "booking assets").

These esoteric arguments, however, do not even figure on the bank CEO's radar screen – they have their own agenda to gain "critical mass" to browbeat the competition, and have a horde of share analysts badgering them for ever rising quarterly dividends, eager to pounce on the CEO for the slightest hiccup in forecasted results. The CEO will naturally be more preoccupied with these more immediate concerns (to his job safety) rather than the more esoteric questions of economic philosophy.

For most banks, the public message is that they exist to "ensure the safety of their depositors' funds and to maximise the value of the organisation to its shareholders". For publicly traded banks, this means maximising the return on and market value of its publicly traded stock. For banks that are not publicly traded, the usual yardstick for performance is its performance in achieving profitability and controlling risk.

It is important, however, not to confuse prudent management theories with reality. The excerpt in Box 1.2 from a *New York Times* article on the Enron shenanigans and bogus posting of loans by Citigroup provides a useful contrast.

Regarding the safety of depositors' funds, it seems akin to asking one to believe in fairy tales when reading about real life bank failures (see Section 1.3 on the "four aces").

Indeed one can recall four major cases of excessive risk taking by banks in the last 20 years:

- The massive lending to LDC (lesser developed countries) in the 1970s as a way of recycling the glut of petrodollars arising after the 1973 Yom Kippur war and OPEC oil boycott
- The mergers and acquisitions and leveraged buyout fever of the 1980s
- The boom and bust in property lending in the late 1980s/early 1990s (Canary Wharf, La Défence)
- The emerging market speculative ventures which came undone in the volatile 1990 markets (Asian crisis/Barings)

Ultimately the players all know that in the event of bankruptcy, the "flyover people" will foot the bill as they did in the Reagan era savings and loan crisis bailout. Who are the "flyover people"? Those folks that one flies over when to-ing and fro-ing from New York to Los Angeles.

Still, within the game, there are certain conventions and accepted methodologies used to assess banks.

We shall consider the accepted methodology of analysing these banks with their sophisticated regulations, structures, financial statements, mathematics, and some of their shortcomings, and how common sense can significantly supplement the efficacy of that analysis.

Despite failure, the tools are effective. Acting on the information provided by analysis, however, is another matter, and is beyond the scope of this book.

Box 1.2

July 23, 2002
Citigroup Said to Mould Deal to Help Enron Skirt Rules
By RICHARD A. OPPEL Jr. and KURT EICHENWALD

Senior credit officers of Citigroup misrepresented the full nature of a 1999 transaction with Enron in the records of the deal so that the energy company could ignore accounting requirements and hide its true financial condition, according to internal bank documents and government investigators.

The relationship between Enron and its bankers has been a focus of investigative efforts since the company collapsed amid an accounting scandal last December. For months, both Citigroup and J. P. Morgan Chase have been repeatedly criticized by investigators and shareholders' lawyers for structuring billions of dollars of transactions for Enron involving entities with names like Mahonia, Yosemite, Delta and Stoneville Aegean.

The *NY Times* said that bankers intentionally manipulated the written record of their dealings with Enron to allow the company to improperly avoid the requirements of accounting rules and the law, thus keeping USD 125 million in debt off its books.

In the 1999 deal, the records show, the bankers knew that a secret oral agreement they had reached with Enron required that the accounting for the transaction be changed. Instead, investigators said, Citigroup left that side deal out of the written record and allowed Enron to account for the transaction in a way that the bankers knew was improper. In other words, the full terms of the deal were left out of the paperwork, with the result being that anyone reviewing it would have no idea that the accounting treatment being used by Enron was not proper.

A spokesman for Citigroup declined to comment, but he stressed that the bank believed that its dealings with Enron were "entirely appropriate."

The transaction and other deals between Enron and the banks are expected to be examined today at a hearing before the Senate Permanent Subcommittee on Investigations. Already, some members of the committee have concluded that the "Roosevelt" transaction violated accounting rules.

"Citibank was a participant in this accounting deception," said Senator Carl Levin, Democrat of Michigan and the panel's chairman.

The subcommittee's ranking Republican, Susan M. Collins of Maine, said the investigation had found that Citigroup was willing to risk its reputation "to keep Enron, an important client, happy."

Mr. Bennett, the Enron lawyer, said the current criticisms by Congress were a result of political pressure to crack down on the appearance of corporate wrongdoing. "What we have here is an incredible amount of revisionist history, which is motivated by the upcoming election," he said. "Most of the problems – not all of them – are things that have been legal and have been acceptable."

1.1.3   Different types of banks and their revenue structures

It is helpful to begin first by considering the fundamental question of what characterises a bank. Basic definitions soon become inadequate, as banks are highly varied in the type of business they do, the types of revenues they generate, and the types of risks they assume in their ongoing operations.

There are several different types of banks and financial institutions. Some may be hybrids and others may be entities specialising in a particular operational niche.

These characteristics obviously affect a bank's risk profile and the risk analysis to be undertaken.

Risk (and return) occurs through financial and non-financial decisions, as well as operational and loan portfolio development strategies. The risks arise from the bank's operations and are all interrelated. We will examine these risks later in the book.

Banks differ widely in the composition of their activities, and can differ widely in culture due to their historical development. Merchant banks (or investment banks) differ considerably from other types of banks such as agricultural banks or cooperative banks. The differences in culture immediately become apparent in a merger, such as the merger of Crédit Agricole, initially an agricultural cooperative bank, with Banque Indosuez, a merchant bank with a colonial heritage.

While to an outsider, banks may appear to be only in the business of taking and lending money and issuing credit cards, this view is only skin deep.

The primary categories of revenue generation for banks, which we shall examine in further detail later, are:

- Interest income (from loans)
- Trading income (from currency and financial instruments)
- Fee/Commission income (income from setting up deals, providing advice and services)
- Investment income (from associates or subsidiaries)

The "mix" of these activities defines what sort of institution the bank is: namely a commercial bank, investment bank (also known as merchant bank), or other specialised institution. The wave of mergers witnessed, however, has resulted in a blurring of these categories.

These categories moreover help to define the bank's behaviour with respect to matters such as:

- Chasing fee income (setting up deals to collect the fees and offloading the assets to second tier banks that do not have the ability to underwrite big ticket loans)
- "Stuffees" (the ability to underwrite deals, collect the fees, and "offload the assets" to second tier banks)
- Capitalisation ratios (does the bank have sufficient mass and balance sheet size to enable it to underwrite large loans?)
- Syndication ability (how well developed is the bank's marketing to generate loans, and syndications department to place the loans in the market)
- Mergers (is the bank vulnerable and therefore pressured to undertake risky strategies to try to survive?

There is industry standard software which enables comparative analyses of banks to be undertaken. This enables differences in the mix of revenue streams to be identified.

Most banks achieve their profits through a variety of ways, and this tends to define the type of institution they are.

Now, let us consider the main types of banks.

1.1.4   Commercial banks

Commercial banks are also known as "retail" or "clearing" banks (or in Europe "universal banks"). These are typically banks that provide a "full" range of services via an extensive branch network and receive a large part of their funding from the public in the form of retail deposits. Their clients range from individuals to major corporations.

Typical examples of commercial banks include Barclays and NatWest in the UK, Deutsche or Dresdner Bank in Germany, Crédit Agricole in France, ING and ABN Amro in the Netherlands, UBS in Switzerland, Chase, Citicorp, and Bank of America in the USA (see Table 1.1).

These are all very large banks with large retail depositor bases. They also all have specialised merchant banking or investment banking operations in the world's major financial centres as well as international networks of bank branches worldwide.

Consider Figure 1.1 produced by the World Resources Institute.

This figure depicts the organisation and workflows in a typical commercial bank involved in project financing. There are other types of banks with differing structures – mortgage banks, investment banks, for example.

Deregulation and competition has meant that commercial banks have diversified in recent years from their core business of deposit and lending, into new areas such as instalment finance,

Table 1.1

Mark	Bank name	Total assets USD 000 last year	Equity USD 000 last year	Net income USD 000 last year
1	Citigroup Inc.	1 051 450 000	89 425 000	14 213 000
2	HSBC Holdings Plc	748 890 000	58 959 000	7 116 000
3	Bank of America, National Association	551 691 000	53 311 000	6 664 000
4	JP Morgan Chase & Co.	693 575 000	46 233 000	1 746 000
5	Royal Bank of Scotland Group Plc	649 376 878	43 584 710	5 169 046
6	Mizuho Holdings Inc.	1 099 018 041	42 247 748	−7 430 180
7	Crédit Agricole CA	609 502 571	35 990 135	2 585 791
8	Deutsche Bank AG – US GAAP	795 735 124	35 021 513	416 623
9	BNP Paribas	745 413 999	33 542 869	3 815 720
10	Wachovia Corporation	330 452 000	31 533 000	1 619 000
11	UBS AG – IAS	854 211 326	30 751 428	2 795 979
12	Wells Fargo & Company	307 569 000	29 686 000	3 429 000
13	Bank of China	406 149 599	26 712 135	985 043
14	Mitsubishi Tokyo Financial Group Inc.	702 874 610	26 124 625	−1 003 003
15	Merrill Lynch & Co., Inc.	447 928 000	25 533 000	2 513 000
16	Santander Central Hispano	334 799 461	24 943 540	2 923 287
17	Barclays plc	637 833 159	24 670 226	3 626 552
18	UFJ Holdings Inc.	575 574 324	23 819 069	−9 038 288
19	ING Group-Int'l Nederlanden Groep	751 778 781	23 442 124	5 070 836
20	Industrial Commercial Bank of China	524 234 608	23 309 371	754 398
21	Morgan Stanley	529 499 000	23 161 000	2 988 000
22	HBOS Plc	512 148 144	22 895 633	3 342 875
23	Rabobank Group	393 241 683	22 139 784	1 531 116
24	Credit Suisse Group	688 422 651	21 074 709	−2 405 439
25	FleetBoston Financial Corporation	203 638 000	20 558 000	934 000
26	Bank One Corporation	268 954 000	20 226 000	2 638 000
27	Bayerische Hypo Vereinsbank AG IAS	711 869 031	20 156 365	−900 409
28	Sumitomo Bank Ltd	527 891 856	19 633 575	707 829
29	Société Générale	526 041 557	19 529 856	1 565 747
30	US Bank National Association	166 949 094	19 431 199	1 801 600

Source: DC Gardner Training, 2003.

trade finance, mortgage lending, insurance, leasing, trust agencies, and investment banking. This has had the impact obviously of diversifying revenue streams to the point where such banks can be said to be comprised of several discrete profit centres.

Such diversification has also had the effect of increasing the portion of non-interest income activities, which has placed them in direct competition with investment banks. Indeed, the consolidation trends in the market have meant that several merchant banks have been absorbed by major clearing banks, such as the Chase Manhattan–JP Morgan merger or the Deutsche Bank takeover of Banker's Trust.

Another effect of these realignments of course has been to reduce the number of players in the market, which has had an impact on mechanisms to dissipate credit risk such as the syndicated loan.

While there are of course differences, commercial banks such as Citigroup in the USA, Crédit Agricole Indosuez in France, Deutsche Bank in Germany or ABN-AMRO in the Netherlands broadly follow similar characteristics: large retail depositor bases, a widespread network of

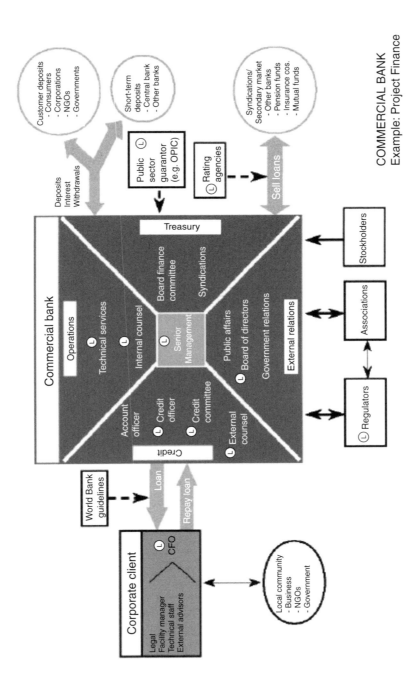

Figure 1.1

© World Resources Institute – Guide to the Private Financial Services Industry.

COMMERCIAL BANK
Example: Project Finance

branches in its home country, a far flung network of branches abroad, and a large portion of revenues generated by interest income (although fee/trading income is on the rise).

1.1.5   Investment banks

Investment banks historically were primarily active in the financing of international trade. Dwarfed by the vast balance sheet size and branch networks of the clearing banks, the investment banks have continued to prosper by exploiting various market niches, and competing through innovation, flexibility, and a willingness to participate in equity ventures, as well as a wide and specialised variety of banking services.

Such banks are now very much involved in areas such as mergers and acquisitions, corporate finance, underwriting, funds management, foreign exchange, investment management, financial advisory services, and Euromarket business. In addition, many investment banks have diversified, either through subsidiaries or substantial stakes in associated companies. These activities can include equipment leasing, hire purchase, factoring, insurance, insurance broking, shipping, property development and management, and real estate.

Having no significant retail depositor base, investment banks' main deposit taking activity has been via wholesale deposits for periods varying from one day to a year or more. Obviously, wholesale short-term funding is more volatile or "confidence sensitive" than a retail depositor base and represents a higher element of risk.

While investment banks' involvement in direct lending has virtually disappeared over the past few years, they are suppliers of corporate finance, concentrating on medium-term lending. In this connection, important aspects are the provision of funds for companies growing towards the size where they can consider a public flotation, medium-term finance for major UK exports backed by export guarantee (ECGD), and Eurocurrency loans.

The financial revolution associated with the UK's "Big Bang" in 1986 resulted in several UK investment banks acquiring major stock exchange firms in an effort to become "integrated security houses". The UK merchant banks have progressively become more like the US investment banks, and most of them have been acquired by the large European "universal banks" or US "investment banks".

US investment banks such as Salomon Brothers or Morgan Stanley were primarily involved in corporate finance. However, during the past 10 years, and especially since 1985, the growth of investment management and securities trading has been increasingly emphasised. Several banks like the US's Citibank and major European banks such as UBS and Deutsche Bank have exemplified this trend towards "universal banking" in London's internationally oriented markets. These mergers have tended to blur the differences between these types of institutions, and it is helpful to consider the differences as this understanding will be useful when we come to the financial analysis of a bank.

1.1.5.1   Historical background

In the 1930s the collapse of the US stock market and the consequent losses suffered by the US investment or securities institutions prompted the US regulators to split financial institutions into investment banks and commercial banks.

With the enactment of the Glass-Steagall Act, banks were split; JP Morgan became a commercial bank and Morgan Stanley an investment bank. The Japanese financial markets have been modelled on the US with commercial and investment banking separated by law.

In the UK merchant banks started out as trading banks financing high risk ventures overseas but today are very similar to the US investment banks.

In Europe investment banking has generally been an integral part of the activities of the major "universal banks"; this separation and specialisation of activities has not occurred and so we have institutions such as UBS and Deutsche Bank covering the whole range of financial activities (Figure 1.2).

1.1.5.2   Key activities of investment banking

Investment banking activities typically comprise:

- Underwriting, issuing, broking and trading government, bank and corporate debt securities. (These can be divided into short-term instruments such as treasury bills, certificates of deposit and commercial paper or long-term instruments such as fixed rate bonds, floating rate notes, medium-term notes.)
- Underwriting issuing and trading and broking equities.
- Research analysis: many investment houses provide research papers for existing investors or sell to interested parties their analysis of the future prospects of securities in the markets in which they operate.
- Providing and trading derivative products.
- Trading in foreign exchange and commodities.
- Corporate advisory services; mergers and acquisitions and corporate restructuring.
- Bridge finance (loans to be taken out by a subsequent bond or equity issue).
- Investment management.

1.1.5.3   The key risks

The key risks relating to investment banks are different than commercial banks. Investment banks are transaction-driven organisations while commercial banks are loan-driven entities. The key risks are:

- Where will next years profits come from? Investment banks do not have the regular income flow provided by a loan portfolio with staggered maturity schedules over time. Investment banks' income comes from fee income – from setting up deals. Obviously, deals are generated on a one on one basis. Investment banks therefore have to find their income every year.
- Operational risks – the trading environment in investment banks can be extremely complex and not understood by auditors or management, resulting in the problems encountered by Barings and Daiwa.
- Proprietary trading risks – much of the activities of investment banks is position taking in securities and other instruments which is inherently speculative and therefore highly risky. The losses suffered by several houses in 1994 were caused by an unexpected rise in dollar interest rates and a collapse in bond prices.
- Conflicts of interest – loss of confidence in investment bankers can result from selling investments which are complex and inappropriate as happened with the Orange County and Bankers Trust. Recent scandals show that supposedly "impartial" research has been little more than "advertising" as a means of selling an investment banks' high inventory of securities. Similarly the separation of corporate finance advisory work and trading activities is extremely sensitive. Indeed recent scandals have resulted in waves of departures of analysts

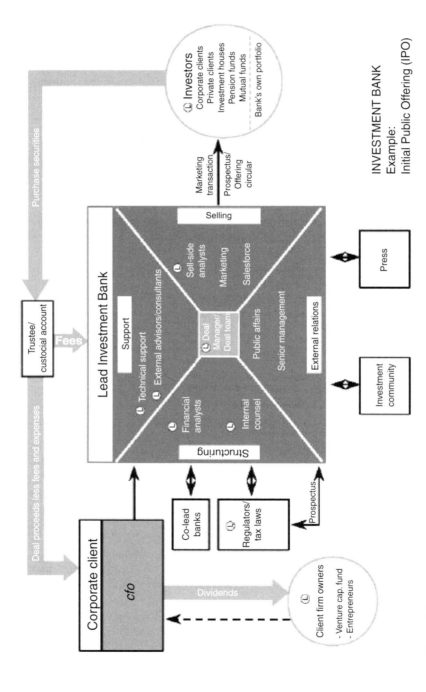

Figure 1.2
© World Resources Institute – Guide to the Private Financial Services Industry.

INVESTMENT BANK
Example:
Initial Public Offering (IPO)

Investors
Corporate clients
Private clients
Investment houses
Pension funds
Mutual funds

Bank's own portfolio

Marketing transaction
Prospectus/ Offering circular

Purchase securities

Trustee/ custocial account

Fees

Deal proceeds less fees and expenses

Selling

Lead Investment Bank

Support

Technical support

External advisors/consultants

Deal Manager/ Deal team

Sell-side analysts

Marketing

Salesforce

Financial analysts

Internal counsel

Public affairs

Senior management

Structuring

External relations

Press

Investment community

Co-lead banks

Regulators/ tax laws

Prospectus

Corporate client

cfo

Dividends

Client firm owners
- Venture cap. fund
- Entrepreneurs

and their managers at brokerage houses such as Merrill Lynch, and scandals which have led to laws requiring analysts to sign off assuming responsibility on the "research" they produce.

- Management risk – the salaries and bonuses earned in the securities industry are extremely high and the need to ensure an open and team culture is paramount. Failure to manage this well has led to mass defections of key players making investment banks vulnerable to sudden losses of business.

1.1.6 Risk profile of investment banks

The main activities, in ascending level area of risk, are:

- Asset management – this has typically targeted retail and wholesale investors, although the big firms, at least prior to the beating shares have taken during 2002–03, have tended to do best selling mutual funds to individuals. This business pays annual fees rather than generates one-off returns, which makes them very attractive to firms whose other businesses are inherently cyclical.
- Broking – a commission-generating activity – a business in which firms appeal to customers mainly on price.
- Investment banking or corporate finance – this includes underwriting of new issues, advisory work, and mergers and acquisitions. Underwriting typically contributes around four-fifths of the fees earned in this area, although all elements of the business are highly cyclical, as they are deal driven. M&A activity, though unreliable and cyclical, can be very profitable due to the lucrative underwriting fees.
- Trading, which thrives on volatility and has been growing in importance as firms have committed more capital and resources.

1.1.7 Broking is a competitive business

The other key consideration in broking in various markets throughout the world is the ability of the counterparties to settle real time. Significant risks can exist where there are intrading settlement or delivery open positions or when the margin calls on an exchange are insufficient to cover a collapse of the market. Documentation and the legality of ownership of pledged assets in the repo market are issues which need to be analysed closely on a country-by-country basis.

1.1.8 Derivatives trading and AAA subsidiaries

Many major investment houses, which have developed a strong derivatives capability, have found that their ability to trade these long-term instruments have been constrained by the acceptability of their creditworthiness.

They have therefore set up Derivatives Product Companies (DPCs), subsidiaries which have been structured to give them an enhanced AAA rating. This has been done by the parent guaranteeing pools of collateral which are available to these DPCs, theoretically making them "bankruptcy remote". The collateral is marked to market by an outside firm of accountants and regularly reviewed by credit rating agencies and supervisors.

If a financial group's credit was to deteriorate, the capital and collateral available to the AAA subsidiary would still be available to it but could detract from the overall financial strength of the group.

1.1.9 The regulation of investment banks

Investment banking activities may be carried out by a number of different types of companies and it is important to understand their status.

- A triple AAA derivatives company is protected by collateral that is monitored accordingly to central bank regulators and the monitoring of this is constantly reviewed by the rating agencies.
- A bank will be regulated by the Bank of England in the UK, the Fed in the US and the central bank or government supervisory authority in each country. The structures of supervision, competence of the authority, degree of control and willingness to provide support will be crucial to the confidence one may have in any bank.
- A broker – in the US the regulations of the Securities Exchange Commission are extremely rigorous and this will afford protection to an investor or lender.
- "Other" investment banking subsidiaries may not be regulated and may at short notice have their capital divided out to other parts of a "group" and should therefore be viewed with great circumspection.
- Holding companies: are vulnerable to double leverage.

1.1.10 "Analyst of the year" Awards

In Box 1.3, three press articles illustrate the conflicts of interest and scandals regarding inappropriate behaviour of share analysts attempting to "churn" or "offload" their inventory of securities. While highly amusing to read, these articles are indicative of the pressures on investment bankers to "manage the bottom line", some of the contortions they get into in pursuit of this goal, and some of the difficulties in regulating these activities.

Box 1.3

BBC NEWS | Business | Merrill settles in share tipping row
Tuesday, 21 May 2002, 16:21 GMT 17:21 UK
Merrill settles in share tipping row

Investment bank Merrill Lynch has said it is to pay USD 100m to settle an investigation by the New York attorney general into allegations its analysts misled tech stock investors.

The bank, which is not admitting any wrongdoing, will pay USD 48m to New York state and USD 52m to other US states, Merrill said in a statement.

Under the deal, Merrill Lynch has agreed to sever all links between analysts' pay and investment banking revenues.

Merrill, one of Wall Street's most prestigious names, has also issued a public apology to its clients, shareholders and employees.

Merrill stock rises

New York attorney general Eliot Spitzer told reporters the agreement should help to overcome "inherent tensions" within US investment banks.

"If necessary, firewalls have to be constructed," he said.

But he rejected suggestions that affair showed evidence of corruption on Wall Street.

The new regime at Merrill Lynch will be overseen by a "compliance monitor," whose appointment must be approved by the attorney general.

In New York, Merrill Lynch shares closed 47 cents higher at USD 43.85 on Tuesday, off earlier highs.

Regrets

The affair stemmed from allegations that Merrill Lynch analysts tipped stocks they privately disparaged so as to keep open the possibility of gaining investment banking business from the companies concerned.

One Merrill analyst allegedly described one such stock as "a piece of ****" in an internal e-mail.

"We sincerely regret that there were instances in which certain of our Internet sector research analysts expressed views that at certain points may have appeared inconsistent with Merrill Lynch's published recommendations," the bank said in a statement on Tuesday.

The settlement also requires Merrill analysts to state whether the companies they are rating are also investment banking clients.

Troubles ahead

Attorney general Spitzer is pressing ahead with investigations into similar alleged conflicts of interest at other major US brokerages.

And Merrill is still facing up to two dozen private lawsuits from investors who claim the bank's investment advice lost them money.

"Sadly, our reputation has been impacted, and it's something we're going to work hard to re-establish," said Merrill Lynch chairman David Komansky.

He added that he did not believe the affair had compromised the integrity of Merrill Lynch's research.

BBC NEWS | Business | Salomon "next on Spitzer hit list"
Sunday, 28 July, 2002, 15:17 GMT 16:17 UK
Salomon "next on Spitzer hit list"

New York attorney general Elliot Spitzer, fresh from an inquiry into allegations that Wall Street brokerage Merrill Lynch issued misleading stock tips, may investigate Salomon Smith Barney next, according to press reports.

Mr Spitzer is expected to decide whether or not to bring charges against Salomon Smith Barney early next month, the *Observer* newspaper reported.

Mr Spitzer is spearheading an investigation into Wall Street analysts, accused of issuing glowing reports on firms they privately disparaged so as to keep open the possibility of gaining lucrative investment banking business from them.

Many investors backed firms which later went bankrupt on the strength of the reports, racking up heavy losses.

Analyst under scutiny

Two months ago, Wall Street giant Merrill Lynch paid USD 100m to settle an investigation led by Mr Spitzer.

Any inquiry into Salomon Smith Barney is likely to focus on the activities of its star analyst Jack Grubman, who was closely associated with bankrupt telecoms giant WorldCom.

US regulators are already investigating upbeat research reports that Mr Grubman wrote on bankrupt US telecoms firm Winstar Communications.

Last week, a group of independent stock analysis firms formed the Investorside Research Association, which aims to provide investors with an alternative to stock research from Wall Street investment banks.

BBC NEWS | Business | SEC tightens rules on analysts
Thursday, 6 February, 2003, 21:29 GMT
SEC tightens rules on analysts

Wall Street analysts are facing new rules. Wall Street analysts will have to state that the opinions given in their research are their own under new rules passed by the US stock market watchdog, the Securities and Exchange Commission (SEC).

The move follows allegations that, during the 1990s tech stock boom, some analysts gave unreasonably favourable reports on companies to help their employer win investment banking business.

"Simply put, we want analysts to say what they mean, and mean what they say, and to sign their name to that," said SEC commissioner Cynthia Glassman.

Last December, the main banks and brokerages on Wall Street paid more than USD 1.4bn in order to settle stock-tipping allegations with US regulators.

Informing investors

Under Regulation Analyst Certification, or Reg AC, share analysts will have to certify that the research they publish is truly their own personal view.

They will also have to vouch that they received no payment that could influence their buy or sell recommendations on shares and bonds.

"It's . . . important that investors be fully informed of compensation arrangements and other conflicts that could influence an analyst's recommendations or views," said the outgoing SEC chairman Harvey Pitt.

Mr Pitt resigned from the SEC in November but is staying on until his nominated successor William Donaldson is cleared by Senate.

SEC commissioner Harvey Goldschmid said: "The modifications we have made . . . are sensible" within an analyst system that "is badly broken."

But some people said the new regulations would make little change.

"I'm not sure what it adds to the mix," said Saul Cohen, a partner at the law firm of Proskauer Rose.

"But if it makes some people more comfortable, fine."

1.2   PRIMARY CAUSES OF BANK FAILURE

Although the banking industry is one of the most closely regulated and controlled of all industries in terms of financial health, it has suffered from failures ranging from the smallest one branch bank to the largest international institutions.

What is particularly fascinating about bank failure is that after a major bank failure, post mortems and mea culpas are inevitably performed with a quasi religious solemnity, but as soon as the dust settles, a new crisis is in the making.

Finally, what tends to be forgotten in these bank failure crises is that the money is never "lost". It merely "changes hands".

A cynic might attribute this to the infinite creativity of the human mind to find new solutions to problems; in this case, ways to work around the new legislation designed to prevent preceding crises. These loopholes and the search for new ways to find them and exploit them render bank failures unexpected and unique in their nature but utterly predictable as a phenomenon. Indeed, one could say it's inherent in the nature of the business.

Most bank failures can fall into broad sets of categories.

If we are going to analyse banks it is important to see what are the causes of failure, what is the incidence of these failures, what are the warning signs and what losses depositors with the bank or counterparties of the bank might suffer.

1.2.1 Types of failures

There have been several well-publicised instances of bank failure or fraud in the past 15 years. The following are among the more important ones:

1970	US Penn Central Bankruptcy	Market liquidity
1973	US Secondary Banking	Credit bank failures following trading losses
1974	Franklin National	Poor credit control
1974	Bankhaus Herstatt Germany	FX overtrading credit/payments system
1980s	Johnson Matthey UK	Poor credit controls
1982	LDC Debt Crisis	Bank failures following loan losses
1983	Penn Square USA	Industry concentration, excessive revenue generation
1984	Rumasa	Intergroup lending, nepotism
1984	Continental Illinois	Industry concentration, poor credit controls
1985	Canadian Regional Banks	Bank failures following loan losses
1986	FRN Market	Collapse of market liquidity and issuance
1986	US Thrifts	Bank failures following loan losses
1987	Stock market crash	Price volatility after shift in expectations
1989	Collapse of US junk bonds	Collapse of market liquidity and issuance
1989	Australian banking problems	Bank failures following loan losses – credit
1990	Norwegian banking crisis	Bank failures following loan losses
1990	Swedish commercial paper	Collapse of market liquidity and issuance
1991	Swedish banking crisis	Bank failures following loan losses
1991	Finnish banking crisis	Bank failures following loan losses
1991	Southeast Bank, Florida	Real estate concentration
1992	Japanese banking crisis	Bank failures following loan losses
1992	ERM crisis	Price volatility after shift in expectations
1992	BCCI	Fraud, ambiguous domiciliation
1992	ECU bond market collapse	Collapse of market liquidity and issuance
1993	Crédit Lyonnais	Excessive expansion, political corruption, inadequate controls
1994	Bond market reversal	Price volatility after shift in expectations
1995	Barings	Poor management controls
1995	Mexican crisis	Price volatility after shift in expectations

1997	Asian crisis	Price volatility following shift in expectations
		Bank failures following loan losses – market, credit, sovereign
1998	Russian default	Collapse of market liquidity and issuance
1998	LTCM	Collapse of market liquidity and issuance
2001	Allied Irish Banks (USA)	Rogue trader

Information from BIS and http://www.brunel.ac.uk/depts/ecf/lectures/5007/5007-4.pdf

1.2.2   Causes of losses

The causes of bank losses are as important as their value. A 1988 study by the US Comptroller of the Currency found that US bank failures could be attributed as follows:

- Poor asset quality (98%of cases)
- Poor management (90%of cases)
- Weak economic environment (35%of cases)
- Fraud (11%of cases)

In developing countries the economic environment may play a larger role but probably not more than, say, 50%. In many financial crises – including severe decade-long cases (as in Argentina) – private banks with good management survived, indicating that bank losses are not inevitable and can be avoided through good risk management and adequate capital.

Banks incur losses as a result of poor credit policies, bad debt, operational losses, speculation, inefficiencies, and fraud. Such losses adversely impact the bank's asset quality, funding profile, equity base, and operations. When such losses exceed the bank's total capital and reserves, bank insolvency occurs. While losses can often be controlled or minimised with quality management, some variables such as taxes and exchange rate or interest rate controls are outside a bank's control.

Understanding bank insolvencies therefore requires analysing the behaviour of bank management, borrowers, depositors, and policymakers in response to external shocks, policy changes, and sectorial imbalances, as well as the internal workings, operations, and management of the bank. It requires understanding management attitude towards business risk and protecting the funds of their depositors or clients.

A letter from the SEC (Box 1.4) illustrates well the role of regulatory agencies, and the contrast between business school management theories, the reality of running an investment bank, and importance of management attitudes in running a clean and above the board operation.

These factors obviously are subjective and therefore mean that you cannot assess a bank's financial health purely in terms of its financial statements. Other subjective factors are linked to poor asset quality and poor management.

Analysing a bank's financial health requires setting objective standards of measurement, obtaining independent verification of bank operations (through auditors or supervisors), and providing full disclosure of results to all parties involved in bank restructuring: depositors, shareholders, bank employees, management, and supervisory authorities. Often, this is not possible.

During the 1980s severe bank losses appeared in both industrial countries (Norway, Spain, the United States), and developing countries for a variety of reasons.

Main event categories leading to bank failure are as follows:

Box 1.4

UNITED STATES
SECURITIES AND EXCHANGE COMMISSION
WASHINGTON, D.C. 20549

April 30, 2003

Mr. Philip J. Purcell
Chairman and Chief Executive Officer
Morgan Stanley & Co. Incorporated
1585 Broadway
New York, NY 10036

Dear Mr. Purcell

I am writing about today's *New York Times* report of your comments concerning the Commission's and other regulators' recent enforcement action against Morgan Stanley. I know you have already spoken to our Director of Enforcement about the report, but I wanted to give you my own thoughts.

I am deeply troubled that you would suggest that Morgan Stanley's conduct, so described in the Commission's complaint, was not a matter of concern to retail investors. My concerns are two-fold. First, your statements reflect a disturbing and misguided perspective on Morgan Stanley's alleged misconduct. The allegations in the Commission's complaint against Morgan Stanley are extremely serious. They include charges that Morgan Stanley paid other firms to provide research coverage, compensated its research analysis, in part, based on the degree to which they helped generate investment banking business, offered research coverage by its analysis as a marketing tool to gain investment banking business, and failed to establish adequate procedures to protect research analysts from conflicts of interests. In light of these charges, your reported comments evidence a troubling lack of contrition and lead me to wonder about Morgan Stanley's commitment to compliance with the letter and spirit of the law and the high standards of conduct all investors have a right to expect from their brokerage firms.

Second, I wish to remind you that among the terms of the settlement to which Morgan Stanley agreed is a requirement that the firm, and those speaking on its behalf, do not deny the Commission's allegations. Like every term of the settlement, this is a legal obligation assumed by the firm (and certainly applicable to you as CEO), that is enforceable by the court. I caution you that the Commission would regard a violation of that obligations as seriously as a failure to comply with any other term of the settlement.

Please let me or our Director of Enforcement know if you would like to discuss these matters further.

Yours truly,

William H. Donaldson
Chairman

..2.1   Asset quality

y far the major cause of bank failures has been problems of asset quality, also known as "bad
ending". Overexpansion or excessive growth, driven by a desire to be "the biggest bank",
ıeads almost inevitably to a compromise on credit quality standards and consequent losses.
  Poor asset quality generally results from the following:

- **Lax credit standards** – usually associated with rapid loan growth and/or heavy exposures
  to speculative industries and sectors of the economy (property, oil industry). Notable victims
  are Continental Illinois, Penn Square Bank, Southeast Bank. This cause accounts for 40%
  of bank crises.
- **Loans to owners, other insiders, or their companies** – this phenomenon was especially
  prevalent in the western hemisphere, but worldwide is present in 40% of failures. An example
  of overextension of loans to owners/insiders is the case of a leading bank in one of the Gulf
  oil states in 1990. Here, accounting ambiguities manifested themselves with respect to loans
  equal to a large proportion of the bank's net worth. Recent manifestations of this tradition
  are seen in countries with weak banking regulatory environments and "crony capitalism"
  structures such as Indonesia (Andromeda Bank), Russia (Avtovazbank) or indeed even the
  United States (Enron/Bush). As Lind notes: "Crony capitalism is the only kind familiar
  to the southern oligarchs, descendants of planters who could not balance their books and
  adventurers who despised mere trade. The lesson of the Enron and WorldCom scandals is not
  that capitalism is unworkable. It is that capitalism only works where there are capitalists."
  This applies equally to banking.[2]
- **Misrepresentation, corruption, unauthorised investments, fraud** – fraud, for example,
  can consist of events such as loans being extended with no guarantees being taken or "properly verified" or "incomplete loan documentation". These factors figure in bank failures
  such as BAII (Banque Arabe et Internationale d'Investissement, a Franco-Arab consortium
  bank). More importantly, these factors were particularly apparent in the more serious crises,
  i.e. those which ultimately resulted in losses to creditors and depositors (BCCI – Bank of
  Credit and Commerce International).

Obviously, these factors are not mutually exclusive – many crises can reflect a combination of
the above factors. We treat the subject of asset quality analysis in further details below and in
section 2.4.1 of this book.

Credit losses

Bank losses cannot be attributed solely to external shocks. Countries such as Algeria, India,
Kenya, and Pakistan all enjoyed several decades of uninterrupted growth, but each country's
banking system has suffered problem loans for a variety of reasons. In India and Pakistan the
credit allocation policies of state-owned banks played an important role. Banks were expected
to maintain a large number of loss-making branches, particularly in rural areas, and to lend at
below-market rates for economic and social welfare purposes. In Algeria, banks were expected
to lend to loss-making state enterprises as they were thus supporting the state's full employment
policy. Such policy-based lending has been responsible for a significant volume of loan losses.
Banks made loans according to policy directives and were lax in their credit evaluation because
they believed that the state would underwrite the loans.

---

[2] New America Foundation, Article 1186 – "The Texas Nexus" – Michael Lind): http://www.newamerica.net/index.cfm?pg=
article&pubID=1186.

Maintaining such a policy over time would result in countries with loan portfolios where 60% of the loans would be considered as non-performing. Weak management skills and fraud, an inability to set and maintain healthy credit policies, coupled with the fact that banks are owned by political factions, led to the failure of several smaller institutions. These institutions were subsequently consolidated under the supervision of the central bank.

Connected lending

Banks in Argentina, Chile, Colombia, and Spain suffered from a system in which banks were owned by large economic groups that also owned enterprises, with substantial bank lending to finance activities within the same group. The largest failure of such a group was the Rumasa group in Spain, which was nationalised in 1983. Rumasa was a diversified conglomerate active from wine trading to tourism and construction, and expanded via the acquisition of small Spanish regional banks that were absorbed into the Rumasa structure and managed by friends or family of the charismatic "prime mover", Ruiz Mateus. Many of these banks ended up lending over 70% of their total credit exposure to Rumasa group companies (which numbered some 300 subsidiaries). The whole edifice ended up being nationalised by the Spanish government in 1983, as a measure designed to head off collapse.

Inherited portfolios

A number of banks created during the transition of national banking systems from centrally planned economies to market-based economies such as the Czech and Slovak Republics, Hungary, and Poland, inherited large portfolios of non-performing loans to state-owned enterprises – effectively the government subsidising enterprises which were loss-making ventures.

The quality of most of these loans was substandard but it was difficult to accurately estimate the losses in the absence of stable prices. In 1990–91 many of these enterprises suffered trade shocks from the collapse of the trade arrangement through the Council of Mutual Economic Assistance, creating large loan losses for the banks.

Commodity shocks

Banking systems with reasonable supervision standards in economies that depend on commodities – such as Malaysia, Norway, and Texas in the United States – also suffered severely in the wake of the collapse of oil and gas prices in 1984–85.

In the USA, this was illustrated by the case of Penn Square Bank offloading oil exploration loans in Oklahoma "upstream" to Continental Illinois (which went bust) as well as to Chase Manhattan Bank. In the decade before the collapse, banks in these areas enjoyed high profits as business boomed. The boom created a bubble in real estate and other asset markets as speculation in property and shares surged, financed by banks in pursuit of higher profits. (The quest for high profits in discrete industry sectors resulted in two errors – that of industry concentration at the expense of sane portfolio diversification, and – that the quest for easy profitability via these "easy decisions" was a way to avoid dealing with more important and deep-seated causes of the bank-impaired profitability.)

Governments intervened through the central bank or a state deposit insurance fund. In the case of Continental Illinois (as with Crédit Lyonnais in France), the impaired assets were split off from the bank and placed in a special purpose vehicle to be managed separately (and enable the orderly sale or disposal of the healthy portion of the truncated bank).

1.2.2.2   Excessive overhead

Banks in developing countries incur high administrative costs through overstaffing, excessive branching, and wasteful expenditures, all the result of seeing banks as vehicles for the implementation of state policy and the provider of employment. Prior to restructuring, banks in Ghana incurred non-interest operating costs equivalent to 6% of total assets, compared with an average of 1 to 2% in OECD banks. These costs were more than 75% of total interest income. Banks in Algeria are also said to be overstaffed by 40%, despite the fact that profitability is weak, over 40% of lending is said to be impaired and cheques take up to four weeks to clear. The problem in these countries is that there is no political will necessary to address these problems by writing off the dud loans, firing the excessive employees and replacing them with a younger generation of managers free from the inherited values of a state planned economy, and implementing a commercially driven loan portfolio policy. Until there is a demand to address these issues, excessive overheads will be a characteristic of such banking systems.

1.2.2.3   Interest rate mismatch

A second cause of bank failure is mismatching of the tenor of loans and deposits. Mismatching occurs, to a certain extent, in almost every bank and if there is a positive yield curve, i.e. long-term interest rates always higher than shorter-term rates, banks can make money if they take short-term deposits and make longer-term loans.

The crucial point is "to what extent". This is what indicates whether the mismatch is due to normal "friction" where curing the situation requires more effort than living with it, or speculation, where the bank is effectively betting the farm on a favourable interest spread and hoping it stays there. This can work in the short term but certainly not in the long term. The US savings and loan crisis was caused primarily by the maturity mismatch in the balance sheet of savings and loans, which invested in 20-year or more fixed rate mortgages but relied on short-term deposits at flexible rates to fund this activity. Speculation, in other words. Over a period of two years interest rates rose substantially. An initial profitable 10% fixed rate loan became significantly loss making. After short-term rates rose in 1980–81 the thrift industry had an estimated net insolvency of about USD 100 billion in 1982 (US Treasury Statistics 1991[3])

1.2.2.4   Foreign exchange mismatch

Banks are involved in buying and selling foreign exchange, bonds, derivatives and a variety of financial products as market makers. They earn a spread or profit on the difference between the buying and selling price. This can be relatively safe if controlled and if they do not speculate or become involved in proprietary trading.

This is highlighted by the chief dealer at Bankhaus Herstatt who took a position in the USD/DEM market which effectively wiped out the bank's equity and bankrupted it. The 1974 failure of Herstatt Bank in Germany highlighted the dangers of mismatches in foreign currency positions. Inadequate management attention to such dangers could lead to large speculative losses. In Poland and Yugoslavia, for example, banks took substantial amounts of foreign currency deposits from residents but surrendered these funds to their national banks.

---

[3] US Treasury Statistics 1991.

Since foreign exchange reserves were considerably less than external debt during most of the 1980s, these banking systems suffered large losses when the domestic currency was devalued.

Similarly, Nick Leeson, the 28-year-old futures dealer of Barings Bank, took huge positions in equity futures on the Singapore futures exchange (and extended his exposure in an effort to cover his position) and wiped out the capital of Barings. The problem of the incompetent, overambitious, or dishonest dealer is compounded if, as in the above case, there were not proper management controls.

1.2.2.5   Excessive diversification

This is another cause of bank problems. This occurs when financial institutions believe that another part of the financial marketplace, about which they know very little, is very attractive. They then make a relatively large acquisition. This leads to disaster because they generally pay too much, or buy a company just as it is getting into difficulties, or fail to control it. For example, merchant bank Henry Ansbacher acquired a US investment house which was relatively large compared with itself. In six months, this investment wiped out Ansbacher's net worth. Ansbacher was only rescued by an equity injection from the Pargessa Group and BBL. Similarly TSB Group acquired Target Group and Hill Samuel Bank, which involved them in significant losses; the losses were fortunately not so large as to destroy TSB's enormous equity base.

The essence of a bank's continued existence is the confidence of its depositors. If this is lost, queues of depositors appear at the bank's branches and a run on the bank occurs. This occurred with Intra Bank Beirut and the liquidity crises when cash ran out, developed into a solvency crisis, and the bank closed down.

1.2.2.6   Fraud

Fraud is the least obvious cause of bank failure, although one can often detect unsavoury odours from such entities in the marketplace. Fraud, often in conjunction with other causes, typically brings about the destruction of banks such as the case of BCCI.

Early cases of fraud such as Banco Ambrosiano (Italy, 1982), Johnson Matthey (United Kingdom, 1984), and BMF Hongkong (Malaysia, 1982) seem small compared with the spectacular closure of the Abu Dhabi-owned – Luxembourg-incorporated – and London-based BCCI – Bank of Credit and Commerce International in 1991, where fraud and mismanagement are estimated to have caused losses of USD 10 billion out of total assets of USD 20 billion. In Guinea five of the state-owned banks – accounting for the bulk of the banking system's assets – were closed in 1985 when 78% of their assets were found to be fictitious. Even in traditionally orderly markets such as Japan, cases of forged deposit certificates have caused large losses to the smaller trust banks.

1.2.2.7   Flawed liberalisation policies

Many of the banking problems of the 1980s can be traced to poorly designed financial liberalization processes. Liberal entry rules and the expansion of new banks and deposit-taking institutions in the absence of adequate capital and managerial skills and sufficient supervision were responsible for failures in Argentina, Chile, Kenya, Spain, and Uruguay. The lifting of credit ceilings and deregulation of interest rates enabled banks to take excessive risks in areas where they had no prior experience, such as real estate. This connection between poorly implemented financial reform and crises derives from an unstable macroeconomic environment, unsound liability structures of borrowing entities, and weaknesses in the institutional structure for banking.

1.2.2.8 Understanding the big picture

As we have seen, banking failure has no single cause. To blame solely management failure, policy mistakes, or a business cycle tendency to focus into new unknown areas of speculation and risk does not suffice either.

A proper diagnosis of bank failure calls for a thorough understanding of the policy and economic environment, the institutional framework, banking practices, the quality of bank supervision (if any), and the structure of incentives acting upon the bank. Indeed, a "top-down" analytical framework is absolutely essential as analysing a bank's financial statements in isolation is only going to yield part of the overall picture necessary to assess all the risk and environmental elements and how they interact.

Policymakers are becoming increasingly aware that perverse incentives (e.g. deregulation and lifting of credit ceilings leading to a "gold rush" effect where banks all head for the new "eldorado" (e.g. real estate) like lemmings) can lead to bank failure if left unchecked. For example, evidence suggests that it was moral hazard (greed coupled with opportunism) – not simply bad luck or delayed closure – that led to the US savings and loan crisis and increased its cost.

Excessive tax incentives to real estate, for example, can artificially stimulate a property boom which ultimately leads to oversupply and results in heavy real estate loan losses in US or French banks.

While there is general agreement that effective supervision and enforcement are required to maintain stability in a financial system, even the most sophisticated bank supervisors in advanced OECD countries have not been able to prevent bank failures completely. This is due to the infinite creativity of bankers to find workaround solutions to regulatory measures enacted to control "yesterday's" problems. Bank supervision is thus a necessary and constantly evolving framework, but an insufficient condition in itself to ensure bank stability.

Supervisory authorities must therefore pay greater attention to issues of sector and national imbalances that may destabilise the banking sector and monitor these guidelines more closely. This implies beefing up the accounting framework, allocating resources to the supervisatory authorities, and most importantly, having the requisite political will to render these measures effective. After all, the savings and loan debacle in the USA, the collapse of Crédit Lyonnais in France, and the wave of corporate scandals to hit the press in the USA in 2002 are all the fruit of government policy accumulations more euphemistically known as a "pro-business" environment. And as is typical in these cases, it is rarely the perpetrators which are stuck with the bill, it is that universal sucker who foots the bill in most countries – the taxpayer.

1.2.3 Warning signals in predicting bank failure

Having seen what the prime causes of bank failure are, below are some warning signs that can help the analyst to identify problems and possible failure. We focus on the micro aspects, moving out towards the macro.

1.2.3.1 Excessive loan/asset growth

This is a key indicator. A bank which aggressively increases its loan portfolio growth rate may be assuming greater lending risks. (For example, in the early 1980s, Continental Illinois attempted to become one of the top 10 US banks through an aggressive programme of loan growth funded on the wholesale markets. This loan growth occurred in the oil and gas industry in Oklahoma: when this sector, following stagnant oil prices, experienced a protracted downturn, the bank experienced a liquidity crisis which broke it.) Loan growth should be viewed not only in the context of the bank's historical growth rates but also against its competitors: if it is growing faster than its competitors, you should try to establish the reasons why. After adjusting for inflation, double digit percentage loan growth indicates a possible deterioration in asset quality.

1.2.3.2   Excessive lending concentrations

Excessive lending concentration in particular economic sectors is one key factor behind many recent bank problems. Banks that exceed prudent lending limits to certain industries or geographical locations are vulnerable to changes in economic conditions. Areas like property, shipping or agriculture which dominate a bank's loan portfolio can be extremely vulnerable, such concentrations are potentially dangerous. How this typically arises is that the bank has some ambitious goal (to be the biggest bank on the block) and therefore has to compromise its lending policy since there are only so many good assets to go around and if you want to grow at a higher than average rate, you will need to lower your lending criteria. The result is that the bank may expand into oil and gas exploration, shipping, or real estate, for example. For a while, this works as the bank's loan portfolio grows; however, once the overbuilding manifests itself and you end up with high vacancy rates in office buildings, for example, and the loans enter in the repayment phase, that's when the chickens come home to roost. And the bank goes bust as with Continental Illinois or Crédit Lyonnais.

1.2.3.3   Deteriorating financial ratios

From year to year financial ratios may fluctuate but a prolonged deterioration in the profitability, liquidity and capital ratios are a warning sign. One of the leading indicators of problems is an increase in non-performing assets and provisions.

1.2.3.4   Tracking loan recoveries to gross loan charge-offs

Tracking loan recoveries to gross loan charge-offs is another indicator of credit quality. The history of loan losses is of extreme importance. A low recovery rate probably indicates that the bank is harbouring problem credits beyond reasonable time frames, as opposed to writing them off as losses. To place the above in context, you should try to assess the effects of a protracted downturn in a particular economic sector in which the bank may be exposed. If the bank is exposed to the oil or real estate sectors and there is a protracted downturn in those sectors, what effects will this have on the bank's portfolio, provisions, and earnings stream? Are these exposures partially mitigated by the fact that they may be extended to state-owned authorities, which may provide some additional element of security? These are questions that you should be asking as you are assessing the bank's asset quality.

1.2.3.5   Deposit rates higher than market rates

Many banks attempt to attract retail deposits by offering higher deposit rates than competitors in the market. This needs to be closely watched. For example, the new and privately owned

Khalifa Bank in Algeria during 2002 offered retail depositors higher rates of interest than the state-owned banks (up to 17%).[4] Khalifa's explanation for this is that as a new bank, the government encouraged the growth of the bank by rendering retail deposits in the new bank "tax exempt" for a five-year period following the establishment of the bank. The obvious question in this case is to ask yourself what will happen once the tax grace period is ended and the bank must then compete for retail deposits with other older and more established banks benefiting from the perceived security of being a state-owned bank. Not surprisingly, Khalifa Bank was shut down in mid 2003 by the Algerian authorities – ostensibly for fraud but actually for politically related clan infighting reasons related to laundering money embezzled by corrupt officials in Algeria's military backed government. Depositors, of course, can wait for hell to freeze over before recovering their deposits.

1.2.3.6   Off-balance sheet liabilities

Contingent liabilities should also be thoroughly analysed. While contingent liabilities (which represent an attractive source of fee income) do not appear on the balance sheet, they have amortisation schedules, and impact solvency ratios; if they crystallise, the bank can be liable for substantial payments to third parties (e.g. performance bonds relating to overseas construction contracts). Consequently, a breakdown of contingent liabilities and an examination thereof is important in determining overall asset quality.

1.2.3.7   Creative accounting

If a bank chooses not to provide adequate information in its accounts, changes its accounting policy or its auditor, or is known to window dress its balance sheet (borrow on the interbank markets and park the funds in ST assets as a way of boosting the balance sheet's liquidity position) this is very often symptomatic of problems which it is trying to obscure.

1.2.3.8   Delayed financials

In many instances annual reports and audited accounts tend to be produced well after the year end. Generally lateness is an indication of inefficiency or a lax attitude to reporting. The more worrying occurrence is when reports are significantly later than the norm for the particular bank or country. This is not usually "a problem with the printers" but a problem with the auditors. Rather, the auditors have a problem with the bank and wish to qualify their accounts. Johnson Matthey's accounts came out five months later than usual, unqualified, and the bank was closed down three weeks after that. The auditors subsequently were sued for incompetence. In the case of European Arab Bank the auditors signed off on the accounts as a going concern only after the shareholders had guaranteed a £100 million standby line of credit, some six months after the normal date.

1.2.3.9   Change in auditors

This problem is closely related to the preceding – when a bank chooses to change its auditors, there is usually a compelling reason, and it is fair to say that this reason is not typically related to price. It is crucial to get to the bottom of the reason why the bank will have changed its auditors

---

[4] Time Magazine, 22 Sep 2003, vol 162, no. 11 – "Crash and Burn".

and not be put off with lame excuses. Typically, this will be due to a major disagreement on the interpretation of accounts, and the new auditor may be willing to certify the accounts in order to win the business.

1.2.3.10 Change in management

Abrupt resignations may indicate the removal of an incompetent or fraudulent executive. Equally worrying can be the death or departure of the chairman or CEO who may have run a "one man band". The orchestra can collapse if a competent understudy has not been groomed for succession. Similarly, rapid staff turnover can also be an indication of problems at the bank, as mid-level executives and staff leave what may be a sinking ship.

1.2.3.11 Use of political influence

In the case of banks with close ties to the existing governmental regime, the bank may try to gain favourable treatment under the regulatory authorities by pulling political strings. This is known to be the case in countries with "crony capitalist" systems where the government places its people in key industrial and banking groups. Such countries include the Philippines, Indonesia, Algeria, etc. In such places, the government is seen as the hand dispensing favours and largesse to its children (the industrial and bank groupings controlled by its appointees). In such cases, it is virtually impossible for any entity to be run on purely business principles and as a result, politically motivated transactions typically manifest themselves to be unviable on business criteria, and are carefully "rolled over" ad infinitum or buried in the balance sheet and carried on it from year to year. It is not difficult to identify entities using political connections because upon meeting the bankers in such banks, they will usually with pride tell you how well connected they are with such and such a minister in an effort to impress you, not realising that they are merely confirming the fact they are the managers of nothing and have absolutely no clout or autonomy to run a concern along sound business practices.

1.2.3.12 Rumours in the money market

"I heard it on the street": dealers and other banks can be very useful sources of information about problems or unsavoury practices in banks.

1.2.3.13 Share price volatility

Often the market analysts may have a more real appreciation of the value of a bank than what the annual report may indicate. Beware of banks whose market capitalisation is lower than book value or whose share price suddenly collapses.

1.2.3.14 Deteriorating economy

If the economy into which a bank is lending is experiencing severe disruption or recession this will generally presage company failures and increase banks' loan losses.

Many of these signals may merely be indicative of transitory difficulties which a bank may be experiencing; however, they are more often than not a glimpse that all may not be as it appears and that the institution in question may be experiencing severe difficulties. In such cases, you may want to supplement your inquiry via other "unofficial" avenues such as market rumours and word of mouth.

1.2.4 Rescuing the bank!

Having looked for these signs and determined whether a bank may be in trouble the next thing to consider is whether it is likely to be rescued if it is. If one has concerns about a bank but has confidence that it will receive support thereby ensuring that depositors or counterparties do not lose out this will enhance its creditworthiness.

It should be noted that Fitch (the Fimalac-Euronotation-ICBA-Fitch-Duff & Phelps-Thompson Bankwatch collective), in addition to giving a performance rating, also gives a support or legal rating for the banks that it rates. This legal rating scale ranges from 1 ("A bank for which there is a clear legal guarantee on the part of its home state to provide any necessary support or a bank of such importance both internationally and domestically that support from the state would be forthcoming if necessary") to 5 ("A bank which cannot rely on outside assistance").

A bank may be rescued either by the state nationalising or recapitalising it, as it may be taken over by another bank, with or without the prompting and assistance of the regulatory authority. Alternatively there may be a national support package where all the other banks assist in the rescue by providing finance or liquidity, this will generally have to be seen in the national interest and usually encouraged by the central bank.

Some observers of the banking scene will describe banks as "too big to fail". Generally larger banks are more likely to be rescued than smaller ones – witness Crédit Lyonnais compared say to Banque Worms or Al-Saudi Bank in France. In considering the likelihood of rescue one has to look at the past history of regulatory intervention in different countries, the resources available, the likely political reaction to a rescue or collapse and the motivations of all the interested parties.

In Europe and the USA, out of some 40 major bank failures over the past 20 years, only four have involved losses by large non-bank depositors. These were Schroder Munchmeyer Hengst, BCCI, Penn Square and First City.

1.2.4.1 Costs of the bailout

One of the most difficult tasks of a bank supervisor is deciding whether or not to wind up a bank. This means establishing the costs and benefits of a bailout versus a closure.

In the mid-1980s governments rescued large problem banks because of the "too big to fail" principle, thus effectively extending deposit insurance coverage to almost 100% of the deposit base.

The pendulum has since swung back and there is generally the belief that only banks that are crucial to the payments system, and whose failure could have knock-on effects in the economy should not be allowed to fail.

This means that banking supervisors would focus on a core of "mission critical" banks that are directly involved in the high-value, time-critical payments transfer and clearing system.

Smaller banks and non-bank financial intermediaries on the other hand, whose failure would not jeopardize the payments system, should be allowed to fail, to rid the market of inefficient institutions.

What this means in effect is that there would be a two-tier banking system, with the second tier being higher risk and not benefiting from government support. Such a policy naturally begs a host of new questions, such as is it decreasing perfect competition and fostering the creation of an oligopoly?

There are also arguments claiming that functioning institutions may have a higher market value (and thus a lower cost of bailout) than that realised by immediate closure (the phenomenon of asset shrinkage, where value realised in a liquidation tends to be lower than under normal business conditions). The criteria for such a decision obviously vary from country to country based on the characteristics of the institutional mechanisms present.

The decision to rehabilitate or close the bank therefore depends on the institutional framework, the legal powers and resources available to intervene, and the ultimate cost to the government. While there are no rules, precedent cases can orient one's line of inquiry.

The typical line of inquiry includes:

- Determining the size of bank losses.
- Calculating the net deficit (estimating the time required and assuming that new capital is available).
- Determining loss allocation to shareholders, the need (and costs) of staff retrenchment, and the burden to be borne by the restructuring agency (central bank, deposit insurance agency, or ministry of finance).
- Estimating the fiscal impact of depositor bailout, assuming that government will engage in either a carve-out or flow solution.
- Is there a franchise value in the bank's brand or branch network? If so, this value can be added as goodwill to the capital of the insolvent bank.
- Is there a market for bank shares with other banks or new shareholders?

The resolution process typically starts with a diagnosis, typically involving an information package and asset valuation review. After this, an information meeting is arranged with potential acquirers of the failed bank or the remaining assets, with those interested performing a "due diligence" examination of the failed institution.

1.2.4.2 Various support mechanisms

UK model (Lifeboat Fund 1974)

- Funded by large clearing banks and the Bank of England.
- Initial liquidity support for viable secondary banks.
- Failed banks liquidated.
- Bank of England took over a failed bank that was subsequently privatised; losses were borne by the central bank.

US model (deposit insurance)

Federal Savings and Loans Insurance Corporation (until 1989)

- Acquisition or mergers.
- Income maintenance programme.
- Accounting forbearance.
- Phoenix and bridge banks.
- Management consignment.

Resolution Trust Corporation (after 1989)

- Concentration of failed assets in RTC.
- Liquidation or sale of banks to private sector.
- Losses borne by RTC (funded by federal guarantee).

Spanish model (bank "hospital" and carve-out mechanism)

* Accordion principle.
* Joint funding by commercial banks and the Bank of Spain.
* Deposit guarantee fund buys bad assets.
* Provides banks with guarantee and long-term soft loans.
* Sale of banks to private sector.
* Nationalisation of Rumasa group.

Chile variation

* Central bank issues bonds to buy bad assets, with buyback schedule.
* Central bank loans to banks converted into equity.
* Sale of banks to private sector.

1.2.5   Credit rating agencies

The press has highlighted certain issues and problems regarding credit rating agencies predictive capabilities.

Box 1.5

Who knew what?
by BBC News Online's Orla Ryan, Friday 1 February 2002, 10:03 GMT

A suspicious mood has settled on Wall Street in the wake of the Enron bankruptcy.

The collapse of the company feted by investment bankers and politicians has led many to question why no one saw it coming. As the US Congress debates the role of those who kept the energy giant company, attention is also turning to the credit-rating agencies. The Enron collapse has highlighted the role of these agencies, who provide guidance to investors on a borrower's creditworthiness.

"Lots of people were there at the time beyond auditors. There were rating agencies reporting up to a very short time before the collapse of Enron," Andersen UK's managing partner John Ormerod told the BBC's World Business Report.

While Andersen's excuses may seem lame, as the auditor tries to deflect attention from its own role, other critics are making similar noises.

Blame game

The analysis provided by rating agencies is influential in determining the interest rates that borrowers pay on their debt. Rating agencies such as Moody's, Standard & Poor's and Fitch grade borrowers – both companies and countries – as to their creditworthiness.

Who knew what

Moody's dismisses suggestions they were in a better position to know than other analysts. "Largely, the financial information on which we base our ratings is publicly filed information," Moody's Fran Laserson said. "We also have meetings with the issuers, who may choose to share issues with us, it is up to them, they will choose their level of disclosure," she added.

The three big agencies have already indicated that they are looking at tweaking the way they do business. Even as the job descriptions are being tweaked, Fitch's Bob Grossman is clear that agencies provide "leadership."

But in rumour-driven markets, prices rise and fall, and it can seem that rating agencies take their lead from traders, rather than the other way around.

"If they are only reacting to changes of risk that markets have already priced in, they become less useful," Bank of America's Juliet Sampson said.

The agencies – more highly visible than other analysts and hence more vulnerable to criticism – cannot be seen to be reacting to market whim.

Deja vu

The tricky point for the agencies is that we have been here before. The rating agencies also faced criticism for acting too slowly at the time of the Asian and Russian crises.

Bank of America's Ms Sampson believes that country rating changes have less impact than before, partly due to "a loss of credibility in the last round of crises" in Russia and Asia. For some investors, the agency's word is a rubber stamp and nothing else.

"Most city analysts don't think much of rating agencies is the truth of the matter they use rating agencies as an insurance device," one seasoned market watcher said.

"If things go sour, the pension fund administrator can say we checked with the rating agency and they gave it a clean bill of health, in other words it is not our fault."

1.3   BANK FAILURES – THE FOUR ACES

Before considering the classic approach of bank risk analysis with the typical staid regulatory, analytical, financial analysis, ratio analysis, and country risk analysis methodologies listed in classic textbooks, we provide for the sake of illustration, the stories leading to four major bank failures, each with a substantially different context but all with broadly similar characteristics.

That is to say, banks that "lost their way", and abandoned their role of being well-managed financial intermediaries focusing on prudent credit principles, for agendas driven by politics, corruption, megalomania, or excessive ambition. We select banks that were brought down by sick cultures rather than the antics of an isolated rogue trader.

These stories do not make pleasant reading but are included in this book not for cynical voyeurism, but to illustrate what is actually involved in bank failure and how avenues of inquiry must be broader than the static checklists, methodologies, and ratio number crunching of classic financial analysis.

These stories of failure illustrate the importance of understanding the nature of the business in question, and how to focus to the maximum extent possible all of the tools of questioning and inquiry in order to maximise the chances of producing a relevant analysis with accurate conclusions based on facts, and not what the market wants to hear.

Indeed, the panoply of financial analysis tools is merely the starting point. Understanding banks and their underlying motivations requires a good dose of psychological analysis as well as a dollop of cynicism and street cred.

1.3.1   Bank of Credit and Commerce International

This section quotes extensively from the Congressional report on the BCCI Affair: A Report to the Committee on Foreign Relations United States Senate by Senator John Kerry and Senator Hank Brown, December 1992.

New York Times columnist William Safire called it the "megascandal of the underworld bank". *Time* magazine described it as "the largest corporate criminal enterprise ever, the biggest Ponzi scheme, the most pervasive money-laundering operation and financial supermarket ever created". And New York District Attorney Robert Morganthau called it simply "the largest bank fraud in world financial history".

The subject of course is BCCI – Bank of Credit and Commerce International (or Bank of Crooks and Criminals Incorporated, or Bank of Crack and Cocaine Incorporated), which went bust in 1990–91. The bank was a Pakistani managed, Abu Dhabi owned, Luxembourg incorporated, and London Head Office based bank.

BCCI's unique criminal structure – an elaborate corporate spider-web with BCCI's founder, Agha Hasan Abedi and his assistant, Swaleh Naqvi, in the middle – was an essential component of its spectacular growth, and a guarantee of its eventual collapse. The structure was conceived by Abedi and managed by Naqvi for the specific purpose of evading regulation or control by governments. It functioned to frustrate the full understanding of BCCI's operations by anyone.

Unlike any ordinary bank, BCCI was from its earliest days made up of multiplying layers of entities, related to one another through an impenetrable series of holding companies, affiliates, subsidiaries, banks-within-banks, insider dealings and nominee relationships.

By fracturing corporate structure, record keeping, regulatory review, and audits, the complex BCCI family of entities created by Abedi was able to evade ordinary legal restrictions on the movement of capital and goods as a matter of daily practice and routine. In creating BCCI as a vehicle fundamentally free of government control, Abedi developed in BCCI an ideal mechanism for facilitating illicit activity by others, including such activity by officials of many of the governments whose laws BCCI was breaking.

The Congressional report notes that:

> BCCI's criminality included fraud by BCCI and BCCI customers involving billions of dollars; money laundering in Europe, Africa, Asia, and the Americas; BCCI's bribery of officials in most of those locations; support of terrorism, arms trafficking, and the sale of nuclear technologies; management of prostitution; the commission and facilitation of income tax evasion, smuggling, and illegal immigration; illicit purchases of banks and real estate; and a panoply of financial crimes limited only by the imagination of its officers and customers.
>
> Among BCCI's principal mechanisms for committing crimes were its use of shell corporations and bank confidentiality and secrecy havens; layering of its corporate structure; its use of front-men and nominees, guarantees and buy-back arrangements; back-to-back financial documentation among BCCI controlled entities, kick-backs and bribes, the intimidation of witnesses, and the retention of well-placed insiders to discourage governmental action.
>
> BCCIs' systematically relied on relationships with, and as necessary, payments to, prominent political figures in most of the 73 countries in which BCCI operated. BCCI records and testimony from former BCCI officials together document BCCI's systematic securing of Central Bank deposits of Third World countries; its provision of favours to political figures; and its reliance on those figures to provide BCCI itself with favours in times of need.

The BCCI scandal seemed to ripple out in ever wider and wider circles. From internal bank measures, to auditors, and regulators, the bank's web enlarged to encompass characters such as the splendidly uniformed Lt. Col. Oliver North and various arms traffickers running armaments to the Afghan mujahideen.

The US Justice Department failed to investigate and prosecute the bank's officials to the full despite strong evidence of wrongdoing. Various sources in the press claimed that the Justice Department did not follow up on leads, including eyewitness accounts that the bank was involved in widespread corrupt activities, including money laundering, drug trafficking, illegal arms deals, fraud, and bribery.

In 1991, the Bank of England took the unprecedented step of shutting down BCCI. This closure was coordinated with closures in Luxembourg, where the bank was incorporated. Soon afterwards, the District Attorney of Manhattan, Robert Morganthau, handed down criminal indictments against top officials of the bank.

Soon, the popular media were filled with tales of drug-money laundering, bankrolling of Middle East terrorists, underwriting of Saddam Hussein's quest for a nuclear bomb, etc. BCCI was linked to some of the Persian Gulf's wealthiest sheiks, and was described as a secret slush fund for the Central Intelligence Agency. *Time* magazine even quoted CIA head Robert Gates, referring to BCCI as the "Bank of Crooks and Criminals International".

Two rather critical facts, however, were invariably left out of the story – even during the lengthy soap opera trial of former BCCI attorney Robert Altman. Namely that BCCI was able to operate in London by having links with some of Britain's most powerful financial houses, and that BCCI was closely linked by the press with the management of covert funds that poured into the secret war in Afghanistan.

Hardly any mention was made of the fact that BCCI was in the middle of the Afghan effort – serving as the de facto central bank for a multibillion-dollar Golden Crescent illegal arms-for-drugs trade that mushroomed during 1979–90.

During the decade of the Afghan War, BCCI's assets had grown from an initial capitalisation in 1972 of USD 2.5 million, to USD 4 billion in 1980, to an astounding USD 23 billion at the point that the Bank of England moved to shut it down. The bulk of the USD 23 billion disappeared and to this day is still unaccounted for.

During its meteoric rise in the 1980s, BCCI was anything but a "Third World bank". Nominally founded in 1972 by Pakistani banker Agha Hasan Abedi, it was initially capitalised by the British-run Sheik Zayed of Abu Dhabi, incorporated in Luxembourg, and conducted all of its real business in London.

Abedi was closely allied with the Pakistani military, especially with Gen. Mohammed Zia-ul-Haq, who took power in 1977; and BCCI was used as a laundromat for the narcotics traffic in Pakistan's North West Frontier Province that processed Afghan opium and smuggled it onto the world market. Likewise, BCCI was the central bank for the British and American arms flows to the Afghan mujahideen.

BCCI became a "crown jewel" in the British offshore hot money system because of its convenient location in the City of London.

BCCI's Swiss, London, and Caribbean branches were an essential part of the cash pipeline for the Bush-led "covert operations" of the 1980s. According to congressional testimony, Lt. Col. Oliver North and British arms dealer Leslie Aspin opened up four joint bank accounts in BCCI's Paris branch.

Former Senate investigator Jack Blum summed up the BCCI case in a 1991 testimony before a congressional committee: "This bank was a product of the Afghan War and people very close to the mujahideen have said that many Pakistani military officials who were deeply involved in assisting and supporting the Afghan rebel movement were stealing our foreign assistance money and using BCCI to hide the money they stole; to market American weapons that were to be delivered that they stole; and to market and manage funds that came from the selling of heroin that was apparently engineered by one of the mujahideen groups."

When BCCI was closed down in July 1991 by regulators in numerous jurisdictions, some one million depositors around the world lost their money.

In their congressional report on the BCCI affair, US Senators John Kerry and Hank Brown concluded that a unique criminal structure, comprising a network of corporate entities, was an essential component of BCCI's spectacular growth. "The structure was conceived and managed for the specific purpose of evading regulation or control by governments", reads the report. "It functioned to frustrate the full understanding of BCCI's operations by anyone."

Being owned by Abu Dhabi shareholders, incorporated in Luxembourg, headquartered in London, with branches in exotic Caribbean locales, it is hardly surprising that BCCI was able to operate virtually free of government control, which facilitated illicit activity involving billions of dollars: money laundering in Europe, Africa, Asia and the Americas; bribery of officials in most of those locations; support of terrorism, arms trafficking and other financial crimes.

The report found that BCCI officers and directors took advantage of offshore laws to disguise their activities and throw off any suspecting regulators." Among BCCI's principal mechanisms for committing crimes", reads the report, "were its use of shell corporations and bank secrecy, layering of its corporate structure, use of front-men and nominees and the retention of well-placed insiders to discourage government action." Investigation efforts were hampered by a lack of cooperation by foreign governments and a lack of coordination among regulators, highlighting the need for integration of regulatory efforts in the international financial services sector.

While most analyses of BCCI saw it as a banking scandal, Beaty and Gwynne in their book *"The Outlaw Bank: A Wild Ride into the Secret Heart of BCCI"* offer an interesting proposal – that the BCCI scandal provided the deepest and most detailed glimpse anyone has so far had into the real workings of the underground economy.

1.3.2   Continental Illinois

Chronological dates/statistical data provided by Professor Ingo Walter of Stern Business School, New York University.

The Penn Square/Continental Illinois bank failure is a classic in US financial history. The rise and fall of Penn Square and Continental Illinois was described in extensive and hilarious detail in Mark Singer's book *Funny Money*. Penn Square's head office was based in a shopping mall in Oklahoma City and moved in just a few years from financing new patios and lawn mowers to a point where the repercussions of its collapse, in 1982, could have brought down the whole US economy.

What makes the Penn Square saga so strange is that its decline was not brought about by greed, fraud, megalomania, or corruption. Rather it was a conspiracy of circumstances aided by a large dose of stupidity. The prime ingredients were: the OPEC oil price increases of the early 1970s, the supposed oil and gas deposits in Oklahoma, the mechanisms of finance in the oil business, the Oklahoma "can-do" spirit, some "old college boys", and a brace of oddball characters.

The founder William "Beep" Jennings, and Bill "Monkeybrains" Patterson, the bank's lending officer, were eventually sent to jail for their abuses. The chief lending officer at Penn Square had spent his college years hanging nude from lamp posts, and he brought a similar professionalism into the boardroom, occasionally wandering in with a Nazi stormtrooper helmet. Penn Square lending staff allegedly drank beer out of their cowboy boots. As Penn Square escalated the scale of its loans, it was common for a deal to be concluded within 20 seconds if the borrower was small fry – i.e. only needed a million dollars – with a "yeah, you look okay to me".[5]

---

[5] Mark Singer, *Funny Money* (Knopf, 1985).

These small banks like Penn Square were able to lend beyond their means by selling the loans "upstream" to bigger banks. The goings-on at Penn Square eventually involved Continental Illinois and even the massive Chase Manhattan.

This upstreaming of loans fits in well with Continental Illinois' rapid growth strategy: during 1975–81 based on loan growth; in assets held (CGR = 15% 1975–81). Continental Illinois' objective was to become the largest bank in the USA, and the steady stream of oil exploration loans from Penn Square in Oklahoma provided welcome growth to the loan portfolio. Continental Illinois grew to be the sixth largest US bank from eighth, and was recognised at the time as one of the five best managed American companies (shades of Enron?).

Continental Illinois' good loan loss records, "streamlined" loan approval process, focus on energy loans (in the wake of the OPEC oil boycotts) made the bank the darling of Wall Street analysts in June 1981.

Chase could well have known exactly what was going on at Penn Square Bank because Chase was a major participant in Penn Square's loan portfolio. Penn Square was more of a packager of deals for Chase, Continental and a few others rather than a bank. They would go out and find loans and offer participations to their good friends. The people at Chase were good friends.

Penn Square had done quite well collecting finder's fees from their associates, but the loans weren't very good. Some USD 2 billion of Penn Square loans were in default. Almost 200 credit unions and savings and loans had deposits with Penn Square, magnetised by a return of two points more than their competition. These loans were not insured.

In 1982, however, Penn Square Bank failed. Ultimately, Treasury Secretary Regan gave instructions to the Comptroller of the Currency and Federal Deposit Insurance Corporation to close it down. The date was 30 June 1982, the same day that the Federal Reserve gave some more money to the Mexican Central Bank to keep it going a little longer.

Continental Illinois was identified as holding over USD 1 billion in loans to Penn Square (on a balance sheet of around USD 45 billion).

Continental Illinois, with limited access to retail depositors, manoeuvred to defend itself against "run on the bank" (withdrawal of deposits) by using the Euro CD market as a principal source of deposits – this became 40% of the bank's entire funding. High funding costs ate into high loan spreads, making the bank on balance less profitable than peer banks. But this was made up by low overheads and non-interest expenses. The bank moreover was becoming increasingly reliant on "confidence sensitive" funds (bank lines which can be cut overnight).

By the end of 1981 the bank's ROA was falling strongly. In Feb 1984 Continental Illinois replaced its CEO. At this time, non-performing loans on Continental Illinois' books more than tripled. To raise cash, Continental Illinois sold its credit card business to maintain its May 1984 dividend.

No question that Chase's problems had problems. As we know, Chase survived but not their sometimes partner, Continental Illinois, at least not in the same form that it was in then. On 9 May, 1994, an announcement issued by the Commodity News Service conjectured at rumours that had been circulating regarding a Japanese bank taking over Continental. The Japanese translator translated "rumours" as "disclosure" and this translation error "hit the fan". This precipitated a run on foreign deposits.

The Office of the Comptroller of the Currency issued a report denying the rumour. The bank borrowed USD 4 billion from Chicago Fed (1/2 daily funding requirement) and announced a consortium of 16 major US banks will provide LOC.

In an effort to restore confidence, the Federal Deposit Insurance Corporation (with Federal Reserve Board and Office of the Comptroller of the Currency) extended the FDIC guarantee to "all depositors and general creditors of the bank". FDIC extended capital infusion of USD 2 billion mid-May 1984.

A major run on the bank developed. Not that Continental hadn't been in big trouble for some time, but rumours sometimes became prophesies, which more often than not become self-fulfilling in times such as these. Continental's sister bank, First Chicago, was a mess, Bank of America had big real-estate troubles and Manufacturers Hanover was strangling on its Latin debt. There were probably a dozen of the top 20 banks in the United States in an equal or greater mess than Continental, but Continental is where the run started.

By 1 July 1984, USD 20 billion in deposits had run off. Federal officials admitted that the run on deposits had continued despite efforts to restore confidence, and they therefore moved to take over the bank. The bank was too big to fail – as the knock-on effects would have harmed the banking system as a whole, Federal officials therefore "guaranteed everything".

Because the failure of one could set off a domino effect, the Federal Reserve reluctantly agreed to bail out the bank. The Fed pumped in over USD 8 billion before they were through, making it the largest bank reorganisation in the history of this country. Ultimately, it probably ranks in the global big three along with BCCI and Crédit Lyonnais.

The FDIC split Continental into a "good" bank and (a new subsidiary) "bad" bank. The FDIC bought the bad loans with a face value of USD 3 billion for USD 2 billion, and committed to buy up to USD 1.5 billion more of bad loans over three years at book value.

The FDIC took over the bank's debt to the Chicago Fed, provided an additional USD 1 billion investment in preferred stock, and replaced the Continental Illinois board and management team.

The cost of the rescue to the FDIC is estimated at USD 1.7 billion. By December 1990 (six years later) the bank had assets of USD 27 billion and ranked 27th in US.

There was little or no interest by the other banks in a shotgun marriage with Continental Illinois as analysis proved the loan portfolio was in far worse shape than even the most pessimistic projections had indicated. Within months, Continental went from the seventh largest bank in the country to the thirteenth and became a ward of the government.

The bank went public again and FDIC was able to recover about USD 800 million of its costs.

The Continental Illinois intervention is seen as very successful, and a model for others, when one considers the damage control measures were meant for the banking system as a whole. S&L liquidations were later to follow during the Reagan Administration. Also further commercial bank failures forced banks to merge with others instead of being taken over by FDIC. For the US government, this meant not having to foot the bill and for the acquiring bank, although the purchased bank might be a dud, it enabled a circumventing of the prohibition against interstate banking.

1.3.3 Crédit Lyonnais

The background details and chronology of this bank failure are extracted from an article written by Joseph Fitchett, (*International Herald Tribune*, Thursday, 3 October 1996, page 13).

Once France's flagship bank, Crédit Lyonnais (aka "Crazy Lyonnais" or "Debit Lyonnais") is now better known as the country's worst financial scandal this century. Once considered a monument to bad management, the case is increasingly seen by parliamentarians and others investigating operations at the state-run bank as involving something much more serious.

Beset by the biggest amount of bad debts ever amassed by a bank – 125 billion francs (USD 24.22 billion)[6] – Credit Lyonnais has survived only because the French government bailed it out.

Fitchett noted in 1996 that government rescue efforts topped 10 billion francs, and outside experts predict that the total cost will ultimately reach 100 billion francs.

Both the French government and the European Commission, in authorizing the subsidies (bailouts), have insisted on a price: Crédit Lyonnais will have to spin off most of its subsidiaries, trim staff and curtail its once-lofty ambitions.

As part of that price, Minister of Finance Mr Arthuis noted on behalf of the government that criminal charges would be pressed against Crédit Lyonnais' former management, though he did not name specific individuals. Moves against the elite civil servants who run state businesses was unheard of in France, most likely to avoid exposing embarrassing public scrutiny of how these companies are often used as economic instruments of France's political power.

Much of the Crédit Lyonnais story has been hidden from the public. Gradually, however, often-overlapping sources have produced a broad outline of what happened at Crédit Lyonnais.

The design for Crédit Lyonnais began when Mr Mitterrand was re-elected in 1988. Alarmed by growing German power in an increasingly integrated Europe, the government chose Crédit Lyonnais (its two main rivals, Société Générale and Banque Nationale de Paris, had been privatized) – as the bank that would be helped to surpass Deutsche Bank AG, Europe's leading financial house.

Mr Haberer, who was appointed to run the bank in 1987, had unimpeachable credentials. At 56, he was a superbly well-connected elite bureaucrat whose résumé included upper-echelon positions in the Ministry of Finance and the private offices of cabinet ministers. Members of this elite have interlocking careers, hiring and promoting one another, and putting their leaders' grand designs into effect.

Mr Haberer accordingly expanded the bank's activities at breakneck speed. Too savvy to let itself appear partisan, Crédit Lyonnais extended its almost limitless-seeming credit (the bank's slogan was "the power to say 'yes'") to a cross-section of French business. It backed the Matra-Hachette defence and publishing conglomerate, Francois Pinault, then an entrepreneurial new-comer and now a department-store king, Canary Wharf, the ill-fated London docks project touted by Prime Minister Margaret Thatcher, and Bernard Tapie, the flamboyant French maverick entrepreneur and Mitterrand protégé who saw his credit grow unquestioned despite his increasingly conspicuous business difficulties.

To accelerate the bank's expansion, Mr Haberer acquired a string of subsidiaries and let them operate on a loose rein. Almost all lost money for the bank, especially Mr Haberer's personal choice, Altus Finance. According to a French government audit, Altus actually ran up losses between 1989 and 1993 in excess of 20 billion francs. But until 1993, Altus' results were concealed, apparently by false balance sheets, according to the recent government audit. Whether or not he realized what condition Altus was really in, Mr Haberer continued to extol Altus' CEO's performance, on one occasion famously calling him "the Mozart of finance".

Other clients of Crédit Lyonnais included Giancarlo Parretti, an Italian businessman who set up shop in Paris in 1989. He had started his career as a money man for the Italian Socialist Party in Naples, where he left a criminal record for fraud. Proof of his conviction in Italy was

[6] Fitchett, IHT, 3 Oct 1966

obtained by French parliamentarians in 1990. Parretti may have seemed like a gate crasher at a party but he came to occupy a large place in Crédit Lyonnais' lending – and eventually the downfall of the bank stemmed from its role in financing his ambitions to become a movie mogul in the United States. As described by Fortune, it was a colossal scam. In the space of two years, Mr Parretti extracted more than USD 2 billion from Crédit Lyonnais, much of it to pay for his extravagant lifestyle. The USD 9 million mansion in Beverly Hills, the brown Rolls-Royce, the private jet – all were paid for with Crédit Lyonnais money.

At that point, Crédit Lyonnais became the largest foreign investor in Hollywood. But the MGM takeover proved to be a deal too far and backfired almost immediately. Barely five months after he acquired MGM, Mr Parretti was confronted by disgruntled creditors who threatened to drive the studio into bankruptcy. The French bankers decided to oust Mr Parretti, a step that they considered dangerous enough to take armed guards to all their meetings with him.

In the end, Crédit Lyonnais got possession of MGM, the sole salvageable asset in the dealings. But the bank was stuck with a white elephant that it took four years to unload.

The MGM scandal provoked the investigations that uncovered the dimensions of the bank's overall losses.

In Paris, no one seemed to be counting as Crédit Lyonnais' investments foundered in sector after sector: not just in real estate, which has hurt most French banks, but also in the film industry, manufacturing and business ventures from US golf courses to waste disposal.

When the French government decided in November 1993 that the mounting losses could no longer be ignored, it raced to stem financial panic. A bailout plan was quickly announced by the Finance Ministry, and the bank's 8 million depositors and 13 000 employees were reassured about their savings and their jobs, while the chief executive, Jean-Yves Haberer, was replaced. Not a centime was to come from taxpayers. The crisis, it seemed, had been circumscribed. In fact, government officials eventually acknowledged that French taxpayers will have to foot the bill.

Today "Crazy Lyonnais", as the bank was called in the title of a recent book about its troubles, has become a symbol of financial disaster.

Mr Haberer's defence, stated during the 1994 hearings, is that he was only carrying out government orders in making foreign investments and putting money into ailing state-owned French industries. In a series of lawsuits and countersuits between Mr Parretti and Crédit Lyonnais, many cases have been settled out of court, with records sealed at what is reported to be the bank's insistence.

Mr Haberer, in his rare statements, has tried to distance himself from dubious decisions by his subordinates; in the parliamentary hearings, he said that he was unaware that the funds – which came from a Dutch subsidiary, Rotterdam-based Crédit Lyonnais Bank Nederland – were being funnelled through shell companies to disguise the amount of money going to a single customer, Mr Parretti.

Asked why he ignored a letter from the Dutch banking authorities admonishing Crédit Lyonnais to reduce its exposure to Parretti-controlled companies, Mr Haberer told the inquiry that he was too busy to keep tabs on every customer – even though Mr Parretti had by this time become the bank's largest single borrower.

The hearing was told that Mr Haberer ignored warnings from officials of other European countries that Mr Parretti was involved in unsavoury activities.

So at the end of the day, what caused the failure of Crédit Lyonnais? One factor is "megalo-mania", on the part of Crédit Lyonnais' management, and the other is "laxity in controls liable to foster abuses", according to the recent auditors' findings.

Megalomania in that rampant ambition and growth projects were not based on any meaningful analysis of the bank's historical areas of strength, or knowledge of the new areas of business it was entering, or indeed clear strategy. At this point, it is not even worth talking about prudent principles of credit management and risk exposure – such mundane concerns were subordinated to the megalomania creed of "being the biggest bank in Europe".

The management style at Crédit Lyonnais seems to have been more "aloof" than "monarchic". Managers had to stand during staff meetings to discourage tedious, pedestrian speeches liable to bore superior intellects. In practice, no one looked over Mr Haberer's shoulder. Cabinet ministers were too busy or did not dare, and his fellow mandarins in the bureaucracy obeyed a code of silence against calling into question the competence of a member of their caste.

1.3.4   Rumasa

The background details and chronology of this bank failure are based on interviews provided by Mr Peter Gooch, Publisher of the "Valencial Life" magazine.

Rumasa was a diversified holding company headed by a charismatic entrepreneur called Jose Maria Ruiz Mateos. Graduating with a professorship in Mercantile Commerce, Jose Maria Ruiz Mateos started work in the businesses of Jerez – sherry production. At this stage, he negotiated the biggest contract ever undertaken in the history of Jerez wineries, with the English company Harvey for a duration of 99 years.

He also managed to obtain the management of the export department of many Jerez manufacturers and that led him to the Barcelona wine makers and the vineyards of La Rioja, where he hammered out similar agreements.

Just six years later, the company Jose Maria Ruiz Mateos SA was worth over half a million pounds, and his brothers joined him in Barcelona to help improve his ever-expanding business interests.

The company grew to such an extent that by 1969 it had acquired 54 other companies producing 14 different product lines. As a result of these acquisitions, the Ruiz Mateos Company – now called Rumasa – soon started to have close links with the government of the day, and it was these links that enabled it to acquire the group's first bank – Banco Atlantico – in 1975.

In the seven years that followed up to 1982, the Rumasa empire spread and expanded, acquiring sherry companies, wineries, insurance companies, liquor manufacturers, as well as pharmaceutical companies, food producers, various hotel chains and nine banks. Another company that was bought by Rumasa was the giant Hispano Aleman construction company.

The company soon began expanding outside Spain, and obtained projects all over the Arabian and Latin American subcontinents. By the time it became an integral part of Rumasa, Hispano Aleman was carrying out 250 different works projects in 130 cities across 35 of the provinces of Spain as well as having building projects in Jeddah and Caracas. Hispano Aleman was also involved in the extension and remodelling of five football stadiums including those of Madrid, Barcelona and Seville.

Ruiz Mateos next set his sights on his most ambitious project to date – a chain of department stores. Ruiz Mateos managed to purchase the chain of Galerias Preciados stores, putting yet another feather in the Rumasa cap. This acquisition meant that just 22 years after his business career started in earnest, Jose Maria Ruiz Mateos and his Rumasa group controlled over 600 companies, employed 60 000 people, had an annual turnover of some £1250 million, with assets worth over £1000 million.

However, this long road towards conglomerateship did not come without critics, who were constantly decrying the business practice of Rumasa, alleging that it had no real assets at all.

They claimed that the group used one company as collateral when buying another, and that the entire empire was built up pyramid fashion, with the least little slip threatening the collapse of the whole, with subsequent disastrous consequences.

It was also claimed that the group was using its own banks to secure advantageous loans for mergers and acquisitions outside the norms established by Bank of Spain, which on more than one occasion demanded an accounting from Rumasa. This was almost always met with stonewalling on the part of the Rumasa directors, which did not sit well with the Bank of Spain, particularly as they believed that there existed a 150 000 million peseta 'hole' in the accounts that could cause innumerable problems in Spain.

In 1982, Mr Ruiz Mateos had his sights on another acquisition – another ship to join his Galerias Preciados chain. This was the branch that the US retailer Sears Roebuck had set up in Madrid's Calle Serrano, practically next door to the United States embassy. Rumasa offered what Sears considered a fair price. There was one proviso, however. Sears wanted payment in the United States in dollars, and while Rumasa did not balk at this condition, it sent alarm bells ringing in the corridors of government as such an acquisition would require governmental approval, and a further permission was required to export so much money from Spain.

In talks with the Prime Minister at the time, Leopoldo Calvo Sotelo, Mr Ruiz Mateos was told of the rumour that it was expected that the upcoming elections would be won by the new Socialist Party headed by Felipe Gonzalez, and that as a result any international dealings of the kind envisaged by Rumasa should be put on hold until after the elections.

Falling back on a mixture of Andalucian pride, his own personal self esteem which is considerable, and the belief in the very power the Rumasa group represented, Mr Ruiz Mateos ignored all the warnings and went ahead with the deal.

Unfortunately for Jose Maria Ruiz Mateos, he was to be proved wrong, for if the Rumasa group viewed the new Socialist government as a group of dunderheads, Mr Gonzalez and his first Finance Minister Miguel Boyer thought that Rumasa was a hotbed of far-rightist thinking as well as a left over from the days of General Franco – whose ideals Mr Ruiz Mateos embraced – and as such should be stopped.

It was late on the evening of 23 February 1983 when Eduardo Sotillos, the official government spokesman disrupted the late night TV news to read an official statement:

> The Government, in order to guarantee fully several bank deposits, jobs, and third party rights, which it considers to have been gravely threatened, has approved a Royal Decree of Law of the Expropriation of the banks and other companies that make up the Rumasa Group. The reasons for this decision that was made at today's Cabinet meeting are the considerations of public utility and social interest as set out in Article 33.3 of our Constitution. In this way, the State Patrimony will take charge of the businesses, thus absolutely assuring the rights of both the depositors and employees.

By this time, the Rumasa empire had turned into a holding of 700 companies. To get some idea of the size of the conglomerate, it had some 31 different companies in the tourist sector, such as hotel and travel agencies; 11 in agriculture; 8 in food production; 21 banks (with 1300 branches); 56 drinks manufacturers; 4 insurance companies; 15 financial service companies; the Almacenes Jorba and Galerias Preciados chains of department stores; 3 mining companies; 8 construction companies; 85 real estate companies; 1 publicity agency; 19 commercial companies in various sectors; 2 chemical companies; 4 textile companies; 2 boat manufacturing companies; and 65 other companies.

At the time of expropriation, the company employed 65 000 people on direct contracts, and 300 000 people worked indirectly for Rumasa. Annual sales volume reached 350 000 million pesetas (or 2% of Spain's GNP at the time), and a net worth of 650 000 million pesetas.

The expropriation of Rumasa sent shock waves through practically every Spanish business, as many thought that they might be next on the Socialist hit list. The directors of several of these companies also expressed disbelief at the measures stating that it was hardly in line with the newly democratic country that Spain had just become.

Following the Expropriation Order, the entire Rumasa empire was handed to a government administrator, Javier del Moral, who was put in charge of selling off the various bits that had been expropriated. The conditions of sale of the Rumasa components met with widespread criticism, as the sale prices were allegedly far lower than the value of the businesses, but that is another story.

1.4   THE MACROECONOMIC ENVIRONMENT

1.4.1   Banking system and industry risks

While conventional banks worldwide face similar operating risks, there are also enormous differences in the function and organisation of banking systems. For example, the USA has 9000 banks, while several large industrialised countries have only 10 or fewer major banks.

No country has ever designed a banking system from the ground up or implemented a banking system from a textbook. Banking systems are the result of historical events: they reflect national differences and ongoing evolutionary processes. The risks faced by banks in any given country will accordingly be greatly influenced by the structure of the banking system.

For example, US banks in the 1920s and 1930s faced enormous risks in the areas of liquidity and speculation in securities due to the combination of commercial banking and securities trading activities under one banking structure. This resulted in traditional depositors being exposed to the more speculative trading activities undertaken by their bank on the financial markets.

The Depression in the 1930s resulted in the US government enacting the Glass-Steagall Act, which forbade commercial banks to engage in securities trading, effectively splitting the banking function into "commercial banking" and "investment banking" (e.g. Morgan Guaranty being split into JP Morgan, the "commercial bank" and Morgan Stanley, the "investment bank"). US commercial banks in the 1950s by comparison faced negligible risks in these areas.

In Europe, by contrast, the division between investment banks and commercial banks was never enshrined in law because Europe never implemented a series of measures as did the USA in the 1930s, and the relationships between banks and major industrial groupings were different.

The point is that despite increasing globalisation and the implementation of convergence such as standardised capitalisation ratios, "banking" can vary considerably from one country to another, and gaining a clear perspective on this issue (not to mention communicating it to someone else) can be exceedingly difficult.

A detailed explanation of the history of a banking system in a given country is the starting place, when identifying the role of banks versus other financial intermediaries in the economic system. In some countries, commercial banks may provide only short-term working capital financing, while in others they may be a short-term lender, long-term lender and provider of equity.

Some of these distinctions may result from regulatory legislation; however, to a large degree they have been influenced by the distribution of wealth in the society, and the patterns through which the holders of wealth have channelled their resources into capital investment. These distinctions will affect not only the risks which banks face, but the type of credit facilities which it may be appropriate to extend to them based on their role in the economy.

Within the definition of conventional banks, there usually exist numerous categories of banks which are formally (or informally) recognised based on common factors such as:

- Function (commercial/savings/cooperative)
- Ownership (government/public/private/foreign) and
- Scope (international/national/regional)

The number of categories will vary in each country, but an overriding objective should be to identify specific groupings of banks which serve different roles in the economy and which will be treated differently by the regulatory authorities. These groupings should be compiled carefully, for they will be the basis for subsequent comparative analysis.

Specific categories might be the "big five" or the "eight major regionals", or whatever is appropriate to the particular environment. However, in the case of bank failure, there should be a distinction drawn between banks of national importance which "cannot fail" (e.g. Crédit Lyonnais, the French clearing bank which was "bailed out") versus banks of "lesser" stature (e.g. Al-Saudi Bank, a French-based consortium bank which was allowed to fail) whose existence is not critical to the country's economy or its international reputation. As the size of banks increases via mergers and the potential costs of bailouts increases, it becomes increasingly important to draw the distinctions between the "too large to fail" and "not too large to fail".

In defining the different categories of banks, the customary and permitted activities of each category should be identified, including topics such as the following:

- Lending versus investing activities
- Length of commitments (how long are loan maturities being taken or extended?)
- Lending policies (e.g. trade financing versus capital expenditure financing)
- Foreign exchange activities
- Legal system's treatment of banks – use of security agreements, guarantees, etc. as well as their effectiveness and enforceability in practice (i.e. how much clout do banks have – do the courts strongly protect their rights or do they favour the delinquent debtor?)
- Funding sources, interbank markets
- Degree of cooperation among banks – are there certain "members of the club" (and certain non-members)? Is there a banking cartel or is there cut-throat competition?

It may be necessary to cover some topics on an individual basis if there are substantial differences among banks within the same category, or perhaps the number of categories should be expanded.

As stated previously, banking systems are always evolving; they possess dynamic characteristics. The specific aspects (and accompanying risks) must be considered on a country-by-country basis, this would include an evaluation of the following elements:

- Concentration – the number of conventional banks is shrinking through mergers and acquisitions. The future will undoubtedly bring a smaller number of larger banks.
- Internationalisation – banks in general are expanding their geographic scope.
- Universal banking – the distinctive functions of different categories of banks (e.g. commercial, savings, cooperative) are eroding as banks offer wider ranges of services previously available only at a different category of bank.

This should not be considered an exhaustive list, but if these trends are evolving gradually and steadily in a given country, the overall banking environment may be very favourable. However, if such changes are taking place quickly and chaotically, the risks must be identified as the environment could prove hostile to some institutions.

1.4.2 Economic environment

While country risk issues are addressed later in this book (Chapter 6), certain elements of country risk analysis are worth mentioning here since the policies, regulation, and administration of the economy have a profound effect on the behaviour and success of its banks.

The loan portfolio of a conventional bank will often represent a cross-section of the economy as a whole; however, concentrations in speculative sectors as we have seen contribute frequently to bank crises. Real estate lending, for example, has been seen as a panacea to cure thin margins and overstaffing costs. In France, for example, many banks dived headlong into the "lucrative" real estate market in an effort to compensate for their inefficient structures; when the oversaturated real estate market collapsed, provisioning and managing this situation became a real drag on French banking profitability despite efforts to discount the gravity of the situation.

As a result, speculative sectors (or depressed regions) should be identified so that banks with portfolio concentrations in these sectors can be examined with greater than usual care (and whether banks in depressed areas are more likely to receive support from the regulatory authorities).

Macroeconomic conditions have other implications as well. The volatility of the money supply and ability for depositors to shift their savings into more remunerative instruments are factors which will impact the liquidity position of banks.

Hence, certain risks to banks are indeed external rather than internal, but it would be dangerous to overrely on this viewpoint. While a strong economy can assure the success of almost all banks, a sole ailing bank can hardly blame all of its problems on a troubled sector of the economy. The economy may be a large contributing factor, but poor credit decisions usually constitute a larger contributing factor.

1.4.3 Industry competition and its impact on banks

The impact of harmonised capital ratios, cross-border trading, and unified trading blocs lowering internal barriers such as the EU, the implementation of the Euro enabling a unified pan-European market in large ticket syndicated loans and debt issues, the increasingly generic nature of banking products due to harmonisation trends in the business as well as impact of information technology hardware/software systems all point the way to increasing competitiveness across a "level playing field". Moreover, the cost savings and restaffing trends in banks arising from these issues all point the way forward to a dynamic, indeed tempestuous, climate for banking.

While great emphasis is placed on analysing banks from a financial viewpoint in order to understand the future health and viability of these banks, it is vitally important to place this trend in context of the business environment in which banks operate.

What does all this mean? Simply put, it means that banks are increasingly required to focus on issues of competitivity and customer satisfaction.

In other words, instead of purely focusing on capital adequacy ratios or loan recovery rates or industry portfolio concentration, one should also focus on the bank's strategy in terms of market position, and mergers and acquisitions as competitive issues.

1.4.4   Technology

Similarly, the use of and investment in information technology – both for "dashboard functions" (analysing product lines and profitability and exposures in real time) as well as "competitive advantage" functions (use of client-based accounting systems as well as traditional accounting-based systems for improved market targeting) – should not be overlooked. The bank which boasts of saving costs by cutting down on IT and management control systems may indeed well be heading towards deep trouble. And this will not be reflected in any set of ratios or accounts in the annual report.

In an increasingly homogenised marketplace, competitivity will increasingly be found in the adoption of appropriate information technology and customer relationship management – centric databases and systems.

Therefore, it is best to know intimately how the bank functions in its home market, how it keeps track of its domestic activities as well as international activities, and whether it can monitor exposures across the board of all its subsidiaries on a real-time basis so that management decisions (e.g. optimally effective asset liability management policy) can be taken quickly and effectively, and effective measures adopted if required.

Indeed, the author recalls having to compile exposure reports from a major bank's overseas network manually from a pile of disorganised microfiches, computer printouts, and telexes. Running a bank with such archaic systems is like trying to fly an aircraft blindfolded with no instruments.

It is important to establish if the bank has a hostile or friendly attitude to IT issues or indeed is aware of them, as this can give clues as to how forward looking the bank's management is in assessing the future. Indeed while the investment in such systems and staff retraining are large, the competitive advantage achieved in virtually all cases more than offsets the investment in such systems.

2
The Rating Framework

You know, Mom and Pop can read these public documents, and it seems that what we are learning from all of this is that there is really not much value-added for the average investor in looking at either what the analysts are saying or what the raters are doing; that when you have a complex set of documents, that you don't really go behind the documents, even though you have a right to.[1]

The ratings agencies track record as seen by the *Figaro*, 3 June 2002

2.1 WHAT IS A RATING?

A rating is an assessment by a rating agency of the likelihood of a borrower's making timely repayment of principal and interest on a debt security. It is therefore a measure of credit risk in a particular issue of securities. Standard & Poor's (S&P), Moody's, and Fitch (the Fimalac-Euronotation-ICBA-Fitch-Duff & Phelps-Thompson Bankwatch collective) are the best known rating agencies.

While ratings typically concern risk assessment of banks, corporates, and some of their debt instruments, ratings are also issued to countries and supranational entities.

Note that a rating is not a recommendation to buy a security and the agencies stress that it should be only one factor in an investment decision. As stated the rating is based upon the

---

[1] Sen. Fred Thompson, Rating the Raters: Enron and the Credit Rating Agencies, United States Senate Hearing Before the Committee on Governmental Affairs, 20 March 2002.

rating agency's view of the future ability of an issuer to make timely payment of principal and interest, the nature and provisions of the specific obligation and the level of legal protection afforded to the holder in the event of bankruptcy or other events affecting creditors' rights.

A rating is usually awarded with respect to a particular issue, allowing for its specific terms and conditions. A rating does not measure liquidity, market, trading or foreign exchange risks and ratings are subject to change, suspension or withdrawal at any time.

2.2   THE DEVELOPMENT OF RATINGS

John Moody established a rating system for railroad bonds in 1919, while S&P has been rating long-term debt since the 1930s and commercial paper since 1969.

US investors have placed considerable emphasis on a reputable and credible rating system. Ratings are required for borrowers accessing the US domestic market.

Until the 1980s, the rating of non-US companies was limited to those seeking to borrow on the US domestic markets. Non-US issuers quickly found that a rating was a prerequisite for gaining access to US investors.

In the last decade, the growth of the international capital markets has seen ratings become widespread for many different nationalities of issuers as name recognition may no longer be enough to attract international investors.[2]

Ratings are used by borrowers to gain ready recognition from investors, by investors to make an assessment of the quality of individual securities and of their portfolios, and by banks as a marketing tool to help sell paper to potential investors.

The use of credit rating agencies by financial regulators[3] forms part of their efforts to fulfil their obligations to protect investors and regulate the banking system. As we saw in the previous section, however, there is healthy debate on whether they are effective in doing so.

2.3   BACKGROUND TO RATING AGENCIES

Credit rating agencies have received a lot of press coverage lately, in large part due to the extravagant claims made by the rating agencies regarding the high degree of professionalism and the importance of the public service role attached to their pronouncements. The gap

---

[2] Frank Partnoy, University of San Diego School of Law, Law and Economics Research Paper No. 20. The Paradox of Credit Ratings, Chapter IV: "Beginning in the mid-1970s, the credit rating industry began to become more influential and more profitable. The changes were dramatic. In 1980, there were 30 professionals working in the S&P Industrials group (even by 1986, there still were only 40); today, S&P and Moody's employ thousands of professionals In 1975, only 600 new bond issues were rated, increasing the number of outstanding rated corporate bonds to 5,500; today, S&P Moody's rate 20,000 public and private issuers in the US, $5 trillion of securities in aggregate. Perhaps the most important change in the credit rating agencies' approach since the mid-1970s has been their means of generating revenue. Today, issuers – not investors – pay fees to the rating agencies. Ninety-five percent of the agencies' annual revenue is from issuer fees, typically 2 to 3 basis points of a bond's face amount. Fees are higher for complex or structured deals."

[3] US Securities and Exchange Commission Report on the Role and Function of Credit Rating Agencies in the Operation of the Securities Markets as Required by Section 702(b) of the Sarbanes-Oxley Act of 2002, Section 2B, Jan. 2003: "The term 'NRSRO' was originally adopted by the Commission in 1975 solely for determining capital charges on different grades of debt securities under the Net Capital Rule . . . Over time, as marketplace and regulatory reliance on credit ratings increased, the use of the NRSRO concept became more widespread. Today, NRSRO ratings are widely used for distinguishing among grades of creditworthiness in federal and state legislation, rules issued by financial and other regulators, and even in some foreign regulations. The Commission itself has incorporated the NRSRO concept into additional areas of the federal securities laws . . . In addition, Congress has incorporated the NRSRO concept into a wide range of financial legislation . . . Finally, a number of other federal, state, and foreign laws and regulations today employ the NRSRO concept . . . In addition, several state insurance codes rely, directly or indirectly, on NRSRO ratings in determining appropriate investments for insurance companies. And the use of the NRSRO concept has occurred in foreign jurisdictions."

between these claims and actual performance has resulted in a reassessment of their role by the public and regulatory authorities.[4,5]

Critics have a demonstrably different opinion of their actual market performance and surrounding issues of professionalism and utility. Rating changes, for example, occur so often that one wonders whether they are an indication of future ability to repay debt or an indication of that morning's newspaper headlines.[6]

Industry research undertaken by the Japan Centre for International Finance, Cantwell and Co., Frank Partnoy, Christoph Kuhner, and Andrew Fight has looked at the rating agencies from various viewpoints. There are several key questions, controversies, and shortcomings affecting the role of credit agencies as reliable predictors of bank and sovereign risk, for example:

- How are rating agencies defined?[7,8]
- Declining informational value of ratings versus record profits[9]

---

[4] E.g. see SEC: http://www.sec.gov/rules/concept/33-8236.htm; Concept Release: Rating Agencies and the Use of Credit Ratings under the Federal Securities Laws (Release Nos 33-8236; 34-47972; IC-26066; File No. S7-12-03) Question 16: Should the size and quality of the credit rating agency's staff be considered when determining NRSRO status? Should the Commission condition NRSRO recognition on a rating agency adopting minimum standards for the training and qualifications of its credit analysts? If so, what entity should be responsible for oversight of qualifications and training? How could the Commission verify whether a member of a rating agency's staff is or was previously subject to disciplinary action by a financial (or other) regulatory authority?

[5] Section 702(b) of the Sarbanes-Oxley Act of 2002 requires the US Securities and Exchange Commission to prepare a report re the credit rating agencies as follows (extract of Act).

Sec. 702. Commission Study and Report Regarding Credit Rating Agencies.

(a) Study required.–

(1) In general.–The Commission shall conduct a study of the role and function of credit rating agencies in the operation of the securities market.

(2) Areas of consideration.–The study required by this subsection shall examine–
    (A) the role of credit rating agencies in the evaluation of issuers of securities;
    (B) the importance of that role to investors and the functioning of the securities markets;
    (C) any impediments to the accurate appraisal by credit rating agencies of the financial resources and risks of issuers of securities;
    (D) any barriers to entry into the business of acting as a credit rating agency, and any measures needed to remove such barriers;
    (E) any measures which may be required to improve the dissemination of information concerning such resources and risks when credit rating agencies announce credit ratings; and
    (F) any conflicts of interest in the operation of credit rating agencies and measures to prevent such conflicts or ameliorate the consequences of such conflicts.

(b) Report required.–The Commission shall submit a report in the study required by subsection (a) to the President, the Committee on Financial Services of the House of Representatives, and the Committee on Banking, Housing, and Urban Affairs of the Senate not later than 180 days after the date of enactment of this Act.

[6] See Graciela Kaminsky and Sergio Schmukler, Rating Agencies and Financial: Markets, in *Ratings, Rating Agencies, and the Global Financial System*, edited by Richard M. Levich, NYU Stern, p. 234 "for example during 1990–2000, Brazil received 10 rating changes, Indonesia 13, South Korea 18, Russia 18, and Thailand 10. Moody's changed their ratings 48 times, S&P 75 times, and the smaller Fitch 47 times". These ratings concern long-term sovereign debt but seem to be managed on a short-term basis.

[7] Investment Company Institute letter dated 2 March 1998 to Mr Jonathan G. Katz, Secretary, Securities and Exchange Commission, www.ici.org/statements/cmltr/98_sec_nrsro_defin_com.html, Re: Proposed Definition of Nationally Recognized Statistical Rating Organization (File No. S7-33-97): "...In particular, the proposed amendments would for the first time include within Rule 15c3-1a formal list of attributes to be considered by the Commission in designating rating organizations as NRSROs." These proposed amendments were never adopted.

[8] See, e.g., Testimony of Isaac C. Hunt, Jr, Commissioner US Securities and Exchange Commission, concerning the role of credit rating agencies in the US securities markets before the Committee On Governmental Affairs, United States Senate, 20 March 2002, http://www.senate.gov/~gov_affairs/032002hunt.htm: "In 1994, the Commission did, however, issue a concept release soliciting public comment on the appropriate role of ratings in the federal securities laws, and the need to establish formal procedures for designating and monitoring the activities of NRSROs...The Commission received 25 comment letters, which...recommended that the Commission adopt a formalized process for approving NRSROs." These proposed amendments were never adopted.

[9] Frank Partnoy The Siskel and Ebert of Financial Markets? Two Thumbs Down for the Credit Rating Agencies. A sample of articles from *The Economist* is representative. See, e.g., Credit-Rating Agencies. AAArgh!, ECONOMIST, Apr. 6, 1996, at 80; Credit-Rating Agencies; Beyond the Second Opinion, ECONOMIST, Mar. 30, 1991, at 80; Rating the Rating Agencies, ECONOMIST, July 15, 1995, at 53; Room for Improvement: Ratings Agencies, ECONOMIST, July 15, 1995, at 54; Sovereign Debt; The Ratings Game, ECONOMIST, Oct. 30, 1993, at 88; The Use and Abuse of Reputation, ECONOMIST, Apr. 6, 1996, at 18."

- Opaque methodologies[10]
- No link between ratings and default rates[30]
- Staff turnover and poor service[20]
- Ratings as a post ipso facto phenomenon[11]
- Monopoly[12]
- Predatory pricing[13, 14]
- Unaccountability[15]

To name just a few. This is fully treated in Andrew Fight's book *The Ratings Game* as well as in other research papers by Partnoy and Kuhner regarding the declining informational value of ratings, which are largely based on publicly available information. We look at some of these background issues before considering the rating framework and its pitfalls, and why bank failure still catches everyone "by surprise".

2.3.1   Inconsistent initial foundations

The story concerning the process of appointing ratings agencies as NRSROs goes back to 1970.

In 1970, the Penn Central Railway Co. filed for bankruptcy. Wall Street broker dealers were holding a lot of Penn Central commercial paper and were caught by surprise. This is because the National Credit Office, a subsidiary of Moody's parent Dun and Bradstreet, had more than 600 commercial paper ratings outstanding. All of them were rated prime, the highest rating available to the short-term debt issue.

---

[10] Frank Partnoy, University of San Diego School of Law, Law and Economics Research Paper No. 20, The Paradox of Credit Ratings, Chapter IV: "The agencies never describe their terms or analysis precisely or say, for example, that a particular rating has a particular probability of default, and they stress that the ratings are qualitative and judgmental. This secretive, qualitative process is not the type of process one would expect if the agencies had survived based on their ability to accumulate reputational capital."

[11] Japan Centre for International Finance Characteristics and Appraisal of Major Rating Companies 1999 Focusing on Ratings in Japan and Asia, p. 57 "... only downgraded sovereign ratings when it was obvious the crisis was spreading".

[12] Andrew Fight, *Ratings Game*, pp. 8–11: "The duopoly does not foster competition since there is a tendency for issuers to obtain multiple ratings – eg: ratings from Moody's and S&P. Accordingly, a competitive situation cannot be said to exist since the choice is not to 'get a rating from one or the other' but, 'let's get rated by both in order to satisfy our creditors' needs'. The duopoly is hence sharing a monopoly and has no risk of losing market share to their competitor (each other)... Issuers are often accused of 'rating shopping' if they go to agencies other than Moody's or Standard & Poor's to obtain a recognised rating. The purpose of rating shopping is to get the best possible rating from a rating agency. This suggests that the rating agencies are by no means rivals trying to squeeze each other out of the market. They in fact make clear that the agencies complement each other. If an issuer is already being rated by an agency, rating by another agency helps to make him happier with the first rating. Further ratings thus remove doubts, not only from the investor's perspective."

[13] The Department of Justice has investigated the possibility of anti-competitive practices in the bond rating industry, including the use of unsolicited ratings. See, e.g., Suzanne Woolley *et al.*, Now It's Moody's Turn for a Review, *Business Week*, 8 April 1996, at 116; The Use and Abuse of Reputation, *supra* note 9, at 18; Credit-rating Agencies. AAArgh!, supra note 9, at 80. Moody's also has been sued privately on similar grounds. In October 1995, Jefferson County School District, a local authority in Colorado, filed a lawsuit accusing Moody's of "fraud, malice, and wilful and wanton conduct" for publishing a "punishment" rating on the district's bonds, because the district did not hire the agency to rate it.

[14] See Ibrahim Warde, *Rating Agencies: The New Superpowers?* (visited 30 Nov. 1998); <http://www.idrel.com.lb/idrel/shufimafi/archives/docs/iwarde1.htm>. Issuers typically invite a rating agency to rate their debt, although Moody's has rated debt uninvited. For example, in September 1996, Moody's announced it was preparing to issue an unsolicited rating of Egyptian government debt. See id. Egypt immediately hired Goldman, Sachs to help it comply with certain requirements and ultimately received a very low rating of Ba2, behind Israel, Tunisia, and Bahrain, although ahead of Jordan. The Egyptian minister of state for economic affairs said, "[a]lthough it is better than no rating, it does not reflect the true strength or potential of the Egyptian economy. I am looking forward to soon having another rating from a different agency to put this right". Id.

[15] Investment Company Institute letter dated 2 March, 1998 to Mr Jonathan G. Katz, Secretary, Securities and Exchange Commission, www.ici.org/statements/cmltr/ 98_sec_nrsro_defin_com.html, Re: Proposed Definition of Nationally Recognized Statistical Rating Organization (File No. S7-33-97): "In addition to being free from all but minimal government regulation, the rating agencies are also relieved of any legal accountability for their ratings. NRSROs are shielded from expert liability under Section 11 of the Securities Act if their ratings appear in a securities prospectus."

The resulting panic got the SEC thinking. Rival agencies including Standard & Poor's and Moody's had introduced a credit ranking system into their work in the commercial paper market but the system had not caught on. Who would want to run the risk of a lower credit rating when the National Credit Office was certain to award a Prime rating?

In 1975 the SEC made its first and biggest mistake. In that year, under the Securities and Exchange Act of 1934, the commission adopted Rule 15c3-1, in the net capital rules. Under the rules, broker dealers, when computing net capital, were required to deduct a certain percentage or "hair cut" of the market value of their proprietary security positions.

But the commission also adopted certain qualifications to the rule. Among others, broker dealers' proprietary positions in commercial paper, non-invertible debt securities, and non-invertible preferred stock would be accorded "preferential treatment" if the instruments had been rated "investment grade" by at least two "nationally recognised statistical rating organisations" (NRSROs). In other words, they would get a shorter "hair cut".

The commission did not attempt to define what an "NRSRO" was, but three rating agencies – Moody's, Standard & Poor's, and Fitch – were given the honour.

From such modest beginnings, the use of credit ratings for regulatory and self-regulatory purposes has proliferated rapidly, both within and without the SEC, and in US legislation at the national and state level.

2.3.1.1   What is an NRSRO?

> **Box 2.1**
>
> "NRSRO" is the acronym used in rule 2a-7 to stand for a "nationally recognised statistical rating organisation" as per paragraph (a)(17) of rule 2a-7, as amended. NRSROs are designated as such by the Commission's Division of Market Regulation through the no-action letter process for purposes of the Commission's net capital rule (17 CFR 240.15c3-1).
>
> In more mundane terms, NRSRO status confers upon the agency a quasi official role as one of the "official rite of passage" players for any entity accessing the capital markets in the USA. The mere fact there is a mere handful of NRSROs means that they are all practically guaranteed a slice of the economic pie (as there will always be a need for more than merely two players) and they are in a virtually unassailable oligopoly.
>
> They are in effect de facto market regulators but not agencies of the US government nor are they subject to any particular regulatory control of aspects, for example, such as the qualifications and knowledge of their analysts, either by educational qualifications or some sort of examination such as a bar examination a lawyer is required to pass. The clear inadequacies of the NRSRO nomination and control process lead one to pose the thorny question *"Quis Custodiet Ipsos Custodes?"*
>
> Because of this, NRSRO status has taken on more and more the aspect of a basic condition to be met by rating companies for entry into the US market, as illustrated by IBCA's complicated machinations to enter the market first on its own, and later via expensive acquisitions of second tier US rating agencies, in order to avail itself of the NRSRO status.

By modifying the Investment Company Act of 1940, the commission had incorporated NRSRO terminology to distinguish the types of security that may be issued using simplified registration procedures. In 1991, worried about the stability of money-market funds, the commission put strict credit limits on securities eligible for investment by such firms. Only securities rated in one of the two highest categories for short-term debt by the requisite number of NRSRO would be eligible.

In other words, obtaining a rating became a virtual prerequisite for issuers seeking to access the financial markets. Competition cannot, however, be said to exist due to the spectre being accused of rating shopping[16] or vulnerability to unsolicited ratings.[14,13]

This dependence has also spread to Congress. Struggling with a rapid growth in the mortgage-backed securities market, Congress sought in 1984 to define a mortgage related security. Among other things, it concluded that mortgage related securities must be rated by at least one NRSRO. Again, there was no attempt to define the term.[17]

In the meantime, state authorities, self-regulatory organisations, and great swaths of the US mutual-fund industry have adopted ratings to define, control, and advertise risk appetites and investor behaviour.[18]

All this has occurred without actually defining what an NRSRO is or what the admission criteria are. In other words, the entire foundation of the edifice is based on ambiguous elements.

The SEC's actions have had two main consequences:

- For issuers, particularly in the US Public Markets, obtaining a rating is now practically mandatory. Moreover, because from the very outset the SEC has limited and controlled the number of agencies qualifying for NRSRO status, the agencies' business is closely protected. One could describe it as an oligopoly or "closed shop" with exceedingly high entry barriers,[19] hence not a competitive market. Under the wings of the SEC, the rating agencies have grown in status and influence. "In 1968, we had maybe half a dozen analysts", recalls O'Neill who joined Standard & Poor's in April of that year. "Today, we've got 1200 employees and 15 offices around the world."
- The transformation of the global financial markets, growth in cross-border capital flows, privatisation, and shift from debt-to equity-based modes of financing have all served to fuel this growth in demand for ratings.

With the decline of the traditional bank credit officer, the rating agencies have stepped in to fill the gap in credit analysis. Moreover, many banks are using ratings as a way of delegating (or outsourcing) responsibility and shedding credit department staff.

Together these two secular trends have served to stimulate the growth witnessed in the rating industry.

Nevertheless, in 1975, the SEC gave its chosen agencies an authority, a purpose and, best of all, a captive market: "We used to joke that SEC recognition was a license to print money", recalls one former Moody's analyst. "This is a government sanctioned oligopoly, and the barriers to entry are becoming higher and higher every year."

It is also an oligopoly that is imposing its ideological model and modus operandi in Europe and Asia leading to accusations of the USA "McDonaldising" the planet to the detriment of local cuisines.

But the underlying ambiguity of the NRSRO status continues to remain unresolved like the proverbial "which came first, the chicken or egg" riddle.

---

[16] See note 12, supra.
[17] See note 7, supra.
[18] See note 3, supra.
[19] Lawrence J. White, p. 46, The Credit Rating Industry: An Industrial Organisation Analysis, in *Ratings, Rating Agencies, and the Global Financial System*, edited by Richard M. Levich, NYU Stern: "Regulation, then, is currently limiting entry . . ."

2.3.2 Secretive deliberations

In "Two Thumbs Down for the Credit Rating Agencies" by Frank Partnoy (*Washington Quarterly*), Partnoy notes that the rating agencies could not have maintained their position unless there was no competition over the last 50 years, hence, an oligopoly.

To quote Partnoy:

> The process agencies use today to generate ratings does not provide any obvious advantages over those used by competing information providers and analysts. If agency processes are not unique, one would expect the agencies to do their best to protect these processes from public view. In fact, both Moody's and SP make ratings determinations in secret. The agencies never describe their terms or analysis precisely or say for example that a particular rating has a particular probability of default and they stress that the ratings are qualitative and judgemental.
>
> This secretive qualitative process is not the type of process one would expect if the agencies had survived based on their ability to withstand investor scrutiny in a competitive market. On the other hand, one might expect such processes to thrive in a non competitive market; if the rating process had been public or quantitative (rather than secret and qualitative), other market entrants could have duplicated the rating agencies' technology and methodology.
>
> Consider for example SP or Fitch procedures – when the agency is asked to rate a new bond, representatives of the issuer meet with the agency's analysts and disclose facts they believe are relevant to the rating. After three weeks, the analyst submits a report to a rating committee of up to 10 professionals. The committee meets in secret and then votes. If the lead analyst's recommendation is overruled and he or she protests, the matter can be referred to an "internal appeals court". The issuer can also appeal if it is not satisfied with the rating.

Since the time horizon on a default is longer than getting fired for an "uncooperative and unhelpful attitude", it is clear the analyst has no incentive to buck the trend unless he is enamoured of quixotic ventures. It is difficult to imagine how such a lengthy process could generate timely, valuable information.

S&P and Moody's moreover, have high levels of staff turnover and limited upwards mobility[20,21]. Both agencies have modest salary levels and limited upward mobility.

As Partnoy notes, it is questionable whether any agency could have sustained a dominant reputation for 60 years in a competitive environment, given such a process and organisational structure.[22]

2.3.3 Main source of revenues

Perhaps the most important change in the credit rating agencies' approach since the mid-1970s has been their means of generating revenue.

What this means is that the rating agencies operate in a highly profitable[23] monopoly[24] which is protected by the SEC with tremendous entry barriers.[25,26] For example, Moody's has

[20] Partnoy, Paradox of Credit Ratings, University of San Diego Law School Research Paper No. 20, pp. 11–12: "Both S&P and Moody's have high levels of staff turnover, modest salary levels and limited upward mobility; moreover, investment banks poach the best rating agency employees. These factors limit the ability of rating agencies to generate valuable information."
[21] Richard House, Ratings Trouble, *Institutional Investor*, Oct. 1999, at 245: "Both S&P and Moody's have high levels of staff turnover, modest salary levels and limited upward mobility; moreover, investment banks poach the best rating agency employees."
[22] Partnoy, p. 653.
[23] Senate Committee on Governmental Affairs Report on Credit Rating Agencies, p. 105: "The NRSRO designation has had a significant beneficial effect on the profitability of credit rating agencies."
[24] See note 12, supra.
[25] White, p. 46: "Regulation, then, is currently limiting entry . . ."
[26] Ibid.

operating margins of nearly 50%, more than triple those of other financial services firms, and Moody's financial ratios are more than double those of other firms. Moody's market capitalisation is more than 10% of Goldman Sachs', even though Moody's assets are only 0.1% of Goldman's.[27] Annual rating industry revenues in aggregate are in the range of a billion dollars.

Today, issuers, not investors, pay fees to the rating agencies. This means that the rating agencies derives the bulk of revenues from issuers who need to pay for a rating in order to access the international financial markets, and that the revenues they raise from "selling research" is practically non-existent, in large part due to the factors mentioned above – the information is stale and behind the curve and investors requiring quality research pay market analysts in investment banks.

Hence, the ratings agencies have no more added value than analysts in any investment or commercial bank. Investment banks moreover are on to this. For some investors, the agency's word is a rubber stamp and nothing else as the following quote testifies:

> Most city analysts don't think much of rating agencies is the truth of the matter – they use rating agencies as an insurance device," one seasoned market watcher said. "If things go sour, the pension fund administrator can say we checked with the rating agency and they gave it a clean bill of health, in other words it is not our fault.[28]"

Ninety-five per cent of the agencies' annual revenue is from issuer fees, typically two to three basis points of a bond's face amount. Moody's and S&P have aggressively expanded and now receive most of their revenue from the corporations they rate. Fitch also charge fees to issuers.[29]

Although investors are not paying directly for rating agencies to rate the securities they buy, issuers who pay for ratings pass on the costs of those ratings to investors by paying a lower return on debt issues.

Economically rational issuers will not pay more for a rating than the expected benefit of the rating. Therefore, the issuer must expect that the rating–and the informational content associated with the rating–will lower the issuer's cost of capital by at least the cost of the rating. Put another way, issuers must expect that they are able to save at least two to three basis points on an issue by having an agency rate it.

Issuers also may consider the expected costs of receiving a negative unsolicited rating (this is when a rating agency decides to rate you even if you don't want the rating as a heavy handed inducement to "cough up the ratings fees" in an effort to get a higher "paid for" rating). Yes, it's a protection racket, especially since Moody's makes you pay for the difference but then does not distinguish between the two in its literature as it maintains "they are of equal quality". So why pay? you may ask. Simple – if you're already the focus of a rating agency's attention, you may as well limit the damage.

It is doubtful that issuers (and therefore investors) receive two to three basis points' worth of informational value from a rating. For an issue of modest size, say USD 100 million, the new information from the rating would have to be worth at least USD 20 000. For the multi-trillion dollars of issues rated in aggregate, the information generated by the agencies–if it is in fact information that issuers (and therefore investors) are paying for–would have to be worth approximately one billion dollars.

---

[27] Moody's Corp. 10Q Statements.

[28] BBC News Online, 1 Feb. 2002, Who knew what? http://news.bbc.co.uk/2/hi/business/1786509.stm, Friday, 1 Feb. 2002, 10:03 GMT.

[29] Frank Partnoy, University of San Diego School of Law, Law and Economics Research Paper No. 20, The Paradox of Credit Ratings, Chapter IV: "Perhaps the most important change in the credit rating agencies' approach since the mid-1970s has been their means of generating revenue. Today, issuers – not investors – pay fees to the rating agencies. Ninety-five percent of the agencies' annual revenue is from issuer fees, typically 2 to 3 basis points of a bond's face amount. Fees are higher for complex or structured deals . . . "

The rating agencies' analyses are based on information in the public domain and therefore have little value added, as one Moody's employee admitted:

> Largely, the financial information on which we base our ratings is publicly filed information . . . We also have meetings with the issuers, who may choose to share issues with us, it is up to them, they will choose their level of disclosure.[28]

The fact of the matter is, that information does not reflect this value. Indeed, the whole informational value argument goes out the window in the light of market research which confirms that financial investors do not hold great confidence in the rating agencies' pronouncements. So why do issuers pay to get rated. Simply put, because they have to. It's an entry ticket to the financial markets – a toll so to speak.

2.3.4   Generating value

How could credit rating agencies generate information of such enormous value in a competitive market, given their limited resources? Credit rating agencies do not independently verify information supplied to them by issuers, and all rating agencies get the same data.

The rating agencies claim it is how they interpret such information that draws distinctions among them in how they rate debt. These claims at best are dubious, given the above points on personnel movements, salary levels, publicly available information, "secret deliberations" that do not stand the light of scrutiny, etc.[30] As they do not disclose this information on their methodologies.

While some investors no doubt have a blind faith in the ostensible infallibility of the rating agencies, such opaqueness (and chequered track record) in the cut and thrust of the financial services industry certainly would not have stood the test of market credibility had the situation not been a government sanctioned oligopoly.

Despite the fact that there are no obvious interpretive techniques unique to rating agencies, it is undeniably true that rating agency profit margins are high. Although the two largest agencies are subsidiaries of public companies and therefore do not publish separate operating results, McGraw Hill's financial services division has had an operating margin of 29%, and Moody's numbers are thought to be similar. Such margins could not have been sustainable over time in a competitive market.

The above discussion demonstrates two points inconsistent with the reputational capital view:

* First, the view of credit rating agencies as prospering based on their ability to accumulate and retain reputational capital does not explain all of the dramatic changes in the value of ratings over time; it is not plausible that four rating agencies have risen (or fallen) together in lock-step based on their collective ability (or inability) to generate valuable credit information.
* Second, during two critical periods – the 1930s and the mid-1970s through the 1990s – credit ratings increased in importance, each instance paradoxically followed by a series of bond defaults demonstrating the rating agencies' serious mistakes in rating bonds.

---

[30] Fight, p. 244: "The ratings agencies' arguments defending the accuracy of their ratings, based on accumulated historical data of ratings and default rates, are not as quantitative as one might believe. The argument is based on the premise that there is continuity in their research. For this argument to be scientifically consistent and applicable over the entire time frame in question, this would mean that the analytical tools used to analyse economic risks today are exactly the same as those used 30, 40, or 50 years ago, and that today's economy is not more complex or volatile or technologically more sophisticated than it was in the past. Since this is obviously not the case, it means there is no substance to the rating agencies' argument that the strength and accuracy of their ratings are based on the consistency of historical correlation data between ratings and default rates over the time frame of ratings activity because you cannot compare today with the 1950s or 1960s. Each fundamentally different period was analysed using essentially different yardsticks."

The obvious solution as expounded in the book *The Ratings Game* and in Partnoy's article is simple – eliminate the regulatory dependence on credit ratings and let investors assess the risks and bid accordingly on the securities.

Indeed, the SEC seems to have caught onto the problem, as its approach to approving rating agencies as NRSROs has created an anticompetitive situation. For example, Michael Macciaroli, associate director of the SEC's division of market regulation, has admitted the SEC "used to do all this ad hoc [and] it only became a problem when these franchises became more valuable as ratings became encapsulated into the capital-raising function". This statement Partnoy notes (Two Thumbs, p. 712) is a startling admission by a senior and respected SEC official that credit rating agencies are selling valuable regulatory licences.

2.3.5   Growth and the future

From the mid-1970s to today, the growth in credit rating agencies has exploded. The oligopoly (Moody's, Standard & Poor's, Fitch) hence is not competing but sharing a lucrative monopoly, especially since issuers tend to avail themselves of multiple ratings in an effort to reassure the market.

The question is therefore not "Moody's" or "S&P", but "Moody's AND S&P".[12]

The modern credit rating agency is more influential and profitable than at any time this century despite the fact that the rating system hasn't changed in any substantial manner since the 1930s.

Why the sudden growth then? Simply because growth correlates to the SEC granting of NRSRO status, although the defining criteria have never been articulated by the SEC (advantageous if the goal is to block the road to foreign rating agencies!). From such an inconsistent foundation, the term NRSRO has crept into US legislation at the national and state level to the point that the entire US capital markets have become dependent upon a concept that no one has ever defined! Constructive ambiguity indeed! And for the shareholders of these privately owned entities, a highly profitable constructive ambiguity!

Adding further interest to this conundrum is the matter of professional qualifications. For not only has the concept of the NRSRO never been defined, there is no formal training, educational qualification, or professional qualification required or qualifying one to become a rating analyst.

Unlike Certified Public Accountants (CPAs) who certify (and assume a legal responsibility on) the financial statements they have audited and stated to be in conformance with good accounting practice, rating analysts do not have any formal qualifications, do not sign off on statements, nor do they have a legal responsibility to stand behind the opinions they proffer although issuers are legally required to get a rating if they access the US financial markets. Finally, rating analysts work for companies that emit opinions with disclaimers denying all responsibility for the accuracy of information contained in their reports. In other words, a risk-free monopoly position with no legal or professional accountability.

As to progress, the rating scales and methodologies are substantially unchanged since the 1930s (see Table 2.1) which begs the question as to how relevant the model is to today's diversified global economy.

Most interestingly, Moody's, S&P and Fitch are all wholly owned subsidiaries of much larger investment or information and publication corporate parents – Moody's is a subsidiary of Dun and Bradstreet, S&P a subsidiary of McGraw Hill and Fitch of Fimalac. Their status as subsidiaries means not only that they are not required to disclose detailed financial

Table 2.1

Moody's	S&P/Others	Meaning	
Aaa	Aaa	Highest quality	
Aa1	AA+	High quality	
Aa2	AA		
Aa3	AA−		
A1	A+	Strong payment capacity	
A2	A		
A3	A−		
Baa1	BBB+	Adequate payment capacity	
Baa2	BBB		
Baa3	BBB−		INVESTMENT GRADE
Ba1	BB+	Likely to repay: ongoing uncertainty	SPECULATIVE GRADE, NON-INVESTMENT GRADE
Ba2	BB		
Ba3	BB−		
B1	B+	High risk obligations	
B2	B		
B3	B−		
	CCC+	Vulnerable to default, or in default	
Caa	CCC		
	CCC−		
Ca	C	In bankruptcy, or default	
Moody's has no D rating	D		

Source: Partnoy, p. 650.

information about their earnings, revenues, and costs, but also that they do not require credit ratings themselves!

Rating agencies, however, have other uses. The current occupier of the White House, Mr George W. Bush, delivered a National Security Speech in 2002 where he confirmed that the entire arsenal of power available to the USA would be used to foster the development of "market efficient" economies (given US criticisms of the Japanese, French, and German economic models, one assumes "market efficient" means US-style economies). Power includes economic as well as military tools, and it could just be that rating agencies are a tool of the US government in pushing to define the rules of the international financial system and leverage its position in the globalisation agenda. This is why, for example, USAID sponsored the establishment of a credit rating agency in Poland or that Moody's (who has fought tooth and nail for its right to express ratings opinions under the freedom of speech provisions of the US constitution) meekly decided to withdraw ratings on Iran because it was "inconsistent" with the current US Administration's policy![31]

It is to be hoped that other rating agencies be organised in other financial centres, such as the EU, setting up its own euro-based network of euro rating agencies rating euro issues (and appointed by the ECB), and reciprocate the mandatory rite of passage exercise implemented

[31] BBC News article of 3 June 2002, http://news.bbc.co.uk/2/hi/business/2023568.stm, Iran dropped by US rating agency: "International rating agency Moody's has withdrawn its sovereign credit ratings for Iran after pressure from the US Government. President George W. Bush has claimed Iran is part of an 'axis of evil' and has continued to impose economic sanctions."

by the SEC for those accessing the US financial markets. Implementation of the euro means that this is a particularly precipitous time to effect this measure. However, this would require the French speaking bureaucrats in Brussels to wake up and adopt a technique developed in the Anglo Saxon economies, most likely an unacceptable loss of face exercise despite the tangible economic benefits of doing so.

Moreover, for the sake of international credibility, the board of directors of Fimalac, the French parent company of Fitch-IBCA, the self-styled "international agency", may need to wake up to cultural issues outside of France and realise that while running a company like a medieval fiefdom and having one's live in partner collect a USD 10 million bonus for a job valued at USD 50 000 may be considered the "dernier cri" fashion accessory in French business circles,[32] international institutional investors and regulatory agencies will be well interested in questioning the professional competence, business acumen, and ratings reliability of an acquisition-driven rating agency with a corporate culture blending incomprehensibly high salaries to live in partners combined with predictive rating failures in the Asian meltdown. We would like at this point to categorically deny having ever met trainee analysts – related to African ministers being offered scholarships to Harvard's School of Government by rating agencies.

Insiders in the ratings business, however, won't be surprised, as it is commonly known that the Geckoesque Ladreit de la Charrière and his live-in pal Morali are complete outsiders and parvenus to the ratings business – latter-day equivalents to gate crashers in a party. Indeed, Fimalac's efforts to apply pressure on the SEC to obtain NRSRO status by having fellow RPR pal Jean Artuis (Minister of the Economy in the Juppé government) lobby the SEC met with failure, thus obliging de la Charrière to buy his way into the coveted NRSRO regime by paying over the odds to buy NRSRO Fitch. What the folks at Fimalac are realising is that gate crashing a party is one thing, getting to stay is another. No doubt the SEC's ongoing deliberations as to the role of credit rating agencies in the global securities markets in the wake of the Sarbanes-Oxley Act should provide interesting developments.

Table 2.1 shows rating quite similar to the table of rating from 1930.

2.4   THE RATING ANALYTICAL FRAMEWORK

Understanding bank financial statements is an essential part of the analysis process. Financial statements for banks are relatively standardised in presentation although accounting practices as well as the level of disclosure may vary from country to country.

Although financial statements in most countries are prepared in accordance with Generally Accepted Accounting Practice (GAAP), or International Accounting Standards (IAS), they can vary considerably in content and presentation. Balance sheets and income statements for banks, however, usually follow a standardised presentation. Examining what lies beneath that presentation, however, is what provides the main challenge.

---

[32] *Financial Times*, Wednesday 30 July 2003, Questions Raised over Fitch's Credibility, by Jo Johnson in Paris, published: 30 July 2003: "Concern for the reputation of Fitch Ratings, the world's third-largest credit rating agency, is triggering boardroom unrest within the secretive holding company which owns it, the *Financial Times* has learnt. Fitch is owned by Fimalac, a Paris-based industrial and financial services conglomerate." "The trigger for the boardroom unrest was the discovery in June of an €8.7m ($9.98m) bonus payment to Véronique Morali, Fimalac's operating officer. Mrs Morali is vice-chairman of Fitch France and live-in partner of Mr Ladreit de Lacharrière, founder of Fimalac and chairman of Fitch Ratings." "Asked whether the French group was an appropriate owner of a rating agency, one Fimalac director said: 'No, no, no. It is run like a private company.' Fitch Ratings, he said, risked being accused of hypocrisy in opining on the credit-worthiness and corporate governance of other companies when the boardroom practices of its own parent company were so open to parody." "A rating agency should be beyond all reproach," he said. "As soon as I read that, I said to myself, 'Oh no, not this'," said one Fimalac director. "I know that she's been useful, but she is not a Fitch executive. She's just a link person and her value is more like $50,000 a year."

After all, with the difficulties and accounting shortcomings witnessed in the numerous corporate scandals of 2002–03, this highlights the importance of not relying on straightforward financial ratio analysis but rather investigative research as to what lies behind the numbers.

In the USA, financial statements for banks are published in a standardised document known as the "Uniform Bank Performance Report". For banks operating in a variety of countries, their statements will have to be recast in a standardised spreadsheet format which will provide the relevant information.

In the past, bank analysts would receive annual reports and recast them into standardised templates known as spreadsheets. This was a manual and time-consuming process as all of the numbers had to be tracked down in the annual report and manually reconciled.

Now, electronic databases such as the Bankscope CDROM have come into existence. Bankscope provides the financial statements of 9000+ banks in a standardised presentation. While such a tool is a powerful one, enabling historical, peer group analyses, ratio analyses, comparative studies, etc., it poses two problems, at least in the case of bank failure.

- The first one is that the information is relatively stale and so while such data may be useful in running historical trend and peer analyses, it will not reveal the present condition of the bank, which can rapidly succumb to the conditions of interior rot characteristic of problem banks.
- The second is that by relying on outside information, the bank analyst in his bank is not personally undertaking the financial analysis himself and the bank could therefore be accused of not directly practicing its process of credit assessment and due diligence.

The accounting practices defining various account categories, however, may be non-standard and an effort to identify them and highlight the issues should be noted whenever appropriate. Therefore, when spreading bank financial statements, it is a good idea to carefully consider what the accounts actually represent.

The classic approach to bank analysis can be greatly facilitated by placing it within a framework which Moody's rating agency has summarised with the acronym CAMEL.

The CAMEL approach basically emphasises the principal aspects which are of concern in assessing a bank's stability. Before treating the subject of analysing a bank's financial accounts, we shall examine the CAMEL approach in some detail.

Although there is a tendency of viewing the CAMEL elements as independent (e.g. a bank may be described as having "strong capital but poor asset quality"), these elements should be viewed as interrelated variables in assessing a bank's overall safety and soundness.

It should be noted that if a banking institution has significant subsidiaries (brokers, leasing, etc.), the consolidated statements of the group are also an important analytical tool. In addition to an analysis of the bank's financial statements are added those of the group, its principal subsidiaries, and any other significant participations. We shall examine each of these concepts below:

- Capital
  - strong capital base
  - high capital adequacy ratio
  - high quality shareholders
- Asset quality
  - diversification of loan portfolio
  - no excessive loan growth
  - return on loan (product) appropriate to risk

- good, clearly stated credit policy
- low/Adequate provisions (but realistic)
- country risk spread well
- Management
  - management experienced
  - honesty and integrity
  - well-regulated environment
  - good spread of technical and management skills
  - clear and logical strategy
  - size and market reputation
  - well-trained staff
  - good internal/external communication
  - long-term relationships
  - competitive rates
  - high quality service
- Earnings
  - high ROA and ROE
  - stable income stream/little exceptional items
  - good trend/track record of profits
  - controlled expense/income ratio
  - high dividend payout potential
- Liability management
  - stable customer base
  - loans and funding well matched
  - good liquidity

2.4.1 CAMEL, CAMEL B-COM, and CAMELOT

CAMEL has lately loaded up on new options, with CAMEL B-COM in the UK (for CAMEL + Business + Commercial Organisation and Management Risk) and CAMELOT in the USA (CAMEL + Operating + Treasury). It may just be a matter of time before JOE CAMEL makes an appearance (Just in time Operational Equilibrium + CAMEL). If so, say you saw Joe here first.

The Bank of England had already developed its new CAMEL B-COM risk framework (Capital, Assets, Market risk, Earnings, Liquidity and Business risk and Control, Organisation and Management) following the Arthur Andersen Report which had reviewed its supervisory practices after the collapse of Barings in 1995. The objective is to identify and measure all of the main categories of risk (on both a quantitative and a qualitative basis) and generally to set the total risk generated by a particular firm (its CAMEL B) against its control or management capability (COM).

One important development announced by the FSA is its general move to supervision by risk (rather than by firm or function). This will involve extending the more comprehensive supervision by risk initially developed for use in the banking area to all other financial market sectors.

The FSA is working on the development of a new, more general risk-based, supervisory process as part of its proposals to create an appropriate supervisory and regulatory authority for the new millennium. This approach is based on earlier work carried out in connection with the construction of the RATE (Risk Assessment, Tools of Supervision and Evaluation) framework for the supervision of authorised banks.

2.4.2 Capital

Capital, capital adequacy, or solvency, is the measure to which an financial institution's portfolio and business risks are adequately offset with "risk capital" (i.e. equity) available to absorb potential losses. A high level of capital can help an institution ride out a protracted downside cycle, adopt more aggressive strategies, and take larger risks with the possibility of larger returns while a lower level of capital reduces management's decisional flexibility. Capital adequacy is also important because it is the primary measure by which regulatory authorities gauge an institution's financial health.

Hence, in order to assess the appropriate level of capital, it should be viewed as it relates to the bank's business: credit risk, market risk, off-balance sheet (contingent liabilities) risk, and business risks. Accordingly, you should assess the factors which should be included in a bank's true economic capital: net worth, loan loss reserves (specific and general), other reserves, perpetual debt, hidden reserves, hidden assets, and undervalued securities and participations (the "Cooke Ratio", which is discussed elsewhere) are an attempt to define a minimal common basis for assessment but, based on the regulatory variations in effect, it is useful to include other variables in the assessment process.

Box 2.2

Bank capital adequacy – key analytical questions

Bank credit analysts should ask themselves key questions when attempting to assess a bank's capital adequacy:

- **Is balance sheet growth outpacing growth in equity**? If the bank's asset base is growing faster than its equity, this can lead to higher leverage and risk. Asset growth should be analysed in relation to equity growth as well as asset growth of peer group competitors. Rapid asset growth can also be an indicator of a lax credit policy.
- **What is the quality of capital**? It is important to identify the key shareholders as this may provide an indication of future support if the bank experiences difficulties. Secondary capital should not exceed 50% of total capital as per the Basle Capital Adequacy guidelines.
- **How does the bank fund itself?** Does the bank have ready access to the financial markets or back-up lines of credit from other banks? Does the bank rely heavily on interbank funding? Who are the main shareholders and do they have the means to inject capital if necessary?
- **What is the bank's dividend policy?** Is the bank retaining adequate levels of retained earnings? If the bank is paying out over 50% of its net income as dividends, this can be indicative of problems – first because the bank will be weakening its capital position but also because to rectify this, further share capital increases will be required, resulting in share dilution. Looking at peer group averages in the country can provide a useful yardstick.
- **How does the bank fit into the national/international banking system**? What is the size of the bank? How does it rank by total assets and equity? Is it a money centre, regional, or local bank? Where do the major competitive pressures lie? How does the bank's capital and profitability ratios compare to peer group competitors?

2.4.3   Asset quality

Asset quality is the most important as well as most difficult element of bank analysis, as it is highly subjective. The majority of bank failures are due to poor quality of "risk assets". The greatest risk in having exposure to a bank is that it can have substantial unrecognised asset quality problems which are not apparent in its accounts and which could eventually crystallise and cause it to fail. Asset quality problems can stem from a variety of causes, we consider six examples:

- **Crocker Bank** in the USA illustrates the case of poor asset quality. The CEO of Crocker wanted to "run the biggest bank in America". Large incentives (and salary bonuses) to corporate "relationship managers" (salesmen) encouraged an expansion of loans of dubious quality. This ultimately resulted in Midland Bank, a major minority shareholder, having to take full control of Crocker, remove the chief executive and, at some cost, restoring the bank to health.
- **Crédit Lyonnais** similarly suffered from a multiplicity of ailments including growth in glamorous albeit unfamiliar areas (film finance) and major branch expansion (planting the flag), in a desire to be the "biggest European universal bank". The resulting massive losses were estimated by *Le Canard Enchaîné* at FFr 9000 for every French taxpayer. The bailout of the bank will have cost French taxpayers well over FFr100 billion (USD 16.9 billion) and possibly more like FFr150 billion.
- **Schroder Munchmeyer Hengst** illustrates the risk in asset concentration, or the principle of not putting all one's eggs in the same basket. This principle has at times been forgotten or ignored by imprudent bankers. Schroder Munchmeyer Hengst, which was one of the most respected German merchant banks, went bust by lending more than its total net worth to one company which went bankrupt.
- **Rumasa (Ruiz Mateus SA)** provides another example of asset quality problems (twinned with autocratic management). Rumasa was a Spanish holding group involved in tourism, construction, banking, and exporting port wine. Rumasa Bank, the group's inhouse bank, overlent to "sister industrial companies" within the "Rumasa Group" and was found guilty of contravening Spanish banking rules. This is a problem that is often encountered in emerging markets where cash-rich trading companies establish in house banks, do not have the requisite banking skills and lend excessively back to their shareholders, be they individuals or companies when they encounter more difficult trading conditions.
- **Penn Square Bank** in Oklahoma (and subsequently Continental Illinois Bank in Chicago) both went spectacularly bust in 1981. Penn Square recklessly concentrated in its lending to the oil exploration industry in Oklahoma and Continental Illinois bought into Penn Square's loans, effectively subordinating its credit policy to the junior Oklahoma bank with the attitude that "If Penn Square thinks it's OK, then we can go in". When the exploration finance resulted in a series of dry wells in the Anadarko basin, Penn Square collapsed, as did Continental. Even Chase Manhattan got stuck with dud loans based on the "Continental precedent".
- **Country concentration** has been problematic for banks lending cross-border to countries with economic difficulties. Libra Bank, Eula Bank (Euro-Latinamerica) and 10 other UK consortium banks lending excessively to Mexico, Brazil and Argentina in the 1980s had to discreetly "close down" when these countries were unable to repay their debts. Similarly Moscow Narodny in London lost in one year more than its equity base when its huge concentration of Russian lending was written down.

The main difficulty in assessing a bank's asset quality is due to the fact that accounting is by nature an activity whose assessments, particularly of the quality of loans which may not be experiencing difficulties at the time of the audit, are subjective. Furthermore, management's allocations of provisions for potential loan losses, based on "experience" is inherently subjective and therefore difficult for auditors to assess. Therefore, the analyst's ability to assess a bank's stability based on financial statements is equally subjective. How can we therefore assess asset quality?

Indicators of risk-asset quality can be obtained from two areas:

- The bank's credit-risk management culture
- Assessing the overall quality of the loan portfolio

Credit risk management is important because it gives an indication of how a bank manages its risk-asset portfolio exposure. These factors basically relate to concentration risks (country as well as industry sector concentration), as well as the reporting systems which enable the bank's management to know its exposure to companies and industry sectors on a global basis. You should also establish whether a bank has a system of classifying its exposure on a risk rating basis for companies as well as countries, whether this forms an integral part of the credit approval process and, if so, how effective the system has been in managing exposure problems in the past. Such information will not be in the bank's annual report and will therefore have to be gained via contact with the bank's management.

Evaluating overall quality of the loan portfolio is somewhat more subjective. However, as noted in the previous section, quantifiable early warning signals do exist and these should be examined when attempting to assess asset quality.

Box 2.3

Credit policy
Some questions you may want to ask yourself about a bank's credit policy which may not appear in financial statements and other such documentation:

- Does the bank have a formal credit policy with written guidelines (credit approval process, approval criteria and procedures, exposure guidelines, reporting guidelines, non-performing loans criteria and recovery methodologies)?
- What role do the bank's internal auditors play and how independent are they? What is their reporting line – to head of marketing and lending or to the bank's board of directors?
- Who is responsible for loan review – loan marketing staff or an independent credit department not subject to marketing pressures?
- Who is responsible for managing loan review and documentation and monitoring?
- Is there a formal lending policy manual in existence?
- What is the bank's policy on limits re industry sectors, outstandings, risk ratings, geography, currency, and tenor? Has this been formally articulated?
- How does the bank handle maturity and interest rate risk? Does the bank have an asset-liability management committee? How often does it meet, what reports does it use, and what is its authority?

2.4.4   Management

One of the most important and yet most subjective areas of bank analysis is the evaluation of management. While one can make certain generalisations about management behaviour, it is important to realise that banks often emerge from different cultures or sectors of the economy and are hence unique entities with their own individual qualities, characteristics, and problems.

Evaluating bank management should therefore be undertaken in relation to the bank's operating environment and credit approval culture. A bank may have all the trappings of a developed sophisticated institution and meet with failure; conversely, a bank may operate in a lesser developed country and yet practise prudent and responsible management.

Management, although highly subjective, is often considered a key issue in understanding the creditworthiness of a bank. This is typically manifest in the area of problem loans where poor management is shown usually to be a main factor in the demise of any bank. It is therefore somewhat surprising that generally, credit presentations made in banks either ignore management issues or treat them superficially. Why is this?

Probably because assessing management is "political" – there are no quantitative ratios or yardsticks to use in rationalising one's opinion. It calls for superior interpersonal skills in questioning, listening, and forming an opinion. Additionally, the banker cannot always understand the full context of a bank's background and operational context, especially if the analyst is sitting at a desk in one country and the bank is in another.

Yet it is often the most important or revealing part of bank credit analysis, as numerous recent bank failures illustrate.

The basics of management assessment are summarised below and subsequently treated in further detail:

* Who are they?
* Where are they now and where do they plan to go?
* Do they have a credible plan to get to where they want to go?
* Are they capable of executing the plan?

2.4.4.1   Who are they?

Banks are typically required to disclose who their directors are in the annual company accounts. Examination of a few years' accounts will reveal if there is any significant turnover at board level. The report and accounts usually do not give much additional information. What sort of information do we require? We need to know how much relevant experience each key member of the management team has. And we need to know how these people are appointed. Lack of relevant experience or cronyism often causes difficulties and can indicate the absence of a coherent business strategy.

Rumasa has already been considered in terms of asset quality problems; this case, however, is closely linked to the quality, nature, and structure of the management. A less incestuous structure might have yielded different results.

The next items to examine are the breadth and depth of management. By management breadth we mean a well-balanced management team – not dominated by the CEO, nor comprised solely of salesmen ("relationship managers"). Also, are the key managers all persons whose prime professional qualification is kinship with the head of state or one of his offshoots?

It is also important to know how the bank's management behaves in the face of risk. On the one hand, a company needs risk takers who can cope with change in the marketplace through innovation. On the other hand, lenders may well want to avoid a management which is prepared to stake the whole future of the bank on the outcome of one event such as a major acquisition, or soaring profitability of, say, the real estate sector (e.g. French banks) or, say, the "Singapore branch" (Barings).

Allied to this concept is the management's outlook. Is it a short-term view at the expense of long-term prospects or vice versa? Or does the company's management achieve the required balance. Finally, we need to know how good the management is at monitoring actual performance to stated objectives and adopting corrective measures (the feedback mechanism).

Questions relating to asset liability management strategy and tools, loan provisioning policies, credit limit policies, accounting for non-performing loans, and investment in computer technology are areas for questioning.

Many banks have failed through inept management (or tacit disregard) of credit control procedures or basic lack of qualified lending bankers. This often occurs when politicians rather than bankers make lending decisions, which is a phenomenon not only in command/post-communist economies but also in developed markets such as Europe and Japan. A rigorous independent credit function is key to assuring asset quality; however, the credit function is not perceived as a revenue centre and accordingly is poorly placed in the power apparatus to influence decision making until it is usually too late. The collapse of Johnson Matthey Bankers, for example, was due to bad lending, and lending decisions not being reviewed by the board of the bank.

In a major review of US bank failures by the Office of the Comptroller of the Currency management lending policies were cited as the major cause in 81% of failed banks.

2.4.4.2   Where are they now and where do they want to go?

Having assessed "who they are", you can then move on to management strategy. Any strategy is affected by the starting position. The industry analysis and competitor assessment is an excellent way to address the first part of the question, i.e. "where are they now?" You also need to find out the management's own perspective of the bank's position. Is there a vast difference between peer group analyses and market positioning, and the management's perspective of their position? If so, you may have certain reservations about the appropriateness of the bank's management strategy.

Having established where the bank is presently positioned, the final part of the question is "where do they want to go?" Economic theory would suggest that every company is attempting solely to maximise shareholder wealth. In reality, many other objectives creep in, either as additional objectives or even replacement objectives to maximising shareholder wealth. You must find out what a bank's overall mission statement is and how clear the corporate objectives are.

2.4.4.3   Do they have a good plan to get there?

You need to examine and understand the bank's future plans or strategies in terms of the "CAMEL" matrix:

- Capital (funding base)
- Asset quality and provisions
- Management (strategy, marketing, controls)
- Earnings (growth, composition of)
- Liquidity (ALM)

You must be satisfied that not only is the plan for each area realistic, but that all the plans can be achieved simultaneously and coherently. Each functional plan should be consistent with the corporate mission statements and the assumptions the management makes about its environment, its industry, its competitors and itself, and should be a development of the company's current strategy.

The decision making and control process is of crucial importance because most bank failures are the result of faulty policy decisions accumulating over a long period of time, which eventually all come to a head. You will want to know who makes credit decisions, and how they are made. Can single individuals make large loans? What is the internal control system like? Are loans extended on an informal basis without any legal documentation being drafted prior to disbursement (you may be surprised to know that this has been known to happen in banks that have failed, BCCI being a case in point!). Is there a limit to loans to single borrowers such as the US concept of the Legal Lending Limit?

2.4.4.4   Are they capable of executing the plan?

Your answer to this last question will depend on the nature of the plan and your assessment of the people concerned. The appropriateness and realism of management plans and strategy can often be better understood in the context of historical financial performance and peer group analyses. In the end, these can augment your ability to judge character.

2.4.5   Earnings

Earnings, or profitability, is the ultimate measure, the "bottom line" in assessing the financial performance of an institution. This measures an institution's ability to create shareholder value and, by adding to its storehouse of resources, maintain or improve capital soundness. It is also a quantitative measure of management's ability to achieve success in the critical areas of asset quality, overhead control, and revenue generation. In analysing profitability, it does not suffice to compare it to historical performance indices, the quality of the earnings stream should also be assessed. Does the bank have a diversified earnings stream or does it have particular dependence on a specific activity? Which areas of the bank have historically generated the bulk of profits: merchant banking fees, FX trading, or loan fees? These all represent sources of revenue in addition and separate to those of the loan portfolio's interest income, and should be included in the assessment.

2.4.6   Liquidity (liability management)

Liability management, also known as "asset-liability management" or "liquidity", is an important element of the overall assessment of the bank's soundness. This involves analysing liquidity and interest rate sensitivity. Illiquidity is often the primary factor in a bank's failure, whereas high liquidity can help an otherwise weak institution to remain funded during a period of difficulty. Liquidity is therefore important, especially in assessing smaller banks, or banks which may not have a large retail depositor base and are obliged to fund themselves on the interbank markets. In assessing liquidity therefore you want to look at an institution's ability to fund itself under periods of stress. For example, does the bank have substantial undrawn but committed lines of credit in the event existing depositors retire their funds?

This is best measured by the degree to which core assets are funded by core liabilities, or to state the inverse, the extent to which the bank is reliant on "confidence-sensitive" funds to finance illiquid assets. You should therefore examine the bank's funding base and view this in light of the bank's asset structure.

Interest sensitivity analysis is an assessment of the degree to which changes in short-term interest rates can impact the profitability of an institution due to maturity mismatch. For example, is a bank which extends loans maturing in three to five years funding itself with one month interbank deposits, or does it have a strong retail base of depositors? Similarly, is the bank in a misaligned position and exposed to currency mismatch risk? You should endeavour to asses the bank's policies in managing its asset-liability and currency matching policies (with respect to tenor, fixed vs floating, and currency).

2.5 HOW THE RATING AGENCIES ANALYSE BANK RISK

2.5.1 What is a rating?

Traditionally, a rating is an assessment by a rating agency of the likelihood of a borrower's making timely repayment of principal and interest on a debt security. Standard and Poor's (S&P), Moody's, and Fitch (the Fimalac-Euronotation-ICBA-Fitch-Duff & Phelps-Thompson Bankwatch collective) are the best known bank rating agencies.

One ratings agency, for example, state that their ratings:

provide an opinion on the ability of an entity or of a securities issue to meet financial commitments, such as interest, preferred dividends, or repayment of principal, on a timely basis. These credit ratings apply to a variety of entities and issues, including but not limited to sovereigns, governments, structured financings, and corporations; debt, preferred/preference stock, bank loans, and counterparties; as well as the financial strength of insurance companies and financial guarantors.

A rating is usually awarded with respect to a particular issue, allowing for its specific terms and conditions. The rating of a senior unsecured debt obligation may only be used as a general measure of a borrower's overall credit quality.

In terms of country risk, a bank cannot have a higher rating than the country where it is located. However, although ratings are now widespread outside the US, they are not a prerequisite for a successful international issue.

Credit ratings are used by investors as indications of the likelihood of getting their money back in accordance with the terms on which they invested. Thus, the use of credit ratings defines their function:

• "Investment grade" ratings indicate a relatively low probability of default.
• "Speculative" or "non-investment grade" categories either signal a higher probability of default or that a default has already occurred.

Rating agencies stress that their ratings imply no specific prediction of default probability. Most credit rating agencies issue a standard disclaimer regarding their ratings. The following disclaimer from Fitch's promotional literature is fairly standard:

Fitch Ratings credit and research are not recommendations to buy, sell, or hold any security. Ratings do not comment on the adequacy of market price, the suitability of any security for a particular investor, or the tax-exempt nature or taxability of any payments of any security. The ratings are based on information obtained from issuers, other obligors, underwriters, their experts, and other sources Fitch Ratings believes to be reliable. Fitch Ratings does not audit or verify the truth or accuracy of such information. Ratings may be changed or withdrawn as a result of changes in, or the unavailability of, information or for other reasons.

Our program ratings relate only to standard issues made under the program concerned; it should not be assumed that these ratings apply to every issue made under the program. In particular, in

Table 2.2   Symbols of the principal rating agencies

Fitch	Moody	Poor	Standard	Majority interpretation
AAA	Aaa	A**	Al+	Highest
AA	Aa	A*	Al	High
A	A	A	A	Sound
BBB	Baa	B**	Bl+	Good
BB	Ba	B*	Bl	Fair
B	B	B	B	Somewhat spaculative
CCC	Caa	C**	Cl+	Speculative
CC	Ca	C*	Cl	Highly speculative
C	C	C	C	Extremely speculative
DDD		D**	Dl+	Low or weak
DD		D*	Dl	Small or very weak
D		D	D	Practically valueless

the case of non-standard issues, i.e. those that are linked to the credit of a third party or linked to the performance of an index, ratings of these issues may deviate from the applicable program rating.

Credit ratings do not directly address any risk other than credit risk. In particular, these ratings do not deal with the risk of loss due to changes in market interest rates and other market considerations.

There are many types of ratings for various categories of entities and the debt instruments they issue. Broadly, they can be spilt into two categories

- Issuer ratings refer to general creditworthiness of an issuer.
- Issue credit ratings refer to the relative preferential position of the holder of the security and reflect the terms, conditions, and covenants attaching to that security.

Some rating agencies such as Fitch moreover use "individual" and "support" ratings.

2.5.2   Rating scale comparisons

Ratings are based upon information from sources the rating agency considers reliable, including in some cases unaudited information.

Following the assignment of ratings, regular information is required from issuers in pre-scribed forms. If this information changes or is not available, the rating may be changed, suspended or withdrawn. Rating agencies provide regular information issuers under review and recent changes in gradings.

The cost of gaining and maintaining a rating can be considerable, so that issuers have to weigh the cost against the savings in yield and the more unquantifiable benefit of widening the investor base. All things being equal, a rated issue should trade at a lower yield than an unrated issue of similar credit quality.

Table 2.2 summarises the various rating as of 1929.

2.5.3   Standard & Poor's ratings

Standard and Poor's long-term and short-term debt ratings scales are summarised in Table 2.3.

Table 2.3

Standard & Poor's Long Term Debt Ratings

AAA	The highest rating assigned by Standard & Poor's. Capacity to pay interest and repay principal is extremely strong.
AA	A very strong capacity to pay interest and repay principal and differs from the highest rated issues only to a small degree.
A	Debt rated A has a strong capacity to pay interest and repay principal although it is somewhat more susceptible to the adverse effects of changes in circumstances and economic conditions than debt in higher rated categories.
BBB	An adequate capacity to pay interest and repay principal. However, adverse economic conditions or changing circumstances are more likely to lead to a weakened capacity to pay interest and repay principal than in higher rated categories.
BB	Debt rated BB and below is regarded as having predominantly speculative characteristics. The BB rating indicates less near-term vulnerability to default than other speculative issues. However, the issuer faces major ongoing uncertainties or exposure to adverse economic conditions which could lead to inadequate capacity to meet timely interest and principal payments.
B	Indicates a greater vulnerability to default than BB but currently issuer has the capacity to meet interest payments and principal repayments. Adverse business, financial or economic conditions will impair capacity or willingness to pay interest and repay principal.
CCC	Denotes a currently identifiable vulnerability to default and dependence upon favourable business, financial and economic conditions to meet timely payment of interest and repayment of principal. In the event of adverse business, financial or economic conditions, it is not likely to have the capacity to pay interest and repay principal.
CC	The rating CC is typically applied to debt subordinated to senior debt that is assigned an actual or implied CC rating.
C	Typically applied to debt subordinated to senior debt which is assigned an actual or implied CC Rating.
C1	The rating C1 is reserved for income bonds on which no interest is being paid.
D	Borrower is in default. The UDU rating is also used when interest payments or principal repayments are expected to be in default at the payment date, and payment of interest and/or repayment or principal is in arrears.

From AA to B a + or − may be added to give two further gradations of risk for each letter.

Source: Standard & Poor's International Creditweek.

Standard & Poor's Short Term Commercial Paper Debt Ratings

A1	The degree of safety regarding timely payment is either overwhelming or very strong. Those issues determined to possess overwhelming safety characteristics are denoted with a plus (+) designation.
A2	Capacity for timely payment is strong. However, the relative degree of safety is not as high as for issues rates A1.
A3	A satisfactory capacity for timely payment, though somewhat more vulnerable to the adverse effects of changes in circumstances than obligations carrying the higher designations.
B	Only an adequate capacity for timely payment. However, such capacity may be damaged by changing conditions or short-term adversities.
C	Doubtful capacity for payment.
D	Issue is either in default or is expected to be in default upon maturity.

Source: Standard & Poor's International Creditweek.

Table 2.4

<table>
<tr><td colspan="2" align="center">Issuer Rating Symbols</td></tr>
<tr><td>Aaa</td><td>Issuers rated Aaa offer exceptional financial security. While the creditworthiness of these entities is likely to change, such changes as can be visualized are most unlikely to impair their fundamentally strong position.</td></tr>
<tr><td>Aa</td><td>Issuers rated Aa offer excellent financial security. Together with the Aaa group, they constitute what are generally known as high-grade entities. They are rated lower than Aaa-rated entities because long-term risks appear somewhat larger.</td></tr>
<tr><td>A</td><td>Issuers rated A offer good financial security. However elements may be present which suggest a susceptibility to impairment sometime in the future.</td></tr>
<tr><td>Baa</td><td>Issuers rated Baa offer adequate financial security. However, certain protective elements may be lacking or may be unreliable over any great period of time.</td></tr>
<tr><td>Ba</td><td>Issuers rated Ba offer questionable financial security. Often the ability of these entities to meet obligations may be moderate and not well safeguarded in the future.</td></tr>
<tr><td>B</td><td>Issuers rated B offer poor financial security. Assurance of payment of obligations over any long period of time is small.</td></tr>
<tr><td>Caa</td><td>Issuers rated Caa offer very poor financial security. They may be in default on their obligations or there may be present elements of danger with respect to punctual payment of obligations.</td></tr>
<tr><td>Ca</td><td>Issuers rated Ca offer extremely poor financial security. Such entities are often in default on their obligations or have other marked shortcomings.</td></tr>
<tr><td>C</td><td>Issuers rated C are the lowest-rated class of entity, are usually in default on their obligations, and potential recovery values are low.</td></tr>
</table>

Note: Moody's applies numerical modifiers 1, 2, and 3 in each generic rating category from Aa to Caa. The modifier 1 indicates that the issuer is in the higher end of its letter rating category; the modifier 2 indicates a mid-range ranking; the modifier 3 indicates that the issuer is in the lower end of the letter ranking category.
Source: Moody's Investor Service

2.5.4   Moody's ratings

2.5.4.1   Issuer ratings

Moody's issuer ratings that are assigned to banks are opinions of the financial capacity of a bank to honour its senior unsecured financial contracts.

Moody's rating symbols for Issuer Ratings (Table 2.4) are identical to those used to show the credit quality of bonds. These rating gradations provide creditors with a simple system to measure an entity's ability to meet its senior financial obligations.

2.5.4.2   Bank financial strength ratings

Moody's financial strength ratings represent the perceived safety and soundness of a bank. Unlike Moody's traditional debt ratings, financial strength ratings exclude certain external credit risks and do not address the likelihood of timely payment. Instead they measure the likelihood of external support and assistance being required by a bank which finds itself in difficulties. However, Bank Financial Strength Ratings (Table 2.5) do not take into account the probability of troubled banks receiving such support.

Factors considered in the assignment of bank financial strength rating include: franchise value, financial fundamentals, and business and asset diversification. Broader factors are also

Table 2.5

	Moody's Bank Financial Strength Ratings
A	Bank has exceptional intrinsic financial strength. Typically major institution highly valuable franchises, strong financial fundamentals and stable operating environment.
B	Bank possesses strong intrinsic financial strength. Typically important institutions with valuable business franchises, good financial fundamentals and stable operating environment.
C	Bank has good intrinsic financial strength. Will typically have valuable and defensible business franchises, better than average financial fundamentals and stable operating environment.
D	Bank has adequate financial strength, but may be limited by one or more of following factors: vulnerable business franchises, weak financial fundamentals or an unstable operating environment.
E	Bank possesses very weak intrinsic financial strength requiring regular outside support or suggesting an eventual need for outside assistance. One or more of the following factors may limit the bank's performance: business franchise of questionable value; seriously deficient financial fundamentals or a highly unstable operating environment.

Source: Moody's Investor Service

considered such as: the structure of the country's financial system, the quality and level of banking regulation, and the strength and prospective performance of the economy as a whole.

2.5.5   Fitch performance and legal ratings

Fitch Ratings (the Fimalac-Euronotation-ICBA-Fitch-Duff & Phelps-Thompson Bankwatch collective) (Table 2.6) cover sovereign (including supranational and subnational), financial, bank, insurance, and other corporate entities and the securities they issue, as well as municipal and other public finance entities, and securities backed by receivables or other financial assets, and counterparties.

Issuer ratings refer to general creditworthiness of an issuer. Issue credit ratings refer to the relative preferential position of the holder of the security and reflect the terms, conditions, and covenants attaching to that security.

2.5.5.1   Short-Term credit ratings

The ratings scale in Table 2.7 applies to foreign currency and local currency ratings. A Short-term rating has a time horizon of less than 12 months for most obligations, or up to three years for US public finance securities, and thus places greater emphasis on the liquidity necessary to meet financial commitments in a timely manner.

2.5.5.2   Individual ratings

The Individual Ratings (Table 2.8), which are internationally comparable, attempt to assess how a bank would be viewed if it were entirely independent and could not rely on external support. These ratings are designed to assess a bank's exposure to, appetite for, and management of, risk, and thus represent our view on the likelihood that it would run into significant difficulties such that it would require support. The principal factors we analyse to evaluate the bank and determine these ratings include profitability and balance sheet integrity (including

Table 2.6

International Long-Term Credit Ratings

Investment Grade

AAA   Highest credit quality. 'AAA' ratings denote the lowest expectation of credit risk. They are assigned only in case of exceptionally strong capacity for timely payment of financial commitments. This capacity is highly unlikely to be adversely affected by foreseeable events.

AA   Very high credit quality. 'AA' ratings denote a very low expectation of credit risk. They indicate very strong capacity for timely payment of financial commitments. This capacity is not significantly vulnerable to foreseeable events.

A   High credit quality. 'A' ratings denote a low expectation of credit risk. The capacity for timely payment of financial commitments is considered strong. This capacity may, nevertheless, be more vulnerable to changes in circumstances or in economic conditions than is the case for higher ratings.

BBB   Good credit quality. 'BBB' ratings indicate that there is currently a low expectation of credit risk. The capacity for timely payment of financial commitments is considered adequate, but adverse changes in circumstances and in economic conditions are more likely to impair this capacity. This is the lowest investment-grade category.

Speculative Grade

BB   Speculative. 'BB' ratings indicate that there is a possibility of credit risk developing, particularly as the result of adverse economic change over time; however, business or financial alternatives may be available to allow financial commitments to be met. Securities rated in this category are not investment grade.

B   Highly speculative. 'B' ratings indicate that significant credit risk is present, but a limited margin of safety remains. Financial commitments are currently being met; however, capacity for continued payment is contingent upon a sustained, favourable business and economic environment.

CCC, High default risk. Default is a real possibility. Capacity for meeting financial commitments is
CC,   solely reliant upon sustained, favourable business or economic developments. A 'CC' rating
C   indicates that default of some kind appears probable. 'C' ratings signal imminent default.

DDD, Default. The ratings of obligations in this category are based on their prospects for achieving
DD,   partial or full recovery in a reorganization or liquidation of the obligor. While expected recovery
D   values are highly speculative and cannot be estimated with any precision, the following serve as general guidelines. 'DDD' obligations have the highest potential for recovery, around 90%–100% of outstanding amounts and accrued interest. "DD" indicates potential recoveries in the range of 50%–90% and 'D' the lowest recovery potential, i.e., below 50%.

      Entities rated in this category have defaulted on some or all of their obligations. Entities rated 'DDD' have the highest prospect for resumption of performance or continued operation with or without a formal reorganization process. Entities rated 'DD' and 'D' are generally undergoing a formal reorganization or liquidation process; those rated 'DD' are likely to satisfy a higher portion of their outstanding obligations, while entities rated 'D' have a poor prospect of repaying all obligations.

Source: Fitch.

capitalisation), franchise, management, operating environment, and prospects. Consistency is an important consideration.

2.5.5.3   Support ratings

Fitch Support Ratings (Table 2.9) are assigned to banks. The term "banks" here includes bank holding companies and bancassurance holding companies, investment banks and private banks and other financial services companies but excludes insurance companies.

Table 2.7

International Short-Term Credit Ratings	
F1	Highest credit quality. Indicates the strongest capacity for timely payment of financial commitments; may have an added "+" to denote any exceptionally strong credit feature.
F2	Good credit quality. A satisfactory capacity for timely payment of financial commitments, but the margin of safety is not as great as in the case of the higher ratings.
F3	Fair credit quality. The capacity for timely payment of financial commitments is adequate; however, near-term adverse changes could result in a reduction to non-investment grade.
B	Speculative. Minimal capacity for timely payment of financial commitments, plus vulnerability to near-term adverse changes in financial and economic conditions.
C	High default risk. Default is a real possibility. Capacity for meeting financial commitments is solely reliant upon a sustained, favourable business and economic environment.
D	Default. Denotes actual or imminent payment default.

Notes to Long-term and Short-term ratings:

"+" or "−" may be appended to a rating to denote relative status within major rating categories. Such suffixes are not added to the 'AAA' Long-term rating category, to categories below 'CCC', or to Short-term ratings other than 'F1'.

'NR' indicates that Fitch Ratings does not rate the issuer or issue in question.

'Withdrawn': A rating is withdrawn when Fitch Ratings deems the amount of information available to be inadequate for rating purposes, or when an obligation matures, is called, or refinanced.

Rating Watch: Ratings are placed on Rating Watch to notify investors that there is a reasonable probability of a rating change and the likely direction of such change. These are designated as "Positive", indicating a potential upgrade, "Negative", for a potential downgrade, or "Evolving", if ratings may be raised, lowered or maintained. Rating Watch is typically resolved over a relatively short period.

A Rating Outlook indicates the direction a rating is likely to move over a one to two-year period. Outlooks may be positive, stable or negative. A positive or negative Rating Outlook does not imply a rating change is inevitable. Similarly, ratings for which outlooks are "stable" could be upgraded or downgraded before an outlook moves to positive or negative if circumstances warrant such an action. Occasionally, Fitch Ratings may be unable to identify the fundamental trend. In these cases, the Rating Outlook may be described as evolving.

Source: Fitch.

Table 2.8

Bank Individual Ratings	
A	A very strong bank. Characteristics may include outstanding profitability and balance sheet integrity, franchise, management, operating environment or prospects.
B	A strong bank. There are no major concerns regarding the bank. Characteristics may include strong profitability and balance sheet integrity, franchise, management, operating environment or prospects.
C	An adequate bank, which, however, possesses one or more troublesome aspects. There may be some concerns regarding its profitability and balance sheet integrity, franchise, management, operating environment or prospects.
D	A bank, which has weaknesses of internal and/or external origin. There are concerns regarding its profitability and balance sheet integrity, franchise, management, operating environment or prospects. Banks in emerging markets are necessarily faced with a greater number of potential deficiencies of external origin.
E	A bank with very serious problems, which either requires or is likely to require external support.
(s)	An Individual rating may be followed by the suffix "(s)", denoting that it is largely based on public information, supplemented by data obtained from the rated entity. In addition, we use gradations among these five ratings, i.e. A/B, B/C, C/D, and D/E.

Source: Fitch.

Table 2.9

	Support rating general definitions
1	A bank for which there is an extremely high probability of external support. The potential provider of support is very highly rated in its own right and has a very high propensity to support the bank in question. This probability of support indicates a minimum Long-term rating floor of "A-".
2	A bank for which there is a high probability of external support. The potential provider of support is highly rated in its own right and has a high propensity to provide support to the bank in question. This probability of support indicates a minimum Long-term rating floor of "BBB-".
3	A bank for which there is a moderate probability of support because of uncertainties about the ability or propensity of the potential provider of support to do so. This probability of support indicates a minimum Long-term rating floor of "BB-".
4	A bank for which there is a limited probability of support because of significant uncertainties about the ability or propensity of any possible provider of support to do so. This probability of support indicates a minimum Long-term rating floor of "B".
5	A bank for which external support, although possible, cannot be relied upon. This may be due to a lack of propensity to provide support or to very weak financial ability to do so. This probability of support indicates a Long-term rating floor no higher than "B-" and in many cases no floor at all.

Source: Fitch

Support ratings do not assess the credit quality of a bank. They are Fitch's judgement on whether the bank would receive support should this become necessary.

A bank's Support rating is an "important contributor" to Fitch's determination of its Long-term and Short-term debt ratings although it is "only a constituent part" of those ratings.

Fitch's Support rating definitions assume that "support" is provided on a timely basis – e.g. that it enables the bank being supported to continue meeting its financial commitments on a timely basis so that it does not default. It does not mean letting the bank fail and then paying our depositors from a deposit guarantee fund.

3

The Regulatory Framework

Challenges facing regulators as seen in the *Financial Times* 2001 (Roger Beale)

3.1 BANKING SYSTEM: STRUCTURE, GOVERNING LAW, AND REGULATIONS

The analysis of a country's banking system should focus on several general areas: the system's structure and regulatory environment, the likelihood and ability for the government to provide support for failing banks, and the accounting standards in force which may affect the presentation of financial statements. An analysis should also address the inherent strengths and weaknesses of a particular system as well as economic and political trends which can have an impact on the performance of the country's banks.

It is important that a bank meets the regulatory authority's standards and maintains their confidence, as much as the confidence of the general public, since the latter will often defer to the judgement of the former.

While the public usually knows relatively little, the financial community are very savvy – there is often "uneasiness" on the part of the financial community preceding a bank failure (such as in the case of BCCI). While this is usually restricted to rumours as opposed to massive deposit run-offs, once the "crisis of confidence" crystallises, the financial community can often precipitate failure by cutting their bank lines (e.g. Continental Illinois) with astonishing rapidity. For example, the Bank of Italy only realised there was a problem after Banca di Napoli reported losses. The deciding blow, however, is almost always struck by the regulatory authority, who should have a much closer appreciation of the real situation in a bank.

The standards of regulatory authorities are dynamic, not static. Many bank crises are the result, not of a change in the bank's situation, but of a change in the regulatory authorities' standards and/or degree of competence. In developed countries, this can take the form of specific policy changes (e.g. the regulatory agencies specify operating conditions and guidelines to manage the Foreign Exchange (FX) markets). In developing countries, it usually results from a broader upgrading (e.g. professionalisation) in all areas but particularly in overall exposure limitations on a group with several subsidiaries.

To understand the regulatory system, the specific participants must be identified, and their functions, competency, and relative power understood. These entities normally include the following:

- Ministry of Finance
- Central bank
- Banking commission
- Bank examiners
- Independent auditors

The regulatory authority normally has a mandate to ensure the soundness of the country's banking system and to carry out specific national objectives. Regulatory authorities determine who gets (and who keeps) a licence to operate a bank. Regulatory authorities also establish the rules and regulations that govern the banking system; for example, it has the power to determine what constitutes "acceptable" financial conditions. The implementation of the "Cooke Ratios" financial guidelines has to some extent succeeded in establishing a degree of financial convergence in cross-border comparisons.

- **Legal existence** – you should be concerned with the bank's charter: the type of legal institution and entity it is. How is the bank chartered? By Act of Parliament, or special law? What do the charter and bylaws of the bank provide for? Is the bank subject to a banking law? Are there special provisions for this type of institution? Have there been any legislative or regulatory changes for banks in the home country? It is crucial that you know that the institution is legally established and has a clear domiciliation (e.g. BCCI, Cayman Islands) as these matters are crucial in a liquidation scenario (as well as ensuring worldwide supervision).
- **Liquidation priorities** – here, you should be concerned with the structure of liabilities in terms of priority of claims. You may want to secure a legal opinion from lawyers in the bank's home country as to the ranking order of liabilities (secured debt, subordinated debt, etc.) in the event of liquidation. Publications by the major accounting firms may be useful in providing information on these matters.

- **Lender of last resort** – perhaps the most important question to answer when analysing a banking system is the likelihood of government intervention to maintain the solvency of various categories of banks, and, as importantly, whether the government has the financial and managerial resources available to undertake such a task. It is therefore necessary to analyse local laws, official announcements, and legal precedents in order to assess the likelihood of support (this may require that you obtain legal opinions on specific matters from legal counsel, usually located in the country in question).

Some countries explicitly provide sovereign guarantees for particular banks while other countries deliberately avoid providing a sovereign guarantee to all government institutions as a matter of principle. In the absence of specific guarantees, government agencies are usually reluctant to openly express support for a particular bank's obligations prior to its encountering financial difficulties.

In all fairness, it should be said that the absence of such explicit government guarantees does not necessarily constitute dereliction of duties. Providing such guarantees can often have a perverse effect by fostering operational ineptitude, since it tends to encourage the attitude "if we get in trouble, the government (the taxpayer) will bail us out".

A point should be made here about state-owned banks. It cannot be assumed that the central government will unconditionally support state-owned institutions if they encounter problems. In Venezuela, foreign creditors were forced to sue state authorities and threaten attachment before the central government agreed to include their debt within the country's sovereign debt negotiations.

This attitude is not limited to developing countries. Foreign countries also had considerable difficulties with Kongsberg Vaapenfrabik, a state-owned Norwegian defence contractor, and FECSA, a state-owned Spanish utility company, when these companies became insolvent. While these entities are not banks, the underlying legal principles would be applicable to banks in the case of failure.

On the positive side, while there may be systems where no explicit guarantee is provided, the record of legal precedents and pronouncements may, in practice, indicate a de-facto commitment to do so such as in Finland, Japan, or Sweden.

3.1.1 Banking supervision

3.1.1.1 The role of the banking supervisor

In virtually every country, banking is one of the most regulated of enterprises. To understand the regulatory system, the specific participants must be defined, and their functions, competency, and relative power understood. This would normally include entities such as the following: Ministry of Finance, the FSA (Financial Supervisory Authority) in the UK, central bank, Banking Commission, bank examiners, as well as independent auditors. (To standardise terminology, regulatory system will include all of the above, while regulatory authority will be reserved for those who formulate policy and establish banking rules and regulations.)

Banking supervision aims to oversee and regulate banks and the banking sector. Unlike corporates, banks occupy a central role in the economy. Banking supervision's raison d'être is twofold:

- To protect depositors.
- To ensure strength of banks and thus the whole banking sector.

Banking supervision can cover a broad area. Responsibilities are many but normally include:

• Entry procedure and restrictions
• Permitted activities
• Capital adequacy
• Liquidity
• Large loans/exposures
• FX exposures
• Provisions inspection/audit
• Deposit protection
• Restrictions on control/ownerships
• Vetting management as "fit and proper"
• Communications with auditors

Harmonisation of bank regulation is progressing worldwide with pressure to produce consistent presentation of accounts, the agreement on capital adequacy rules among the OECD countries and many other banking supervisors and the standardisation of EU rules on banking.

There has been a tendency to underestimate the importance of the regulatory system's policing function, presumably on the basis that bureaucrats and accountants have little impact. This may be true in some countries, where the regulatory system is poorly developed; however, in most countries, the power of the regulatory system is considerable. It is the weakness of the supervisory authority that has allowed more failures to occur in, for example, Russia or Indonesia, than might otherwise have occurred.

3.1.1.2   The role of the regulatory system

The regulatory authority normally has a mandate to ensure the soundness of its country's banking system and to carry out specific national economic objectives. The regulatory authority determines who gets (and who keeps) a licence to operate a bank. In establishing the rules and regulations for the banking system, it has the power to define what constitutes "acceptable" financial condition. For example, in Country A, a bank with a 20:1 leverage, might be declared insolvent and closed down because it violates the maximum 10:1 ratio permitted, whereas that identical institution might be totally viable in Country B where a 50:1 leverage is allowed. But there is a more basic point to be made – the fact that leverage (or other criteria) may not have the same relative importance in various countries. The important criteria are those dictated as such by the regulatory authority. If their major concern is development of specific industrial sectors (such as through a credit allocation programme), then a shortcoming in this area might result in intervention, whereas a violation of a leverage ratio might involve only a moratorium on new deposits. This example may be a bit extreme, but it does illustrate the point that values can differ from country to country.

The power of the regulatory authorities becomes very evident in analysing bank crises. The scenario in which the general public or the financial community anticipate a bank failure, withdraw their deposits, and then cause the bank to close its doors and turn to the regulatory authorities for help is a scenario which almost never occurs. If the general public or financial community sense a problem, they tend to talk about it, period. As long as a bank continues to receive a clean bill of health from the regulatory authority, there will be no panic.

The reasons for this deference to the judgement of the regulatory authorities are fairly obvious. The regulatory authorities are in a unique position to determine the viability of a bank because they get better, more detailed information, and they get it first. Additionally, only they can inspect the portfolio and their opinion becomes binding. It is their full-time job to interpret the rules and their decision is final. Perhaps the best analogy is that of an official at a sporting event – it doesn't matter what the crowd thinks or what the videotape showed – the official's decision will stand.

3.1.1.3   Controls and their value

If used indiscriminately, this power will make it totally impossible to anticipate bank crises. However, if used properly, the power of the regulatory authorities can virtually ensure the safety of the entire banking system. They will always receive information ahead of everyone else, but the important point is to understand their requirements and how effective they are in either preventing violations or dealing with violations which do occur. Points such as the following should be addressed:

- Priorities of the regulatory authority (e.g. liquidity vs credit allocation)
- Formal requirements for capital, leverage, reserves, etc.
- Control of interest rates, likelihood of squeeze on net interest margins
- Regulation of foreign exchange positions
- Required or accepted accounting procedures, with particular emphasis on overall integrity and specific areas such as:
  - delinquencies, charge-offs, and any "gimmicks" used to conceal problem loans (for example, would a partial payment remove an item from the past-due category?)
  - reserves
  - valuations (fixed assets, investments)

Note: The revaluation of fixed assets has always attracted considerable attention and occasional criticism. In reality, however, this practice has become totally acceptable, and it represents yet another point on which the general public and financial community defer to the judgement of the regulatory authorities. If they include revaluation reserve as capital, then it is capital.

- **Examination system** – the competency of the regulatory system in identifying poor credit decisions at an early stage cannot be overemphasised. In many actual crises, the examination system failed to detect a problem until it had gone from bad to worse. The rigorous US system of timely identification of inferior assets with concurrent provision for estimated losses is still a rarity in much of the world.
- **One-obligor limitations** – lack of an effective one-obligor (or single borrower) concept has been a particular problem in those cases where banks had extensive dealings with owners, other insiders, or their companies. In some cases, lending limits "per customer" do not aggregate entities with a common ownership.

Some of this information will be difficult to obtain (a gross understatement), but to the extent that the regulatory system can be shown to function competently, then the need to probe into individual banks will be reduced. A shortcoming in the regulatory system simply implies that a prudent creditor should take additional steps to ensure that a bank is not vulnerable in that area.

Like government in general, regulation is constantly increasing worldwide. In industrialised countries with a professional civil service system, the track record of regulatory authorities in preventing crises is excellent, particularly with respect to banks of national importance.

The great majority of bank crises occur in middle-income, developing countries, where the regulatory system is undergoing professionalisation, moving from a laissez faire posture to one of strict examination and regulation. Practices which had been tolerated in the past cease to be acceptable. The long-term implications of this process are good, but the "weeding out" which accompanies it can bring casualties. In a dynamic environment such as this, it cannot be said that the large banks or the old, established banks are necessarily safe. Size and age are not as important as other criteria, and these will be addressed in the following chapters.

In addition to its policing function, regulatory authorities have a support function as well. Formal procedures might include:

• Rediscount or other credit facilities – lender of last resort
• Deposit insurance
• Moratorium/reorganisation procedures

In general, however, support goes far beyond procedures such as these. The track record of regulatory authorities in dealing with crises should be carefully examined – are problem banks rehabilitated (as in Spain's "bank hospital"), nationalised, forced to merge, or simply left to die? This last option is almost never seen, for the following reasons:

• It is likely to destroy the faith of the outside world in the country's banking system, thereby jeopardising the correspondent network of other indigenous banks and severely restricting the country's import credit lines. A few countries, however, have publicly stated to the outside world that the regulatory authorities will only protect domestic creditors, and that foreign creditors are effectively subordinated, as was the case with a small bank in Guatemala.
• The panic and loss of confidence by domestic depositors and creditors could have even greater political and economic effects.
• It is an open admission by the regulatory authorities that they failed to exercise their policing function to such an extent that the situation became hopeless, with the result that the senior officials of the regulatory authority would most likely be replaced (a rather important consideration for them).

No prudent creditor would put all of his faith in the support function (or more specifically, the bailout prospects) provided by the regulatory authorities, but this remains a final fall-back position.

3.2   CORE PRINCIPLES FOR EFFECTIVE BANKING SUPERVISION

(From Basle Core Principles of Banking Supervision, produced by the Basle Committee on Banking Supervision.)

3.2.1   Core principles for effective banking supervision

1. Weaknesses in the banking system of a country, whether developing or developed, can threaten financial stability both within that country and internationally. The need to improve the strength of financial systems has attracted growing international concern. The Communiqué issued at the close of the Lyon G-7 Summit in June 1996 called for action in this domain. Several official bodies, including the Basle Committee on Banking Supervision, the Bank for International Settlements, the International Monetary Fund and the World

Bank, have recently been examining ways to strengthen financial stability throughout the world.

2. The Basle Committee on Banking Supervision has been working in this field for many years, both directly and through its many contacts with banking supervisors in every part of the world. In the last year and a half, it has been examining how best to expand its efforts aimed at strengthening prudential supervision in all countries by building on its relationships with countries outside the G-10 as well as on its earlier work to enhance prudential supervision in its member countries. In particular, the Committee has prepared two documents for release:
   * a comprehensive set of Core Principles for effective banking supervision (The Basle Core Principles) (attached); and,
   * a Compendium (to be updated periodically) of the existing Basle Committee recommendations, guidelines and standards most of which are cross-referenced in the Core Principles document.

   Both documents have been endorsed by the G-10 central bank Governors. They were submitted to the G-7 and G-10 Finance Ministers in preparation for the June 1997 Denver Summit in the hope that they would provide a useful mechanism for strengthening financial stability in all countries.

3. In developing the Principles, the Basle Committee has worked closely with non-G-10 supervisory authorities. The document has been prepared in a group containing representatives from the Basle Committee and from Chile, China, the Czech Republic, Hong Kong, Mexico, Russia and Thailand. Nine other countries (Argentina, Brazil, Hungary, India, Indonesia, Korea, Malaysia, Poland and Singapore) were also closely associated with the work. The drafting of the Principles benefited moreover from broad consultation with a larger group of individual supervisors, both directly and through the regional supervisory groups.

4. The Basle Core Principles comprise twenty-five basic Principles that need to be in place for a supervisory system to be effective. The Principles relate to:
   * Preconditions for effective banking supervision – Principle 1
   * Licensing and structure – Principles 2 to 5
   * Prudential regulations and requirements – Principles 6 to 15
   * Methods of ongoing banking supervision – Principles 16 to 20
   * Information requirements – Principle 21
   * Formal powers of supervisors – Principle 22, and
   * Cross-border banking – Principles 23 to 25.

   In addition to the Principles themselves, the document contains explanations of the various methods supervisors can use to implement them.

5. National agencies should apply the Principles in the supervision of all banking organisations within their jurisdictions. The Principles are minimum requirements and in many cases may need to be supplemented by other measures designed to address particular conditions and risks in the financial systems of individual countries.

6. The Basle Core Principles are intended to serve as a basic reference for supervisory and other public authorities in all countries and internationally. It will be for national supervisory authorities, many of which are actively seeking to strengthen their current supervisory regime, to use the attached document to review their existing supervisory arrangements and to initiate a programme designed to address any deficiencies as quickly as is practical within their legal authority. The Principles have been designed to be verifiable by supervisors, regional supervisory groups, and the market at large. The Basle Committee will play a role, together with other interested organisations, in monitoring the progress made by individual

countries in implementing the Principles. It is suggested that the IMF, the World Bank and other interested organisations use the Principles in assisting individual countries to strengthen their supervisory arrangements in connection with work aimed at promoting overall macroeconomic and financial stability. Implementation of the Principles will be reviewed at the International Conference of Banking Supervisors in October 1998 and biennially thereafter.

7. Supervisory authorities throughout the world are encouraged to endorse the Basle Core Principles. The members of the Basle Committee and the sixteen other supervisory agencies that have participated in their drafting all agree with the content of the document.

8. The chairpersons of the regional supervisory groups are supportive of the Basle Committee's efforts and are ready to promote the endorsement of the Core Principles among their membership. Discussions are in progress to define the role the regional groups can play in securing the endorsement of the Principles and in monitoring implementation by their members.

9. The Basle Committee believes that achieving consistency with the Core Principles by every country will be a significant step in the process of improving financial stability domestically and internationally. The speed with which this objective will be achieved will vary. In many countries, substantive changes in the legislative framework and in the powers of supervisors will be necessary because many supervisory authorities do not at present have the statutory authority to implement all of the Principles. In such cases, the Basle Committee believes it is essential that national legislators give urgent consideration to the changes necessary to ensure that the Principles can be applied in all material respects.

10. The Basle Committee will continue to pursue its standard-setting activities in key risk areas and in key elements of banking supervision as it has done in documents such as those reproduced in the Compendium. The Basle Core Principles will serve as a reference point for future work to be done by the Committee and, where appropriate, in cooperation with non-G-10 supervisors and their regional groups. The Committee stands ready to encourage work at the national level to implement the Principles in conjunction with other supervisory bodies and interested parties. Finally, the Committee is committed to strengthening its interaction with supervisors from non-G-10 countries and intensifying its considerable investment in technical assistance and training.

3.2.2 Basel committee publications no. 30 (September 1997) on banking principles

Preconditions for effective banking supervision

1. An effective system of banking supervision will have clear responsibilities and objectives for each agency involved in the supervision of banking organisations. Each such agency should possess operational independence and adequate resources. A suitable legal framework for banking supervision is also necessary, including provisions relating to authorisation of banking organisations and their ongoing supervision; powers to address compliance with laws as well as safety and soundness concerns; and legal protection for supervisors. Arrangements for sharing information between supervisors and protecting the confidentiality of such information should be in place.

Licensing and structure

2. The permissible activities of institutions that are licensed and subject to supervision as banks must be clearly defined, and the use of the word "bank" in names should be controlled as far as possible.
3. The licensing authority must have the right to set criteria and reject applications for establishments that do not meet the standards set. The licensing process, at a minimum, should consist of an assessment of the banking organisation's ownership structure, directors and senior management, its operating plan and internal controls, and its projected financial condition, including its capital base; where the proposed owner or parent organisation is a foreign bank, the prior consent of its home country supervisor should be obtained.
4. Banking supervisors must have the authority to review and reject any proposals to transfer significant ownership or controlling interests in existing banks to other parties.
5. Banking supervisors must have the authority to establish criteria for reviewing major acquisitions or investments by a bank and ensuring that corporate affiliations or structures do not expose the bank to undue risks or hinder effective supervision.

Prudential regulations and requirements

6. Banking supervisors must set prudent and appropriate minimum capital adequacy requirements for all banks. Such requirements should reflect the risks that the banks undertake, and must define the components of capital, bearing in mind their ability to absorb losses. At least for internationally active banks, these requirements must not be less than those established in the Basle Capital Accord and its amendments.
7. An essential part of any supervisory system is the evaluation of a bank's policies, practices and procedures related to the granting of loans and making of investments and the ongoing management of the loan and investment portfolios.
8. Banking supervisors must be satisfied that banks establish and adhere to adequate policies, practices and procedures for evaluating the quality of assets and the adequacy of loan loss provisions and loan loss reserves.
9. Banking supervisors must be satisfied that banks have management information systems that enable management to identify concentrations within the portfolio and supervisors must set prudential limits to restrict bank exposures to single borrowers or groups of related borrowers.
10. In order to prevent abuses arising from connected lending, banking supervisors must have in place requirements that banks lend to related companies and individuals on an arm's-length basis, that such extensions of credit are effectively monitored, and that other appropriate steps are taken to control or mitigate the risks.
11. Banking supervisors must be satisfied that banks have adequate policies and procedures for identifying, monitoring and controlling country risk and transfer risk in their international lending and investment activities, and for maintaining appropriate reserves against such risks.
12. Banking supervisors must be satisfied that banks have in place systems that accurately measure, monitor and adequately control market risks; supervisors should have powers to impose specific limits and/or a specific capital charge on market risk exposures, if warranted.

13. Banking supervisors must be satisfied that banks have in place a comprehensive risk management process (including appropriate board and senior management oversight) to identify, measure, monitor and control all other material risks and, where appropriate, to hold capital against these risks.

14. Banking supervisors must determine that banks have in place internal controls that are adequate for the nature and scale of their business. These should include clear arrangements for delegating authority and responsibility; separation of the functions that involve committing the bank, paying away its funds, and accounting for its assets and liabilities; reconciliation of these processes; safeguarding its assets; and appropriate independent internal or external audit and compliance functions to test adherence to these controls as well as applicable laws and regulations.

15. Banking supervisors must determine that banks have adequate policies, practices and procedures in place, including strict "know-your-customer" rules, that promote high ethical and professional standards in the financial sector and prevent the bank being used, intentionally or unintentionally, by criminal elements.

Methods of ongoing banking supervision

16. An effective banking supervisory system should consist of some form of both on-site and off-site supervision.

17. Banking supervisors must have regular contact with bank management and thorough understanding of the institution's operations.

18. Banking supervisors must have a means of collecting, reviewing and analysing prudential reports and statistical returns from banks on a solo and consolidated basis.

19. Banking supervisors must have a means of independent validation of supervisory information either through on-site examinations or use of external auditors.

20. An essential element of banking supervision is the ability of the supervisors to supervise the banking group on a consolidated basis.

Information requirements

21. Banking supervisors must be satisfied that each bank maintains adequate records drawn up in accordance with consistent accounting policies and practices that enable the supervisor to obtain a true and fair view of the financial condition of the bank and the profitability of its business, and that the bank publishes on a regular basis financial statements that fairly reflect its condition.

Formal powers of supervisors

22. Banking supervisors must have at their disposal adequate supervisory measures to bring about timely corrective action when banks fail to meet prudential requirements (such as minimum capital adequacy ratios), when there are regulatory violations, or where depositors are threatened in any other way. In extreme circumstances, this should include the ability to revoke the banking licence or recommend its revocation.

Cross-border banking

23. Banking supervisors must practise global consolidated supervision over their internationally-active banking organisations, adequately monitoring and applying appropriate prudential norms to all aspects of the business conducted by these banking organisations worldwide, primarily at their foreign branches, joint ventures and subsidiaries.
24. A key component of consolidated supervision is establishing contact and information exchange with the various other supervisors involved, primarily host country supervisory authorities.
25. Banking supervisors must require the local operations of foreign banks to be conducted to the same high standards as are required of domestic institutions and must have powers to share information needed by the home country supervisors of those banks for the purpose of carrying out consolidated supervision.

3.3 RISK MANAGEMENT

3.3.1 Generally accepted risk principles

The area of risk management has recently engaged the attention of bank management and supervisions alike. Accordingly, a review panel of bankers and supervisors produced a list of Generally Accepted Risk Principles (GARPs), which are detailed further into various sub-categories and points, and are interesting insofar as they illustrate to the analyst the overall systematic approach one can adopt in assessing the financial health of a bank.

These principles are guidelines for bankers to run their organisations safely and ensure they do not suffer financial collapse. For the analyst, it is difficult to audit the risk management practices of a bank. In reading an annual report of a bank and more importantly by speaking to its management, one can get a clue as to how rigorous its risk management culture is. These GARPs are summarised into the five main categories as follows:

3.3.1.1 Risk management strategy

Risk management strategy concerns the need for the board of the bank to be responsible for risk management. Too often, the culture of risk management does not get the importance it deserves. The message communicating the importance of risk management must come directly and firmly from the top. It is crucial for the analyst to understand how strong the culture is and how professionally risk is monitored. This area is concerned with two issues:

- Risk organisation
- Capital allocation

3.3.1.2 The risk management function

Risk management function concerns how risk management should be a dedicated function with an independent head of risk. The importance of having risk managers being as sophisticated and knowledgeable as business generators and not subject to marketing targets will help ensure that there is more independence of risk assessment and fewer conflicts of interest.

3.3.1.3 Risk management, reporting and control

Risk management, reporting and control requires a quantification of market, credit and liquidity risk and the necessary limits and controls on these. One of the golden rules of management is if it is measurable, measure it, if it is not, make it measurable and thereby control it. The need to do this accurately and comprehensively in banking is critical in terms of credit risk, liquidity risk, and market risk. The failure to measure this accurately or report it vitiated this principle at Barings Bank and brought them down.

3.3.1.4 Operational controls

The need for strong operational controls in the various parts of the bank covering legal, regulatory, reputation, technology and human resources risks are paramount. Operations typically occur throughout the bank. Operations principles are divided into front, middle, and back office and designed to ensure that responsibilities are clearly separated between them, and that appropriate control structures are in place in each of these areas. This includes aspects such as authorisation, decision support, trade processing, reconciliations, and transaction reporting and can be grouped into:

* Front office
* Middle and back office
* Firm-wide

3.3.1.5 Risk management systems

Risk management systems need real-time reliable IT systems that are capable of monitoring and reporting risk. Risk management systems aim to ensure the control of functions such as current and future risk management functions, location of functions, information delivery, data storage and integrity, data ownership and interoperability, backup, recovery, and contingency planning in the IT sphere.

3.3.2 Derivatives and market risk

Many banks use swaps, options, and derivative products, not only as products to offer to their customers, but also as tools to manage their interest rate or currency risk. While such tools can indeed help to manage interest rate risk and cross-border exposures, they can also be used to speculative ends as the Barings débâcle illustrates.

Therefore, in analysing bank risk, it is prudent, indeed desirable, to consider this aspect of bank risk. The following checklist of questions can help you to better assess this risk.

While it may be difficult to ask all these questions, you can most likely delve into a few areas and this should give you an idea of how seriously this area is managed. Indeed, confused or puzzled reactions at some of the more technical questions can, in itself, tell you a lot about how the bank is managing derivatives and market risk!

3.3.2.1 General principles

* When assessing market risk exposure, does the bank distinguish between derivatives portfolios for its own account, for arbitrage, and for risk management?

- What are the main types of derivative products which the bank is party to? Is this exposure assessed in terms of notional and by annual results?
- What are the most extreme daily variations witnessed (largest profit and loss registered)?
- How does the bank classify derivatives trading in the published annual accounts and in internal management accounts? Are there differences between these two sets of accounts? If there is a difference, why?

3.3.2.2   Management risk

- What is the bank's gross and net exposure at year end? What were the highest and lowest exposures posted during the past year?
- How does the bank assess potential risk? Is there any sort of exposure guideline matrix in place to control traders?
- What is the bank's list of major counterparties (banks and corporates, ranked by credit risk)?

3.3.2.3   Market risk

- Does the bank use the VAR (Value at Risk) method? If so,
  - which model does the bank use for its calculations?
  - which historical reference period does the bank use?
  - what confidence intervals (statistical method of calculation) does the bank use?
  - what is the bank's reference period?
  - what was the highest, lowest, and average VAR posted by the bank during the past accounting period?
- Does the bank prepare downside scenarios to assess its current exposure and vulnerability? Can it show a recent example with two or three sensitivity scenarios?
- If the bank does not use these techniques, what sort of assessment and control system does the bank use?

3.3.2.4   Legal risk

- Does the bank have dedicated in-house lawyers specialised in derivative products?
- How does the bank account for the varying regulations from one country to another with respect to netting mechanisms?
- Are all the bank's derivatives contracts subject to standard boilerplate mechanisms such as the ISDA's (International Securities Dealers Association) Master Agreements?
- What measures has the bank undertaken to ensure that clients do not contest or initiate legal actions against the bank?

3.3.2.5   Operational risk

- What role does the bank's board of directors play in the defining and management of derivatives trading activities?
- Are derivatives exposure updates regularly presented to the board of directors?
- What is the typical structure and content of these reports?
- How are derivatives trading limits defined?
- Who monitors derivatives exposure and how is this monitoring done?
- What contingency plans does the bank have in the event that there is a market crisis?

3.3.2.6   European directive ratio

Does the bank calculate European directive ratios with respect to derivatives? Is it possible to see these ratios?

3.3.3   Managing bank limits

3.3.3.1   Defining and managing the limits

Having assessed that the creditworthiness of a potential financial institution as a counterparty is acceptable, the next question to address is to decide what exposure limit your institution is prepared to accept. In deciding this, there are five key considerations:

1. Your own institution's net worth or size
2. The counterparty's net worth or size
3. The counterparty's creditworthiness
4. The nature of the transaction and its inherent risk
5. The return on risk

Some financial institutions only deal with the most creditworthy banks and impose a cut-off point, for example at the top five banks in any country. It is not uncommon for corporates as well to adopt such an attitude. Alternatively, they may look at a benchmark for creditworthiness, e.g. a minimum rating from a rating agency such as Moody's, Standard & Poor's, or Fitch (the Fimalac-Euronotation-ICBA-Fitch-Duff & Phelps-Thompson Bankwatch collective). This is entirely reasonable if the risk is only one sided and the exposure relative to the bank's net worth is relatively small.

Re point 1, the principle of limiting your exposure to a percentage of a bank's capital is the basic concept of not putting all your eggs in one basket, and capital is a bank's measure of solvency. In most countries, this will be legislated normally at a 10%–20% level although in some countries where there are few banks and all their counterparties are large, this may be up to 50%.

Re points 2 and 3, obviously, the size of the counterparty will be significant in how much they need. One would certainly not want to be exposed to a counterparty for an amount over that of the shareholder's equity and a limit of say 50% could be set as a maximum limit. One would also not want to have the same lines to two banks with the same equity bases but very different credit ratings. There are two other factors which are fundamental to defining exposure to another bank; one is whether "it is a sound high performance bank which will not get into difficulties", the other is "should it get into difficulties, would it receive support from its owners or the state". Both of these factors will impact on the critical question "Can I lose money by dealing with this counterparty?"

Re point 4, the next factor is to consider who decides how much to level is the nature of the transaction and the term of the risk.

In general, long-term exposure to financial institutions is limited and two principles might apply here. Either restrict long-term exposure to only the stronger credits, or impose a percentage of say 25% of the whole line for long-term exposure (known as a "sub limit").

Within the general category credit limits there are:

- Essentially pure credit exposure – placings, lending, letters of credit, confirmations, and guarantees.
- Intraday exposure in settlement systems, FX and local currency clearing in payment systems. Here, the full exposure amount is at risk but it is very short term and the integrity of the clearing system is critical.

- Market risk, FX risk, and interest rate risk where fluctuations in the rates will be less than the face value but influenced by the length of the exposure and volatility of the market rates.

Re point 5, finally, one has to make sure that the amount of risk is being appropriately rewarded. In other words, the higher risk lines should produce higher returns.

3.3.4   Generally accepted risk principles risk map

Generally Accepted Risk Principles Risk Map (Developed by Coopers & Lybrand)		
Credit Risk	Direct Credit Risk	
	Credit Equivalent Exposure	
	Settlement Risk	
Market Risk	Correlation Risk	
	Equity Risk	Equity Price Risk
		Equity Price Volatility Risk
		Equity Basis Risk
		Dividend Risk
	Interest Rate Risk	Directional Interest Rate Risk
		Yield Curve Risk
		Interest Rate Volatility
		Interest Rate Basis/Spread Risk
		Prepayment Risk
	Currency Risk	FX Rate
		FX Volatility
		Profit Transition Risk
	Commodity Risk	Commodity Price Risk
		Forward Price Risk
		Commodity Price Volatility Risk
		Commodity Basis/Spread Risk
	Credit Spread Risk	
Portfolio Concentration	Instrument	
	Major Transaction	
	Economic Sector	
Liquidity Risk	Market Liquidity Risk	
	Prudential Liquidity Risk	
Operational Risk	Transaction Risk	Execution Error
		Product Complexity
		Booking Error
		Settlement Error
		Commodity Delivery Risk
		Documentation/Contract Risk
	Operational Control Risk	Exceeding Limits
		Rogue Trading
		Fraud
		Money Laundering
		Security Risk
		Key Personnel Risk
		Processing Risk

	Systems Risk	Programming Error
		Model/Methodology Error
		Mark-to-Market (MTM) Error
		Management Information
		IT Systems Failure
		Telecommunications Failure
		Contingency Planning
Business Event Risk	Currency Convertibility	
	Shift in Credit Rating	
	Reputation Risk	
	Taxation Risk	
	Legal Risk	
	Disaster Risk	Natural Disasters
		War
		Collapse/Suspension of Markets
	Regulatory Risk	Breaching Capital Requirements
		Regulatory Changes

3.4   BASLE CAPITAL ADEQUACY AND INTERNATIONAL CONVERGENCE

3.4.1   Background to the Basle Capital Adequacy regime

One of the key areas of regulatory concern is capital adequacy. This has crystallised into initiatives such as the Basle Capital Adequacy Guidelines.

There are three reasons why a bank must have capital:

- To absorb credit losses
- To provide safety for depositors and creditors
- To satisfy the regulatory authorities' requirements which are designed to protect the stability of the banking system

A strong capital position also enables a bank to absorb unexpected shocks which may be beyond its control. It also enables a bank to maintain operational flexibility (e.g. to be able to underwrite large transactions such as big ticket syndicated loans).

The regulatory framework is closely concerned with capital adequacy. Capital adequacy refers to the amount of equity that is available to support the bank's ongoing operations.

In the past, heterogeneous legislation meant that it was difficult to establish appropriate levels of capital adequacy due to the differing nature of national accounting systems. The amount of capital moreover depends not only on the characteristics of national accounting systems but also on the nature and composition of the bank's balance sheet and loan portfolio. For example, if it holds large amounts of government securities, this is less risky than project finance loans in developing countries. Higher risk therefore requires more supporting capital.

The equity to assets relationship, however, poses a paradox:

- Too much capital results in dilution of retained earnings, meaning that a bank's ROE will be too low.
- Too little capital means that the bank has insufficient "cushion" to make up for unexpected losses or adverse events (but high ROE).

Banks obviously prefer a lower level of capital due to the ability to maximise ROE but also because equity is a more expensive source of financing than debt.

Regulators on the other hand prefer banks to be adequately capitalised to strengthen the stability of banks and the banking system.

These shortcomings in homogeneity need to impose a level playing field on all players, and need to lower international banking volatility led to international initiatives to harmonise methods of measuring capital adequacy and implement level guidelines.

3.4.2   Pressures for change

As far back as the 1970s the Governors of the G10 central banks established the Committee on Banking Regulations and Supervisory Practices whose task was to consider three main areas of work:

- Prudential control (e.g. capital adequacy and liquidity) of the international banking system
- Supervisory arrangements and cooperation between supervisory authorities
- The exchange of information between the authorities

The Committee also published a paper – the "Concordat" – which was updated in 1983 as "Principles for the Supervision of Banks' Foreign Establishments" which established that the host authority is responsible for monitoring the solvency and liquidity of subsidiaries. The solvency of a branch is the responsibility of the home country whereas both home and host nations share responsibility for monitoring the liquidity of branches. The Cooke Committee, as it was known since it was chaired by the Bank of England's Peter Cooke, also agreed various other principles, such as consolidated reporting.

In 1982, the Basle Committee (chaired by Peter Cooke) of the Bank of International Settlements (BIS) was expressing concern about capital standards. A report produced that year for the "Group of Ten" governors (now 12: Belgium, Canada, France, Germany, Italy, Japan, Luxembourg, the Netherlands, Sweden, Switzerland, the UK, and USA) effectively said that "capital standards in international banking have been eroded, and are continuing to be eroded, and should be eroded no further". It thus became clear that it was not enough merely to stop the erosion of banks' capital bases; they had to be rebuilt, especially in light of the Third World Debt Crisis and later of the innovations in international banking and capital markets.

By December 1987, a consultative paper entitled "Proposals for International Convergence of Capital Measurement & Capital Standards" was released by the Cooke Committee of the BIS. It is nothing short of astonishing that these leading banking nations have managed to reach agreement on a common framework for measuring bank capital ratios on a minimal target level.

Several aspects of banks' activities are normally monitored but one of the most fundamental concerns is the amount of capital relative to business undertaken in order to measure the ability of a bank to withstand any losses sustained. This has traditionally been measured as a percentage of assets required to be available as capital in one form or another. This method of measuring the adequacy of capital has, however, been increasingly recognised as unsatisfactory in the context of today's banking market.

Obviously, there are differing opinions in various countries. These focus on matters such as uncertainties over defining loan loss provisions and unrealised gains on investments. Other uncertainties surrounded the issue of "hidden reserves", and defining and attributing "weightings" to various risk categories of assets.

The initial pressures to institute capitalisation requirements for banks were driven by the Bank of England's and the US Federal Reserve Bank's concern that banks would fail. This was due to the increasing worldwide competition in banking, falling profits, and a high level of provisions being experienced in country and corporate lending.

The need for international standardisation of capital adequacy ratios came into the fore following the well-publicised difficulties the banking world encountered with respect to the Latin American/Third World Debt Crisis of the 1980s. This eventually resulted, after much lengthy discussions and incremental refinancing agreements, in a wave of massive "one-off" loan loss provisions (equal to 30% of LDC exposure or the year's profits) by the majority of the world banks following the Citicorp initiative in 1987. They therefore proposed a minimum capital base as a means of avoiding future bank failures.

The growth of disintermediation and innovation in financial markets during the 1980s posed the particular problem of how to measure the extent of a bank's exposure. As an increasing amount of business was being done off-balance sheet, through massive growth in foreign exchange and securities trading and the emergence of the swaps market, simply measuring capital against loan assets did not represent an effective assessment of the full extent of the risks faced by a bank. Although a bank is usually exposed to less than the full principal amount of an off-balance sheet product, the sheer size of the market meant that the risks overall were large enough to merit attention.

The increasing globalisation of the banking industry also meant that banks were competing in various markets around the world but subject to different requirements by their own central banks. This had two implications. First, it is clear that a supervisory regime which had tight capital requirements would make it difficult for a bank to compete against another which did not have to maintain so much capital. The concept therefore developed of a "level playing field" where all banks were subject to similar capital requirements. Second, the nature of many of the new instruments, particularly swaps, transfers risks to counterparties and banks have therefore become more heavily interdependent. This gave cause for concern where there was a question of whether all banks were being sufficiently rigorously policed.

The main significance of these proposals is twofold.

- They provide an element of harmonisation which should render the evaluation of the financial strength of banks on an international basis somewhat less of a subjective exercise.
- They will tend to eliminate the operating advantages offered by national boundaries and legislative systems and create a more level playing field promoting increased competitiveness in global banking (as opposed to national protectionism/obstructionism). In addition, the accord might pave the way for further long-term global cooperation in other matters concerning banking, securities trading, Third World debt restructuring, or monetary policy. Such cooperation could contribute to a more efficient allocation of capital in the global economy.

3.4.3   The BIS paper: the response of the central banks

The first formal reaction from any central banks to these developments came in two discussion papers issued jointly by the Bank of England and the Federal Reserve in early 1987. The first of these focused mainly on guarantees and contingent liabilities, the second on foreign exchange and interest rate related contracts. They proposed that some proportion of the principal amount involved in these instruments should be included when measuring a bank's assets for the purposes of assessing capital adequacy.

Table 3.1 Tier 1 and Tier 2 capital definitions

Tier 1 (core capital)	Tier 2 (supplementary capital)
paid-up share capital disclosed reserves perpetual non-cumulative preference shares	undisclosed reserves, asset revaluation reserves, general provisions/loan loss reserves, hybrid (debt/equity) capital instruments, subordinated term debt

This initiative was overtaken by wider and more far-reaching proposals which were put forward by the Bank for International Settlements (BIS) in December 1987. This paper dealt with the convergence of international standards as well as the appropriate level of provision for off-balance sheet business. These proposals committed the central banks involved to applying a common definition of capital and a minimum capital adequacy ratio by 1992. There was some limited scope for individual authorities to modify the standards to meet local practice, but the intention was to work towards a "level playing field".

The European Community has pursued a parallel initiative to develop a common solvency ratio to be applied to all credit institutions generally, rather than only to banks undertaking international business which are the focus of the BIS regulations. The BIS Committee has maintained close contact with the community with the aim of ensuring "the maximum degree of consistency" between the two sets of regulations.

These regulations have three principal elements:

- Definition of capital
- Weighting of risk assets
- Weighting of off-balance sheet items

The main points are as follows:

3.4.3.1   Definition of capital

Capital is divided into Tier 1, Tier 2, and Tier 3 capital (Table 3.1).

Tier 1 capital must make up at least 50% of a bank's capital base. Normal practice will be to consolidate all subsidiaries in banking-type activities. Where this is not the case, investments in unconsolidated subsidiaries must be deducted. Goodwill must be also deducted from core capital. At the discretion of national authorities, cross-holdings of other banks' capital may be excluded from total capital. Where no deduction is applied, such cross-holdings will attract a 100% weight, and the situation will be closely monitored by the BIS Committee.

Tier 2 capital or Supplementary Capital consists of undisclosed reserves, asset revaluation reserves, general provisions/loan loss reserves, hybrid (debt/equity) capital instruments, subordinated term debt

Tier 3 capital or Additional Supplementary Capital is basically subordinated debt, which can also incorporate special features. To qualify as Tier 3 capital, a bond issue has to fulfil the following minimum criteria:

- Unsecured, fully paid-up and subordinated to senior creditors
- Minimum maturity of two years

- Subject to a 'lock-in' provision which stipulates that neither interest nor principal may be paid if such payment means that a bank's overall capital position would be less than its regulatory (120%) minimum and
- Not repayable before maturity without the agreement of the relevant supervisory authority

Tier 3 capital has a 'lock-in' provision, which can result in the deferral of interest or principal at the behest of regulators if such a payment would reduce a bank's capitalisation below its regulatory minimum.

Because of its short maturity, relatively high creditor status in liquidation (senior to preferred stock), and limited role (it can only be used to support capital requirements arising from a bank's "trading" book), Tier 3 subordinated debt is a relatively weak form of capital. For this reason, some regulators refuse to recognise it.

Tier 3 capital was created by the European Union's (EU) Capital Adequacy Directive (CAD), which came into effect on 1 January 1996. The CAD was introduced to provide a regulatory capital framework for financial institutions' exposure to market risk. As such, it complemented the EU's 1989 and 1990 Own Funds and Solvency Ratio Directives, which established a capital framework for credit risk.

The basic idea behind Tier 3 capital was that it provided financial institutions with a cheap (at least in theory), flexible capital instrument with which to meet the additional capital demands arising from their market risk exposure due to the implementation of CAD. To match the short-term nature of trading book assets, Tier 3 capital was created as a short-term capital instrument. As such, it can only be used to meet the capital requirements arising from the trading book, i.e. market risk. It is not eligible to support the banking book, i.e. credit risk, nor, at the discretion of local supervisors, trading book capital charges arising from counterparty and settlement risk.

The market for Tier 3 has been slow to develop. This reflects a number of factors including the instrument's unfamiliarity, constraints on supply, given that banks have been generally well capitalised since the mid-1990s, and the negative attitude of some rating agencies.

However, the major problem with Tier 3 debt is that when designing it, the regulators failed to sufficiently take into account market realities. Specifically, given its higher risk profile compared to vanilla subordinated debt, spreads on such instruments must exceed the spread of lower Tier 2 debt to compensate investors for the additional risk. As a result, not only is Tier 2 term subordinated debt cheaper, but it is a more flexible capital instrument as it can be used against both trading and banking book exposure and is not subject to the 250% cap.

3.4.3.2   Weighting of risk assets

The BIS Committee acknowledged that different credit risks were attached to loans to different customers. An attempt has therefore been made to recognise relative riskiness by reducing the weighting of "safe" assets held by a bank.

To keep the system as simple as possible the number of weightings were restricted. They are summarized in Table 3.2.

The risk weighted approach is intended to provide a fairer basis for international comparisons between banks, to incorporate off-balance sheet risk easily and not to deter banks from holding low risk assets.

The issue of country transfer risk has been dealt with by distinguishing between claims on OECD and non-OECD entities, rather than a straightforward domestic/foreign split. The

Table 3.2

	Risk weights – summary
0%	cash; claims on own central government and OECD governments
10%	claims on or loans guaranteed by the domestic public sector (0%, 20% or 50% weights can also be applied for these at national discretion
20%	claims on IBRD and multilateral development banks, OECD banks (non-OECD bank up to one year); OECD public sector
50%	most residential mortgages
100%	claims on the private sector; business with non-OECD banks and governments with original maturity of more than one year, fixed assets, and investments

Table 3.3

	Credit risk related exposure Principle credit conversion factors
100%	loan substitutes – e.g. financial guarantees and acceptances; repurchase agreements; asset sales with recourse; forward purchases; forward–forward deposits; partly paid shares with drawdown commitments
50%	transaction related contingencies (e.g. performance bonds); commitments with original maturity over one year (e.g. standby loans and NIFs)
20%	short-term self-liquidating trade related contingencies (e.g. documentary credits secured on shipments)
0%	commitments up to one year and those which can be unconditionally cancelled

weighting applied varies according to the precise type of claim. For example, local currency claims on non-OECD governments attract a lower risk weight than foreign currency claims.

3.4.3.3   Off-balance sheet weightings

Looking only at the assets on a banks' balance sheet is not a valid measure of a bank's exposure to risk because of the level of off-balance sheet business in which banks now engage. The Cooke Committee therefore recommended that a proportion of such business should be included as risk weighted assets to obtain a better estimate of a bank's real risk weighted exposures against which capital is measured. Such business is assigned a 'credit conversion factor' and the resulting amount is then weighted according to the counterparts using the weights described above. There are two types of off-balance sheet exposure which are considered separately – credit risk related business (Table 3.3) and foreign exchange and interest rate related business.

3.4.4   Foreign exchange and interest rate related exposure

Banks are not exposed to the full amount of the principal underlying such instruments but only to the potential costs of replacing the cash flows lost through counterparty default. The extent of the risk will depend on both time and the volatility of the rates on which the instrument is based. Exchange rate risk is greater because this involves an exchange of principal at maturity and exchange rates have a higher volatility.

Table 3.4

	Current exposure method	
Residual maturity exposure	Interest rate	Exchange rate
Less than one year	0.0%	1.0%
One year and over	0.5%	5.0%

Table 3.5

	Original exposure method	
Conversion factors	Interest rate	Exchange rate
Less than one year	0.5%	2.0%
1–2 years	1.0%	5.0%
Each additional year	1.0%	3.0%

- Examples of interest rate contracts are: interest rate swaps, basis swaps, forward rate agreements, interest rate options purchased, etc.
- Examples of exchange rate contracts are: currency swaps, forward foreign exchange contracts (over 14 days), currency options, etc.

Two possible methods of assessing risk are put forward and individual supervisory authorities will be able to choose which method to apply.

3.4.4.1   Current exposure method

The first follows the suggestions in the Bank of England/Federal Reserve paper, which involves revaluing ("mark-to-market") each instrument, known as replacement cost, and then taking a further proportion of the principal amount to cover possible future adverse price movements up to the maturity of the instrument. The exposure for this residual maturity would be calculated according to the percentages shown in Table 3.4.

3.4.4.2   Original exposure method

The second method uses just the original maturity of the instrument to calculate the exposure. This is proposed because some members of the BIS Committee felt that the two-step approach, incorporating a revaluation, was too complex relative to the volume of business in their market. Certainly it will require considerable investment in computer systems to be able to carry out the mark-to-market exercise.

As this second, simpler method does not take account of actual market movements, the weightings need to be more cautious and the levels shown in Table 3.5 have been proposed.

These conversion factors and the "add-one" for the current exposure method may be subject to change as a result of changes in the volatility of interest and exchange rates. It should be noted that the weightings given are intended to be a measure of portfolio risk rather than an assessment of the amount that may be lost on individual agreements. Banks are likely therefore to continue to measure individual credit exposure on a more cautious basis.

Instruments which are traded on exchanges and subject to margin requirements are excluded from the above weightings as the margining in effect provides for likely losses.

3.4.5   Implementation

The minimum agreed 8% capital ratio (with core capital a minimum of 4% of risk weighted assets and off-balance sheet instruments) had to be met by all banks conducting significant cross-border business by the end of 1992. It should be stressed that the 8% is a minimum standard and banks may be required to meet higher ratios. In April 1995 the Bank of England also issued a document implementing a revised Capital Adequacy Directive, setting out revised Capital Adequacy requirements, which came into force 1 January 1996, and amendments to the eligible forms of capital. Some of the issues covered in the April 1995 document relate to the introduction of a "trading book" as a distinct class of business, and new rules for the measurement of risk in the trading book; some amendments to risk weightings for some financial institutions other than banks; calculation of "large exposures" and the introduction of "Tier 3" capital which can only be utilised to meet market (not counterparts') risks.

3.4.6   Impact of the BIS proposals

Banks have, due to capitalisation ratios and market pressures, been obliged to raise more capital or else reduce correspondingly their asset base and off-balance sheet risks. The result of all this has been to impact the pricing of products, and focus bank management's attention on the risk assets ratio and the risk adjusted return on capital ratio for all its business.

The primary weakness in the Basle capital adequacy measures for bank credit analysts is the difficulty for an outside analyst to calculate it, given that the asset category weightings rely on internal information. Indeed, considerable internal management accounting information is needed to break down the various categories of non-risk assets, risk assets, and off-balance sheet items. Typically, this information needs to be obtained directly from the company, which renders the calculation of the Basle Capital Ratios a difficult exercise.

Another weakness is how the asset weightings are defined. Weighting mortgage loans at 50%, for example, is a subjective measure, in view of the levels of losses on real estate lending in various countries.

Accordingly, the BIS are constantly looking at the methodologies used to calculate the Capital Adequacy Ratios, which can lead to changes in categories or weightings.

4

The Analytical Framework

4.1 INTRODUCTION

We have looked at the macro and qualitative aspects of bank analysis, some major bank failures, how to situate a bank in the economy, how credit rating agencies look at bank risk, and how the regulatory authorities manage the framework designed to optimally control bank risk.

All this preliminary groundwork is necessary to understand the environment in which banks operate and the various business and competitive pressures the bank is subject to – economic factors as well as competitive ones.

Once an appreciation has been realised of the positioning of banks in the banking system, one can then consider undertaking an actual "number crunching" of the bank's financial statements. This typically requires recasting the financial information provided by the bank in its annual report into a standardised spreadsheet presentation enabling various comparisons and analytical techniques to be made.

The main tools used here are annual reports, management reports, spreadsheets, and online financial databases such as Bankscope.

4.1.1 The specific nature of bank financial analysis

Bank financial risk analysis differs from traditional corporate credit analysis in that bank financial statements, their structure, and operations are different. Although the need for adequate capital, liquidity and profitability are common to all businesses, the distinct nature of banking requires us to look at these matters in a different way.

Banks, for example, do not manufacture physical items and have inventory and activity ratios. Problems can be concealed in the loan portfolio, rather than manifest themselves visibly (idle inventory, project delays).

Very often with banks but seldom with other types of business, it is assumed that regulatory bodies and "lender of last resort" issues provide an adequate safety net in the event of failure. However, bank failures are becoming increasingly massive and outside support can no longer be considered a certainty. Furthermore, when interior decay begins to become obvious to outside observers and the press, it is usually too late for exposed parties to undertake corrective action to protect their financial exposure.

As we have seen, the past is full of bank failures. While such stories rarely repeat themselves, they can serve as examples of some fundamental problems which are common to most banks and unique to bank analysis. A knowledge of such cases as well as an inquisitive mind in evaluating the future and risks are therefore of crucial importance.

When failure occurs, the sums of money in question can be astronomical for depositors and shareholders. But things just don't stop there. Indeed, in some cases, the contagious effects of a bank failure can be such that the entire banking system and economic stability of a country, as well as other foreign banks, can be jeopardised, and the repercussions can have knock-on effects throughout a country's banking system and economy.

Concern about the financial health of banks has increased in light of the growing signs of instability and volatility which increasingly characterise the financial institutions sector, and this has led to the implementation of international initiatives such as the Basle accords on capital adequacy.

Change and the exchange of financial information is occurring at a rapidly accelerating rate within management structures which may not have kept pace with technology. The ramifications of a major bank failure such as Continental Illinois, BCCI, or more recently Nippon Credit are extensive and far reaching.

To complicate issues further, with the increasing internationalisation of financial transactions, major bank failures can have cross-border effects. Hence, in addition to a comprehension of bank financial statements and operating risks, understanding the regulatory issues in other countries is necessary in order to assess fully the issues relating to a particular bank or financial institution. Therefore, bank analysis typically includes an overview of the banking system of the bank's home country as well as its situation among its competitors (bank peer analysis).

While there is a faith in the solidity of deposit protection schemes such as the FDIC in the USA or in a "lender of last resort" which will "step in at the last moment", this does not eliminate all possibilities of financial loss, nor does it remove the onus of responsibility on a potential depositor to familiarise himself with the characteristics of the institution he is entrusting his funds to.

It is important to realise that banks handle large sums of money, are subject to competitive pressures, and are run by human organisations with management structures. While these structures have systems of checks and counterchecks, conflicts of interest, pressures to perform, and failure of management structures can occur, thus making failure a reality.

To conclude, banks and financial institutions can be the subject of detailed and exhaustive study: entire departments of government and central banks are devoted to the specialised activity of monitoring banks. This book aims to introduce you to the broad framework, methodology and financial analysis tools used to evaluate banks and, in a more general sense, financial institutions.

4.1.2   Sources of information on banks

Before beginning a financial analysis of a bank, you will want to compile all the available information that you can. Aside from the prime source – the bank's financial statements – where can you search? Here are some sources:

4.1.2.1   Information published by or on behalf of the bank

This information is typically produced by the bank, and is the "raw data" for the analyst. It is either destined for an external audience:

These three categories of information can typically be obtained over the internet. Annual reports can be obtained directly from a company's website; statutory filings can be obtained from sources such as the SEC's EDGAR (Electronic Data Gathering and Retrieval) database or the UKs CAROL (Company Annual Reports on line) database:

- Audited annual report and accounts
- Interim statements
- Other statutory statements (i.e. Form 10-K in the USA)

Those having direct relationships with the company can also obtain information directly from the company:

- Economics publications/prospectuses
- Management accounting statements
- Staff newsletters

4.1.2.2   Other published information

Other information in the public domain can help you in your analysis of the bank:

- Directories (bankers' almanac)
- Central bank or Ministry of Finance publications
- Brokers' reports/Reuters/databank/press cuttings
- CDROM databases

4.1.2.3   The internet

The internet can provide interesting country and risk assessment data such as the Center for Strategic and International Studies (CSIS), EximBank (trade finance criteria) or Energy Information Agency (EIA)'s series of country energy reports, all presently free of charge. Many banks have websites, which can be found via search engines such as Google (www.google.com).

Other sources such as *The Economist*, or Open Media Research Institute (OMRI) offer daily emails of focused political and financial news, for example on Eastern Europe, delivered straight to your PC, to keep you in touch with your particular favourite geographic zone and political power struggles.

A brief list of URLs appears in Appendix I.

These sources of information are useful as they enable you to better understand the context and environment in which the bank operates, as well as keep track of matters such as incorporation, registration, and bank directors as they migrate from one bank to the next. Broker's reports can also illuminate activities such as acquisitions, disposals and the financial community's reactions to these developments.

It is important to consider that these sources of free information may sometimes be prepared by a special interest group with its own political agenda. Therefore, while there may be interesting information, one should bear in mind who is preparing the information.

Press cuttings can also provide warning signals: *The Economist*, for example, noted on 8 May 1998 that "Takayuki Kamoshida, a director at the Bank of Japan, in charge of internal investigations into bribery allegations at the central bank, hanged himself, claiming in a note to be 'exhausted'. His is the latest in a number of suicides that have occurred in Japan's scandal-ridden financial sector."

4.1.2.4   Rating agencies

Rating agencies produce information on banks but it is prudent to consider they have their own set of objectives and criteria. In some countries such as the USA, rating agencies occupy a strong position, as all entities accessing the US capital markets are required to obtain a rating from a rating agency approved by the US's Securities and Exchange Commission. In Europe, this situation is less firm as ratings are not required per se (but the advantages in having one render them virtually indispensable).

The "Asian Meltdown" obviously leads the analyst to look towards South Korea and Asia and ask the question "Are ratings accurate?" Moreover, there has been much recent debate on the effectiveness of credit rating agencies and their track record in anticipating problems in banks and banking systems.

There used to be around 10 credit rating agencies – industry consolidations as well as the difficulties in obtaining approved NRSRO (Nationally Recognised Statistical Rating Organisation) status from the SEC means that this number has shrunk into a comfortable oligopoly of three players. They are:

- Standard & Poor's
- Moody's
- Fitch (the Fimalac-Euronotation-ICBA-Fitch-Duff & Phelps-Thompson Bankwatch collective)

Ratings agencies, however, do not rate all banks and cannot therefore be relied on in all cases, especially with smaller foreign banks. Moreover, using their information does not exonerate your bank from undertaking its own independent research.

4.1.2.5   Other

Finally, there are unofficial avenues to explore. While this is not a sanctioning of "credit risk management by newspaper cuttings", other information it can help focus your inquiry into areas not covered by "official" sources of information. Visiting the dealing room of your bank, talking to colleagues in other banks after work, or reading the call memos in the credit file can give you a feel for the client relationship over time. For example, the author recalls meeting with one bank manager who said that the bank's annual report was "delayed at the printer" followed by a brief silence.

Such information can include:

- Share price/stock market ratios
- Word of mouth, especially dealers
- In-house information (i.e. from bank correspondent records)
- Meetings with bank management

4.1.3   Other sources of information

4.1.3.1   Financial press

The best sources of print/online information for bank and country risk analysis are usually current news and opinion pieces from periodicals.

Books and more academic journals are of course important if one is looking at a country in depth or is trying to establish a country risk evaluation system, but are less suited to day-to-day risk analysis.

In general, what you should look for is information that is objectively reported, and analysis by someone with a balanced perspective and expert knowledge. The periodicals listed below are the most useful in these respects.

There are also hundreds of periodicals, newsletters and other material available discussing specific regions and countries which can be accessed over the internet.

These can be useful when one is focusing on a particular country or region.

- *Banker*, the
- *Echos, Les/AGEFI*
- *Economist, The*
- *Euromoney*
- *Far Eastern Economic Review*
- *Financial Times*
- *Foreign Affairs*
- *Foreign Policy*
- *IMF International Financial Statistics*
- IMF publications

- *Institutional Investor*
- *Middle East Economic Digest*
- *Monde Diplomatique, Le*
- *New York Times*
- *OECD Economic Outlook*
- *Wall Street Journal*
- *Washington Post*
- World Bank publications
- World Debt Tables (World Bank)
- World Development Report (World Bank)

4.1.3.2   The internet

The internet and online databases have made finding information much easier. Through services such as Google, you can rapidly search almost the entire universe of online information.

The internet is an unorganised mish-mash of data but several websites can provide interesting country and risk assessment data. For example, sites such as the Strategic and International Studies (CSIS), EximBank (trade finance criteria) or Energy Information Agency (EIA)'s series of country energy reports, all presently free of charge. Most of these US-based websites are affiliated to the government and toe the party line; they can, however, help to orient and broaden an inquiry as long as one remembers the organisations commissioning and uploading this information have their own agendas.

Some of these websites are listed in Appendix I; note the URLs change frequently and may need to be found via a search engine such as Google or Yahoo!

4.2   FINANCIAL CRITERIA – THE KEY FACTORS

4.2.1   Financial statement analysis

Before examining financial statement analysis within the context of spreadsheets and ratios, it may be worthwhile placing this analytical approach within the proper context.

There are certain preliminary points to consider before undertaking the numerical and ratio analysis of a bank's financial statements.

4.2.1.1   Accounting procedures

There have been many accounting scandals during 2002–03 regarding corporate bankruptcies and failures such Enron, WorldCom, Tyco *et al*. (see Box 4.1 for an interesting roundup by the BBC of US accounting scandals during 2002).

While none of these at the time of writing has resulted in a major bank failure, it is important to realise that many of the accounting firms which were colluding in these cases of corporate failure and accounting fraud are also the auditing firms of the major banks such as Chase and Citigroup – banks which fraudulently set up deals to enable their corporate clients to avoid rules (see Chapter 1 – Box 1.2 "Citigroup Said to Mould Deal to Help Enron Skirt Rules").

It is sad to say that these cases of fraud and failure have not only damaged the credibility of the accounting profession, but also adversely impacted the quality and reliability of financial statements on which banks and investors rely to manage their risk exposures.

Using the well-proven computer programming formula GIGO (Garbage In, Garbage Out), this illustrates the almost irrelevant concerns of fine mathematical analysis of financial statements and ratios when one does not know whether or not the accounting statements have been compromised by fraudulent accounting firms. It renders the analysis as little more than a rather elaborate exercise in guesswork.

This is why with respect to a bank's auditors, you will want to know whether the bank has had any recent problems or disputes over material issues with its auditors. Has the bank received any critical comments concerning controls on any areas? Has the bank changed its auditors in the last five years and, if so, why?

Financial statements will continue to be at the heart of any meaningful risk analysis of a bank, but henceforth it would be prudent to bear in mind these accounting scandals and broaden the scope of analytical inquiry to encompass other risk indicators that do not purely rely on accounting data. It renders the analytical task a more difficult and subjective exercise.

Before starting to spread the bank's financial statements and analyse the figures and ratios, it is advisable to consider certain factors in order to place the accounts in proper perspective. Although an understanding of generally accepted accounting procedures is essential in undertaking a meaningful analysis, bank analysis requires particular attention to specific areas. These can include:

- Accounting convention, rules of disclosure in the accounts
- Analysis of contents of accounts
- Exposure management.
- Non-accrual policies (When is a loan considered an impaired, substandard, or non-performing asset? Does the government allow non-accrual loans to be carried at full value for companies in primary economic sectors?)
- Loan loss reserves and provisioning policies – what is the bank's policy in allocating specific and general provisions? (Flat % of total loans, moving average on past experience, or management discretion?)
- Consolidation practices – how are subsidiary operations consolidated? How are parent guarantees issued towards operating subsidiaries?
- Treatment of investments – at book or market value?

This information, which really is tantamount to setting the groundwork for the financial, analysis, will have been gleaned from various sources as well as in meetings with the bank's management.

Any noteworthy or particular items should be noted in the preamble to the financial analysis report before undertaking the actual financial analysis. Remember, analysing figures and ratios is only meaningful when you understand the information you are dealing with.

Box 4.1

BBC Online – Wednesday, 26 June 2002, 10:53 GMT 11:53 UK
Wall Street scandals at a glance
Spotlight on Wall Street

Confidence in corporate America has been shaken by a series of accounting scandals. What started with an admission of false profits by Enron has rapidly become a rout of some of the best known names on Wall Street. Since the Enron scandal came to light, the accounts of many large American companies have been scrutinised and many more scandals have come to light. BBC News Online takes a look at the companies that have dominated the headlines and planted doubts about the integrity of corporate America.

WorldCom

WorldCom has admitted orchestrating one of the largest accounting frauds in history. The company admitted that it had inflated its profits by USD 3.8bn ($2.5bn) between January 2001 and March 2002. The firm was already shrouded in scandal after the departure of its founder and chief executive, Bernie Ebbers, in April. Mr Ebbers borrowed hundreds of millions from the firm to underwrite the inflated prices he had paid for the company's own shares.

Enron

When energy giant Enron reported its third quarter results last October, it revealed a large, mysterious black hole that sent its share price tumbling. The US financial regulator – the Securities Exchange Commission – launched an investigation into the firm and its results. Enron then admitted it had inflated its profits, sending shares even lower. Once it became clear that the firm's success was in effect an elaborate scam – a chorus of outraged investors, employees, pension holders and politicians wanted to know why Enron's failings were not spotted earlier. The US government is now thought to be studying the best way of bringing criminal charges against the company.

Andersen

Attention quickly turned to Enron's auditors – Andersen. The obvious question was why did the auditors – charged with verifying the true state of the company's books – not know what was going on? Andersen reacted by destroying Enron documents, and on 15 June a guilty verdict was reached in an obstruction of justice case. The verdict signalled an end to the already mortally wounded accountancy firm. This wasn't the first time Andersen's practices had come under scrutiny – it had previously been fined by the SEC for auditing work for waste-disposal firm Waste Management in the mid-1990s. The Andersen case raises a wider question about accounting in the US and how it might restore its reputation as the guarantor of the honest presentation of accounts.

Adelphia

Telecoms company Adelphia Communications filed for bankruptcy on 25 June. The sixth largest American cable television operator is facing regulatory and criminal investigations into its accounting. The company has restated its profits for the past two years and admitted that it didn't have as many cable television subscribers as it claimed. The firm has dismissed its accountants, Deloitte & Touche.

Xerox

In April, the SEC filed a civil suit against photocopy giant Xerox for misstating four years' worth of profits, resulting in an overstatement of close to USD 3bn. Xerox negotiated a settlement with the SEC with regard to the suit. As part of that agreement, Xerox agreed to pay a USD 10m fine and restate four years' worth of trading statements, while neither admitting, nor denying, any wrongdoing. The penalty is the largest ever imposed by the SEC against a publicly traded firm in relation to accounting misdeeds.

Tyco

In early June, the US District Attorney extended a criminal investigation of the firm's former chief executive, Dennis Kozlowski. Dennis Kozlowski – the man behind the creation of the Tyco conglomerate – is charged with avoiding USD 1m in New York state sales taxes on purchases of artwork worth USD 13m. The SEC enquiry into Tyco is understood to relate solely to Mr Kozlowski – but there are investor fears the probe could reveal accounting irregularities. Last week, Tyco said it has filed a lawsuit against one of its former directors, Frank Walsh, for taking an unauthorised fee of USD 20m.

Global Crossing

Global Crossing was briefly one of the shiniest stars of the hi-tech firmament. The telecoms network firm filed for Chapter 11 bankruptcy on 28 January. The peculiar economics of bandwidth meant that firms could drum up the appearance of lively business by trading network access with each other. They could effectively book revenues when in many cases no money at all changed hands. US regulators are now looking closely at the collapse, questioning whether it is another case of a company flattering its figures.

Merrill Lynch

In this atmosphere of corporate distrust, the role of investment banks has also faced increased scrutiny. Analysts were suspected of advising investors to buy stocks they secretly thought were worthless. The rationale for this "false advice" was that they might then be able to secure investment banking business from the companies concerned. Merrill Lynch reached a settlement with New York attorney general Eliot Spitzer. The settlement imposed a USD 100m fine upon Merrill but demanded no admission of guilt. Under the deal, Merrill Lynch has agreed to sever all links between analysts' pay and investment banking revenues.

4.2.1.2   Limitations of financial data

Despite the reservations expressed regarding the integrity of financial statements, in most cases, traditional quantitative analytical techniques (leverage/liquidity/profitability) can be useful tools to assess a bank's performance.

However, as a predictor of bank failure, these techniques have not been fully reliable for various reasons:

- Financial data does not always give a true view of the main cause of bank crises – poor asset quality. Impaired assets can be concealed within normal assets – when the impaired assets become evident, it is often too late to take remedial action; as we have seen in the Indonesian and Japanese banking cases.
- The degree of disclosure required varies from country to country. Accounting techniques which are legal (or even mandated) in the bank's own country may be highly unorthodox by international accounting standards, thereby concealing true profitability and asset values.
- By the time financial data becomes available for financial analysis (3–4 months after the closing of the accounts, the information is often too stale to be of use.
- In the case of weak banks, the financial data is likely to be misrepresentative, even by unorthodox local standards.

In the USA, banks destined for failure (i.e. Franklin National) have often demonstrated a drawn-out deterioration process due to rigorous accounting standards revealing deteriorating trends.

Many banks, however, go out with a bang, e.g. Herstatt (FX overtrading), BCCI (ambiguous domiciliation/fraud), Bangkok Bank (Thailand), Hyogo Bank (Japan), Banco Economico (Brazil), and Avtovaz Bank (Russia) since accounting and disclosure standards are less stringent, and in many instances there are no financial warning signs.

Financial accounts show the results of management. While figures alone cannot tell you everything, they can give clues which can help focus an analyst's line of inquiry.

4.2.2   Spreadsheet analysis

Before analysing a bank's financial statements, they should first be cast into a logical and consistent format, which is usually referred to as a spreadsheet (see Figure 4.1 and 4.2).

Spreadsheets provide a straightforward format which greatly facilitates analysis. They also provide a platform for calculating and selecting key ratios, as well as compiling and merging data from various banks for a peer group comparison approach.

Many banks develop their in-house spreadsheet format; however, the development of financial databases on CDROM such as Bankscope provides standardised formats and enables the user to design their own custom summary report formats.

In the three screencaps in Figure 4.1, one can see the Bankscope database listing all the banks in a country by total assets (cap 1). When one selects a bank, that particular bank's summary and financial information appears (cap 2). Clicking on the accounts enables the analyst to "drill down" to see further detail (cap 3).

In the next section, we will examine the main categories appearing in a bank spreadsheet enabling the undertaking of a bank financial analysis. In the next chapter, we will look at Bankscope and its number crunching features in more detail.

Obviously, some judgement will be necessary in classifying certain accounts in order to ensure that there is a consistent approach.

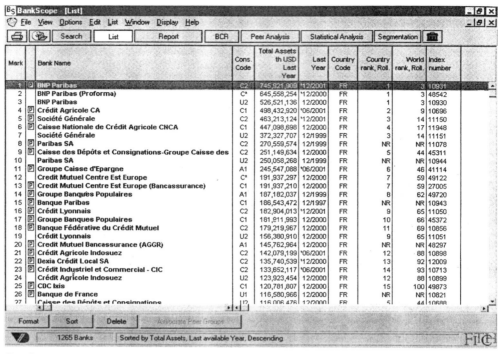

Cap 1

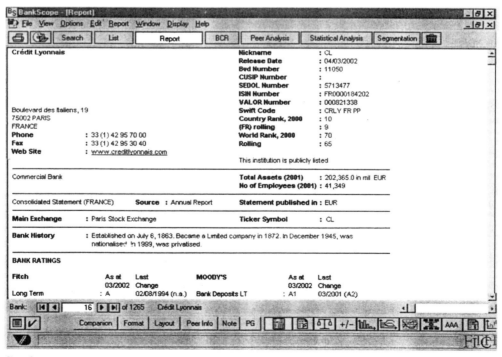

Cap 2

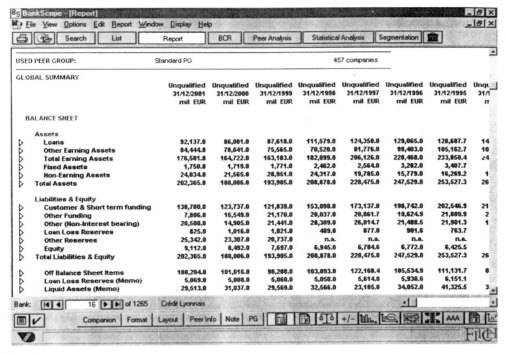

Cap 3

Figure 4.1
Source: BANKSCOPE, Bureau van Dijk, http://www.bankscope.com

4.3   UNDERSTANDING THE BANK'S BALANCE SHEET

4.3.1   Overview

When analysing bank financial statements, the information in them can often be broken down separately in tables and notes to the accounts. The information moreover may not be presented in the same way as the previous year. In such cases, the accounts are said to be "restated". This renders historical comparisons more difficult. It is difficult to understand what is happening with such a disjointed and fragmented presentation.

Furthermore, you may, in your meetings with bank management, be provided with financial information from management accounts (technically these are not audited financial statements), which may provide additional information or highlight specific matters, such as categorisation of problem loans or investment budgets for premises and equipment.

It is important to bear these matters in mind when beginning to recast bank financial statements into a spreadsheet format and begin an analysis.

We therefore shall take a quick overview of the bank's balance sheet and income statement as they are typically presented in a spreadsheet, and highlight the various categories in order to better understand the construction of these statements.

By understanding the organisation of the statements and underlying principles, one will be better prepared for investigating specific accounts in the bank's financial statements and focusing any pertinent inquiry.

A typical summary bank spreadsheet appears in Figure 4.2 although formats can vary.

	NAME	Barings		
	TYPE	Merchant Bank		
	LOCATION	Singapore		
	BUSINESS	Banking		
	AUDITOR	Out to lunch		
	CURRENCY	Pounds Millions		
	ASSETS	**2000**	**2001**	**2002**
1	Cash and due from banks			
2	Due from foreign banks			
3	Government securities			
4				
5	**MINIMUM RISK ASSETS**	0.0	0.0	0.0
6	Marketable securities			
7	Government obligations			
8	Deposits with banks			
9				
10	**LOW RISK ASSETS**	0.0	0.0	0.0
11	Loans/advances < 1 year			
12	Loans/advances > 1 year			
13	Loans to banks			
14	Customers liabilities for acceptances			
15	Other securities			
16	Less reserves (−)			
17	**NORMAL RISK ASSETS**	0.0	0.0	0.0
18	Premises and equipment			
19	Investments/advances to subsidiaries			
20	Intangibles			
21	Other assets			
22	**TOTAL ASSETS**	0.0	0.0	0.0
	LIABILITIES			
23	Bank borrowings and deposits (CDs)			
24	Domestic borrowings and deposits			
25				
26	Customer deposits – Demand			
27	Customer deposits – Time			
28	Customer deposits – Savings			
29				
30	**TOTAL DEPOSITS**	0.0	0.0	0.0
31	Borrowed money + CDs			
32	Customer acceptances			
33	Long-term bank borrowings			
34	Deposits and due to group companies			
35	**TOTAL BORROWINGS**	0.0	0.0	0.0
36	Other liabilities			
37	Bad debts/loan loss reserve			
38	Miscellaneous provisions			
39				
40	**TOTAL NON-CAPITAL LIABILITIES**	0.0	0.0	0.0
41				
42	Subordinated debt			
43				
44	Share capital			
45	Reserves			
46				
47	Retained earnings			
48	**NET WORTH**	0.0	0.0	0.0
49	**NET WORTH AND TOTAL LIABILITIES**	0.0	0.0	0.0
50	**Contras/Contingencies**			
	Crosscheck 49-22=0	0.0	0.0	0.0

	NAME	Barings		
	TYPE	Merchant Bank		
	LOCATION	Singapore		
	BUSINESS	Banking		
	AUDITOR	Out to lunch		
	CURRENCY	Pounds Millions		
	INCOME STATEMENT	**2000**	**2001**	**2002**
51	Interest income			
52	Interest expense			
53	**NET INTEREST INCOME**	0.0	0.0	0.0
54	Fees and commissions			
55	Trading income			
56	Investment income			
57	Other			
58	**TOTAL OPERATIONAL REVENUE**	0.0	0.0	0.0
59	Overheads			
60	**OPERATING INCOME**	0.0	0.0	0.0
61	Extraordinary income (−)			
62	Extraordinary loss (+)			
63	**TOTAL**	0.0	0.0	0.0
64	Pre tax provisions			
65	Bad debt/loan loss provisions			
66	**PROFIT BEFORE TAX**	0.0	0.0	0.0
67	Tax			
68	**PROFIT AFTER TAX**	0.0	0.0	0.0
69	Post tax provisions			
70	Bad debt/loan loss provisions			
71	Dividends			
72	**RETAINED PROFIT**	0.0	0.0	0.0

	NAME	Barings		
	TYPE	Merchant Bank		
	LOCATION	Singapore		
	BUSINESS	Banking		
	AUDITOR	Out to lunch		
	FINANCIAL RATIOS	**2000**	**2001**	**2002**
	Ratios			
73	Total asset growth	na	#DIV/0!	#DIV/0!
74	Loans and advances growth	na	#DIV/0!	#DIV/0!
	Profitability ratios			
75	Net profit growth	na	#DIV/0!	#DIV/0!
76	Pre tax profit/average assets	na	#DIV/0!	#DIV/0!
77	NPAT/average assets (ROA)	na	#DIV/0!	#DIV/0!
78	Net interest income/average earning assets	na	#DIV/0!	#DIV/0!
79	Net interest income/total revenue	#DIV/0!	#DIV/0!	#DIV/0!
80	NPAT/Net worth (ROE)	#DIV/0!	#DIV/0!	#DIV/0!
81	Cost/income	#DIV/0!	#DIV/0!	#DIV/0!
	Liquidity Ratios			
82	Liquid assets/total deposits	#DIV/0!	#DIV/0!	#DIV/0!
83	Total loans/total deposits	#DIV/0!	#DIV/0!	#DIV/0!
84	Liquid assets/total assets	#DIV/0!	#DIV/0!	#DIV/0!
	Risk management ratios			
85	Free capital/risk assets	#DIV/0!	#DIV/0!	#DIV/0!
86	Net Worth/risk assets	#DIV/0!	#DIV/0!	#DIV/0!
87	Total liabilities/net worth	#DIV/0!	#DIV/0!	#DIV/0!
88	Loan loss provisions/average loans	na	#DIV/0!	#DIV/0!

Figure 4.2

4.3.2   Balance sheet

A bank's balance sheet presents the institution's financial condition at a single point in time. Thus, a balance sheet may be prepared on a particular date, say 31 December. The amounts on that date may be different from those on, say, 1 January.

Income statements on the other hand represent the culmination of a year's activities – e.g. net interest revenue represents the total revenues generated during 12 months.

It is important to understand this distinction. Because balance sheets are like a snapshot in time, they can be "window dressed" at the financial year end in order to yield favourable financial ratios. For example, drawing down interbank lines and crediting them to cash in hand is a way of boosting current assets and balance sheet size.

For such reasons, it is a good idea to compare data for several accounting periods, including interim or quarterly statements, in order to gain an overall view of the bank's balance sheet composition, and spot any unusual or incongruous events.

Bank balance sheets provide a summary of a bank's assets, liabilities, and capital. For the sake of clarity, it is perhaps a good idea to reiterate the obvious. Assets represent what the bank owns, i.e. cash, loans and investments; liabilities are what the bank owes, i.e. principally customer (or interbank) deposits; and the capital (equity) accounts reflect the ownership interest in the bank.

Obviously, the balance sheet must balance to the formula:

$$\text{Assets} = \text{Liabilities} + \text{Equity}$$

Bankscope offers a graphical depiction of a balance sheet (Figure 4.3), where these various balance sheet categories are colour coded (assets on the left and liabilities on the right).

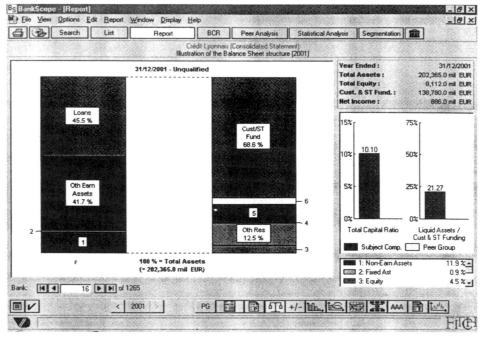

Figure 4.3
Source: BANKSCOPE, Bureau van Dijk, http:// www.bankscope.com

We will now examine the various components of a bank's balance sheet, with most liquid items first and least liquid items last.

4.3.3   Assets

Traditional bank risk analysis recognises four broad categories of assets.

- Liquid "Minimum Risk Assets", "Quick Assets", or "Liquid Assets"
- Relatively liquid "Low Risk Assets"
- The relatively less liquid "Risk Assets"
- Other fixed assets

Analysis of assets focuses on two key factors:

- Liquidity – how quickly can the bank turn assets to cash if depositors require their money back in a hurry or funding dries up?
- Asset quality – what is the risk of not being paid back, e.g. if the loan to or security issued by a company is in financial difficulty?

The example spreadsheet format, whose component accounts are itemised below, follows the pattern of segregating assets as outlined above.

We shall now examine each of the accounts in detail.

4.3.3.1   Liquid/Low Risk Assets

These are assets that are relatively liquid and negotiable in the market. They can represent a temporary liquidity of funds arising from trading activity and temporary investment vehicles.

Obviously, banks are in the business of lending money, therefore you will rarely see banks with the majority of their assets in this category. Generally, all these categories would be defined as liquid but bank deposits which are three months or longer or in countries with transfer risk would not qualify as liquid.

- Cash and due from banks – this item can include cash in till and ATMs, clearing and cash items in process of collection, cash balances with domestic and foreign correspondent banks, money at call at short notice, and bullion. If this item forms a large proportion of the balance sheet, it is possible that non-liquid items such as term deposits with banks have been included.
- Due from foreign banks – if this item is included in the bank's financial statements, it should be broken out separately as it is slightly more risky than domestic bank balances. Interbank assets – assets placed with other banks – can also become problematic, and warrant provisioning.
- Short-term investments or securities – This refers to short-term (ST) high availability corporate or bank securities and includes government bonds and treasury bills. While government bonds are relatively low risk, they should not necessarily be assumed to be liquid. In some countries, banks are obliged to maintain balances of government securities which are a permanent feature of the balance sheet and therefore not so liquid.
- Short-term investments/marketable securities – securities (listed or unlisted) which are easily marketable, i.e. a liquid market exists. "Over the counter" investments and those in

subsidiaries and affiliates do not qualify. The notes to the financial statements should state the basis of valuation (i.e. cost/market) and may give both.

• Deposits with banks and bank CDs purchased – generally considered low risk but may sometimes include support operations for another bank, which portion would be higher risk.

4.3.3.2 Normal Banking Assets

• Loans, or "risk assets", are the least liquid of banking assets, the major source of risk, and the major asset category for most banking institutions. Risk assets are also the primary source of a commercial bank's earnings. Lease financing arrangements substitute for loans in certain types of transactions. For the purposes of analysis, they are included in the risk asset area of the balance sheet (although segregated from the loan portfolio).
• While loans are lumped together under the risk assets category for purposes of ratio calculations, you will want to segregate the bank's loan portfolio by category and tenor, in order to identify the most important characteristics of the portfolio. Detailed information such as the bank's 20 largest borrowers or breakdown of loan maturity schedules can typically be obtained from internal management accounts. Such information is important not only to accurately assess the loan portfolio's characteristics but also in undertaking an appropriate asset liability management analysis re the bank's funding policy).
• Customer's liabilities under acceptances (this item should balance with "acceptances for customers" on the liability side of the balance sheet but may be shown as part of "loans") – generally, the item consists of drafts accepted by the bank under credits established by the bank. It is sometimes shown as a memorandum account which deflates the apparent credit outstanding on the statement date.
• Investment securities – any other stock, bond, etc. not included above with high potential volatility or illiquidity and held for long-term income.

A full analysis of the breakdown of the bank's loan portfolio should be included in order to determine what portion is composed of lower risk loans such as residential mortgages and municipal loans, and which loans fall into higher risk categories.

Any undue concentrations of exposure, in particular industry or geographic sectors, should be noted. In evaluating asset quality, you should give due consideration to the spread or diversification of the assets as well as the overall returns provided by them.

It is important to obtain as detailed a breakdown of the bank's asset portfolio as possible. While some banks will provide this information in a relatively detailed form in their annual accounts, other banks will be less forthcoming, and other avenues of inquiry may be necessary.

Often, such detailed information will not be present in the bank's published financial statements. In certain cases, where disclosure regulations are less than stringent, it may be well near to impossible to obtain such information.

Finally, a major part of asset quality analysis is the bank's track record of loan losses. Loan losses and loan loss provisions can shed light on the overall asset quality of a bank's portfolio, as well as the efficiency of the bank's policy in dealing with loan losses. Information on loan losses and recovery is a key element in enabling analysts to reach an overall assessment of asset quality.

Box 4.2

Asset quality questions:

- What is the annual growth rate of the loan portfolio? What is the forecasted growth for the coming year? How does it compare to peer group averages?
- What is the bank's lending policy? Does the bank have a written credit policy guide and lending guidelines?
- How are loans approved? Is there a committee structure?
- What is the bank's largest client exposure? What are the bank's 20 largest clients?
- Are there any undue concentrations in the lending portfolio (agriculture, real estate, aviation and shipping, telecommunications are but a few categories that have hit banks hard). Any concentrations above 25% of the bank's equity are a warning signal.
- Is there a high proportion of loans to a few firms or a single firm? Are there substantial amounts of intergroup lending as in the Rumasa case? Is there lending to companies that are closely related to the bank's management or shareholders? Such lending can be dangerous and should not be in excess of 15–20% of the bank's equity.
- Is there a high portion of high risk lending? Examples of high risk lending are high or new technology firms, firms losing market share, firms in obsolete industries, highly indebted firms, or sectors that are "overheating" (e.g. property).
- Are there any types of borrowers or industry sectors that the bank avoids? Why?
- What is the level of past due loans? When are past due loans classified as non-accrual loans (30–60–90–180 days)?
- What is the level of non-accrual loans? (non-accrual loans are past due loans in which henceforth no interest income is accrued on the bank's income statement.)
- What is the level of non-performing (past due + non-accrual) loans? It is inevitable that a portion of these loans will be written off as losses.
- What are the bank's provisioning policies?
- Are there any disincentives (e.g. tax related) to full provisioning?
- What is the bank's policy and criteria on writing off loans?
- Who is responsible for managing impaired loans? Does the account officer keep responsibility or is the loan transferred to a specialised problem loans department?

4.3.3.3 Other assets

"Other assets" typically represent assets held by the bank which are not directly related to the core business of lending. However, they can be important in liquidation proceedings and should therefore be identified. The main categories appear below:

- Fixed assets – include bank premises, furniture and fittings, and other real estate owned by the bank. If this latter item is significant, it should be segregated. Check that rates of depreciation are in line with the expected life of the assets.
- Investments and advances to subsidiaries – include interest/dividends earned but not collected.
- Intangibles – unamortised organisational expenditures, goodwill, excess value of acquisitions. These should be deducted from net worth to yield tangible net worth.

- Other assets – include accruals, prepayments, investments in affiliates. Also include "various debtors", "sundry assets", and other such items where further information is not available. It is not unusual for past due items to be hidden under such headings.

4.3.3.4   Assets – summary

Once you have spread the assets side of the bank's balance sheet, you will want to consider the following factors in helping you reach an overall assessment of the bank's asset quality:

- Asset structure/asset quality
- Loan portfolio, sector and exposure distribution
- Classification and definition of non-performing loans

An overall evaluation of asset quality begins with a review of the overall structure of the asset side of the balance sheet. Establishing what portion of the balance sheet is comprised of low risk assets such as government securities and interbank placements, and higher risk assets such as the composition of the bank's loan portfolio is central to this.

As mentioned previously, some effort at standardising the risk weighting of various asset categories has been made in the Basle guidelines. Additionally, classification of various risk asset categories usually is defined by the major rating agencies, and can be provided in their offering circulars describing their rating methodology.

Finally, year to year comparisons can highlight any major rises or falls in the bank's various asset categories. It is a good idea to find out why.

4.3.4   Liabilities

A bank's liability structure is equally as important as asset quality in determining a bank's overall soundness.

Liability structure indicates how the bank's management is funding its loan portfolio, which is why it is closely related to ALM or asset liability management.

To assess the condition of a bank's liabilities structure, you will want to examine issues such as the following:

- What is happening to core deposits? Is there a trend towards a declining portion of interest-free (cheap retail) balances towards more expensive/volatile interbank deposits?
- What is the bank's net position in the interbank markets? Do placements with other banks exceed the funds received from them? Continental Illinois experienced problems due to excessive reliance on interbank deposits to fund its breakneck expansion rather than have a strong and stable retail depositor base to fall back on. When the financial community's confidence in Continental vanished, its bank lines – funding – also vanished and the bank was illiquid. Continental did not have a strong retail depositor base to fall back on as did the major established NY banks. Rabobank Nederland's AAA rating, for example, is not only due to asset quality but also to its large and stable retail base and cooperative cross-guarantee structure, providing a source of cheap and stable funds.
- Asset Liability Management (ALM) refers to optimally managing the matching of liabilities (borrowing at either fixed vs floating interest rates) to assets (the fixed vs floating rate structure of the loan portfolio). ALM also encompasses matching maturity ladders of borrowed funds with those of the loan portfolio.

- What availability/use is made of lines from the central bank? Can the bank function without resorting to funding lines provided by the central bank?
- What is the matching/mismatching as to foreign exchange? For example, is a bank funding its domestic loan portfolio with overseas US dollar funds, thereby increasing its FX risk?
- What long-term debt exists? Is this debt subordinated (i.e. a junior creditor?). If so, this will give greater protection to other lenders or depositors.

Below, we segregate the component accounts which comprise the liabilities side of the balance sheet and identify their key characteristics.

Box 4.3

Asset liability management

Illiquidity, rather than poor asset quality, is the main cause of most bank failures. The analysis of a bank's liquidity position is therefore central in analysing a bank's risk profile. Adequate liquidity can enable an otherwise weak bank to continue operating. Conversely, a healthy bank can be brought down if liquidity weakens or is insufficient.

A bank's asset liability management policy will focus on ensuring that the bank has sufficient operational funds to meet its operational needs as well as satisfy regulatory requirements.

ALM is important for two main reasons:

- Effective ALM should enable a bank to take measures to mitigate the risks of a run on the bank's deposits (particularly interbank deposits), a technical possibility, especially when the markets are increasingly being characterised by volatility. Such runs on interbank deposits have brought banks down as we saw in the Continental Illinois example.
- Liability management can significantly affect profitability as it should optimally match the differences between interest income and funding costs.

Successful liability management (funding techniques) can significantly augment a bank's profitability and reduce vulnerability to volatile funds. Successful ALM requires effective Management Information Systems (MIS) able to quickly generate computerised reports of a bank's asset and liability position at regular intervals (e.g. weekly or daily).

ALM is typically concerned with four risks that must be managed – interest rate, liquidity, capital, and credit risk.

- **Interest rate risk** – analysing interest rate risk uses tools to measure gap, duration, income at risk, value at risk. It concerns managing the relationship between risk and return, the role of deposit and loan products and pricing, and the role of investments and borrowings.
- **Liquidity risk** – this requires understanding the market factors driving how we think about liquidity, and using various measurement tools such as regulatory ratios, sources and uses of funds. The goal is to manage long-term issues of how to fund the balance sheet.
- **Capital risk** – covers analysing the bank's core capital, and evaluating it in function of the Basle II capital adequacy accords.
- **Credit risk** – management is the resultant policy that arises from the ALCO process. It impacts product pricing and loan policy.

The above four points require the implementation of an effective ALCO committee and process, with clearly defined responsibilities and management procedures.

With the growing complexity of the capital markets, asset/liability management has become much more demanding. Investors and asset/liability managers must evaluate a variety of factors including interest rate risk, derivatives risk, complex investment instruments, and liquidity.

4.3.4.1   Deposits

Deposits represent retail and corporate customer deposits, or external wholesale funding on the interbank markets. This includes call money, balances in correspondents' accounts and short-term money market funds. They can be broken down to highlight specific features such as domestic/foreign or tenor conditions.

* Deposits – demand (non-interest bearing)
* Deposits – time or savings (interest bearing)

If broken down into source, domestic is considered as safe as and more liquid than foreign. Also, customer deposits are less volatile than interbank funding and are more likely to remain with the bank in times of difficulties.

Deposits are usually the most stable (and cheapest) form of funding.

4.3.4.2   Funding or borrowings

While borrowings are more volatile (and expensive) than deposits to the bank, they can be of use in funding bank growth and, if ALM is effective, increasing the earnings stream. Banks relying on debt financing moreover have more revenues available for dividends, resulting in a boost to ROE. A bank, however, should not rely excessively on borrowings, and should ensure that it is on a committed basis.

Borrowings can be split into three categories:

* **Short term** – this might be certificates of deposit or other externally generated funds other than deposits. This sometimes includes "acceptances for customers" which should be segregated whenever possible, and may sometimes be deduced by comparing with the assets side of the balance sheet.
* **Long-term borrowings** – this could relate to banks or investors and could comprise actual loans to the bank or bonds issued by the bank.
* **Hybrid capital** – e.g. subordinated debt or borrowings which are long term and have "junior" status in a liquidation.

Box 4.4

Some questions an analyst should ask regarding a bank's funding policy are:

* Does the bank have a diversified funding base or does is it rely on two or three key sources?
* Is there stability and strength in the domestic funding markets?
* Does the bank have the resources, credit standing, and distribution network to change its funding from domestic customer deposits to interbank funding (or vice versa)?
* Is there potential liquidity in the bank's investment portfolio?

Many problems in emerging market banks arise because they tend to rely on interbank funding due to a shallow domestic funding market. For example, the 1994 crisis in Turkey highlighted many Turkish banks' overreliance on international credit lines and syndicated credit facilities from abroad. When credit rating agencies downgraded Turkey's risk ratings, many of these credit lines were cut, which adversely impacted the banks' liquidity position. This moreover adversely impacted retail depositor confidence in the banks, which in turn led to panic withdrawals. Eventually, the Turkish government had to step in and guarantee all deposits to restore confidence and liquidity to the banking system.

While it's fine to say therefore that a strong retail customer deposit base is preferable, the reality is that in many emerging markets, there is not sufficient "depth" in the market to enable banks to rely principally on customer deposits for funding.

4.3.4.3   Non-capital borrowings

- **Loan loss reserve** – this figure may sometimes be found in capital reserves or shown as a deduction from loans on the asset side of the balance sheet. You will want to pay particular attention as to how a bank defines non-performing loans and its provisioning policy with respect to such loans (see questions in Box 4.2.)
- **Other non-capital liabilities** – this includes items such as dividends payable, unearned interest, and accounts payable.

4.3.4.4   Net worth

Net worth is the most important component account used in calculating capitalisation ratios. While we have referred to the subject of capital adequacy, or the harmonisation of their standards, a review of a bank's capitalisation should begin with a comparison with peer group averages and their relation to regulatory requirements.

This information can be obtained from rating agencies' publications which will list comparative data. There is an increasing tendency for a set of standardised guidelines to be set into place on a worldwide basis.

Net worth can be subdivided into:

- **Share capital** – includes fully paid-up, common and preferred shares.
- **Reserves** – the lines can be used for various reserves which it is relevant to itemise (e.g. legal, revaluation, and special reserves). Note that equity reserves are reserves designated for special purposes and are not to be confused with loan loss reserves. Also, capital surplus and any perpetual subordinated debt should be shown separately in this section.
- **Retained earnings** – represent profits ploughed back into the bank's business. In other words, retained earnings represent capital that has been internally generated (as opposed to externally generated – debt or a share issue).

4.3.5   Contingent liabilities

Contingent liabilities, or "off-balance sheet items", as the name suggests, are items which do not appear on the balance sheet. They can form an important part of a bank's business and accounts.

Contingent liabilities represent potential claims against the bank. They are undertakings by the bank to assume liabilities on behalf of another party if a particular set of events occurs (i.e. a performance bond relating to a construction contract in an emerging market country is called). While contingent liabilities traditionally consisted of guarantees issued on behalf of third parties and liabilities under unutilised letters of credit, they can also include commitments arising from swaps, issue of securities, note issuance facilities, etc.

Contingent liabilities can account for a significant portion of the bank's fee income. However, they can be huge and if the liability crystallises, the losses can be as large if not larger than if a large loan goes sour. Because contingent liabilities create contingent risk for a bank, they are under many regulatory regimes included in the calculation of regulatory capital.

Noteworthy characteristics (e.g. major client exposures) should be brought out in the scope of the review.

4.3.6   Income statement

While bank income statements can be presented in a top-down format, as depicted in the bank spreadsheet at the beginning of this chapter, with revenues at the top and net profits at the bottom, some European presentations of the income statement adopt an approach similar to the balance sheet, with all revenues on one side and all expenses on the other.

In the Bankscope screencaps of Figure 4.4, we see in cap 1 the income statement graphically depicted and in cap 2 presented in a classical linear format, with interest received broken down into subaccounts.

4.3.6.1   Breakdown of earnings

Banks provide various services; the key to understanding their operations is to see that they operate on a leverage principle: for a relatively small amount of equity, they can leverage up to 20 or 30 times owner's equity.

This is the key to understanding both their profitability as well as the cause of their difficulties. Banks operate as financial intermediaries in acquiring debt and then using that debt to generate a return higher than the expenses arising from that debt.

There are four principal sources of revenues for banks. The "mix" of those revenue streams can be highly revelatory of the nature of the bank and the types of risks it is dealing with in its ongoing operations.

- **Net interest income** – NII is the difference between interest income and interest expense: a primary indicator of a bank's ability to generate profit on its primary business. Identifying the reasons for any changes in NII is important since this will be a reflection of how the bank's management is managing its credit risks.
  - Interest income arises from loans and deposits and represents the largest source of revenue. This includes income from holding bonds and other marketable securities but is mostly composed of the interest earned on risk assets – loans.
  - Interest expense usually accompanies "interest paid on loans and deposits". The terms and conditions relating to interest expense can be ascertained in the breakdown and analysis of the bank's borrowings (fundings) in the balance sheet.
- **Trading income**, especially from foreign exchange – this includes trading profits from the bank's operations in securities, investments, and sometimes treasury operations. Some

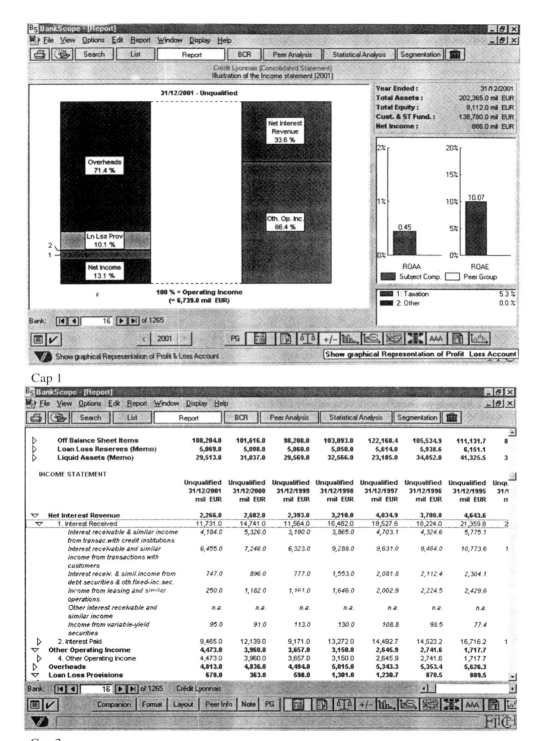

Cap 1

Cap 2

Figure 4.4
Source: BANKSCOPE, Bureau van Dijk, http:// www.bankscope.com

financial institutions specialise in this type of activity. The major part of trading income is foreign exchange or FX trading, but can also include income from trading in bonds, certificates of deposit, treasury bills, and other marketable securities. However, the accounting principles in accounting for FX trading income can vary and you should endeavour to establish how the bank is accounting for this trading income. This should appear in the statement of accounting policies in the notes to the financial statements in the bank's annual report.

- **Fees and commissions** are an increasingly important source of income. Examples are front-end fees for the arrangement of syndicated loans or underwriting of security issues. While commercial banks typically live on their deposits, merchant or investment banks live on their ability to structure and place deals. This leads to an obvious conclusion: if the bank derives a significant portion of its revenues by putting deals together and generating fees and commissions rather than lending money, they can have a better return on shareholders' equity since less equity will be required to support fewer risk assets. Commercial banks are on to this and have their own investment banking operations to generate fee income. The difficulty is that fee income is deal driven and there are no continuous income streams over time as in a commercial lending portfolio. A downturn in activity is therefore dramatic as revenues can be reduced significantly. While the distinction between commercial and merchant banks is becoming blurred, the business cultures are significantly different. Fee income can arise from sources such as the following:
  - letters of credit issued or confirmed
  - underwriting commissions
  - commissions on selling securities to investors
  - custodial services for securities
  - investment/pension fund management
  - mergers and acquisitions advice
  - loan syndication fees
  - guarantees issued
  - standby letters of credit
  - performance bonds issued
- **Investment income** – interest and dividends earned on securities held as investments. Income from associates is fairly common among European and Asian banks but less so with US banks due to historical US banking restrictions on crossing state boundaries and on investing in non-banking subsidiaries. However, for banks which do have a substantial part of their revenues generated by associates, you will want to evaluate the associates' income.

4.3.6.2   Operating income

- **Operating profit** is the intermediary profit/loss figure occurring before (or above) the deduction of extraordinary items and tax. It measures the profit generated by ongoing, recurring operations.
- **Extraordinary income/loss** – any non-recurring income or loss arising from operations such as disposal of a subsidiary or extraordinary profit/loss arising from FX effects such as devaluation; also, transfers from hidden reserves.
- **Provision for loan losses** – these deductions from profits represent loans or portions of loans that the bank does not believe it will collect from distressed borrowers. Provisions may be "general", i.e. where the bank applies provisions on a statistical basis to all loans, and "specific" provisions designed to account for the probability of losses among classified or

problem loans. General provisions are meant to function as a reserve for future problem loans while specific provisions are allocated on a case by case basis to loans that are considered problematic, and whose expected rates of recovery are assessed internally by the bank. It should be noted that it is inevitable that a certain percentage of defaults is expected to occur and one could therefore consider these general provisions as a "cost" of doing business. Because provisions cut into the bottom line, management often has an incentive to keep provisions to a minimum in order to be able to maintain dividend and P/E ratios. Conversely, management may allocate higher than required provisions in order to reduce tax liability or smooth out profits. It is therefore important to realise that the level of provisions allocated can be based on criteria other than that of the bank's loan portfolio.

4.3.6.3 Profit before tax

• Tax can be government, state, and/or local.

4.3.6.4 Profit after tax

• Post tax provisions/disbursements.
• Dividends. Cash dividends declared. Dividends are discretionary payments to common shareholders and obligatory payments to preference shareholders.

4.3.6.5 Retained profit

Retained earnings represent profits ploughed back into the bank's business. In other words, retained earnings represent capital that has been internally generated (as opposed to externally generated – debt or a share issue).

4.3.7 Financial analysis of investment banks

The balance sheet of an investment bank or broker is unique in that the main assets are either "inventory" or securities held for trading purposes rather than the loan book of a bank or the products and fixed assets held on the balance sheet of a manufacturing company.

The quality and liquidity of assets are key factors to analyse, and the volatility of the securities held to movements in interest rates and market conditions have to be analysed.

On the funding side the more equity and long-term debt, the more stable the institution will be and the equity-to-asset ratio will give an indication of this.

Short-term finance is provided by banks on an unsecured basis if the institution is very strong but normally it is provided on a secured basis, with securities as collateral very often through a repurchase agreement.

Spreadsheets for investment banks or brokers will typically have a structure as shown in Figure 4.5.

4.3.7.1 The key activities

Investment banking activities typically comprise:

• Underwriting, issuing, broking and trading government, bank and corporate debt securities. (These can be divided into short-term instruments such as treasury bills, certificates of deposit

Investment bank/broker balance sheet	
Assets	**Liabilities**
1 Cash and cash equivalents 2 Securities borrowed 3 Reverse repurchase agreements	21 Repurchase agreement 22 Securities loaned 23 Securities sold not purchased 24 Other
4 Liquid assets $(1 + 2 + 3)$	**25 Repo funding $(21 + 22 + 23 + 24)$**
5 Due from brokers, dealers, clearing houses 6 Due from customers	26 Bank loans 27 Commercial paper
7 Loans	28 Other
8 Notes	**29 Short-term borrowings $(26 + 27 + 28)$**
9 Others	**30 Short-term funding $(25 + 29)$**
10 Receivables $(5 + 6\ + 7 + 8 +\ )$	31 Senior LT debt
11 Government securities	32 Subordinated LT debt
12 Municipal securities	**33 Long-term debt $(31 + 32)$**
13 Money market instruments 14 Commodities 15 Corporate securities 16 Other securities	34 Preferred shares 35 Ordinary shares 36 Reserves/retained profit
17 Inventory $(11 + 12 + 13 + 14 + 15 + 16)$	**37 Total equity $(34–36)$**
18 Fixed assets 19 Other assets	
20 Total assets $(4 + 10 + 17 + 18 + 19)$	**38 Total liabilities + equity**

Investment bank/broker income statement
39 Net interest revenue 40 Commissions 41 Investment banking fees 42 Principal transactions (trading) 43 Asset management 44 Other revenues
45 Total operating revenues $(39 + 40 + 41 + 42 + 43 + 44)$
46 (Personnel expenses) 47 (Other overheads)
48 Operating profit $(45–46–47)$
49 Exceptional items
50 Pretax profits $(48 + 49)$
51 (Taxes)
52 Net profit $(50–51)$
53 Other adjustments 54 (Dividends paid)
55 Net income $(52–53–54)$

Investment bank/broker capital adequacy ratios	
Equity/total assets (line 37 ÷ line 20)	This capital ratio demonstrates what shrinkage can occur in the banks assets before it is insolvent.
Total liabilities/equity (line 30 + 33 ÷ line 37)	Leverage: another measure of capital adequacy relating liabilities to the equity of the institution.
Investment bank/broker profitability ratios	
Operating profit/total revenues (line 48 ÷ line 45) Operating expenses/total revenues (lines 46 + 47) ÷ line 45) Net profit/equity (ROE) (line 52 ÷ 37) (average of beginning and end of year)	A measure of the profit made relative to total income. Essentially a cost income ratio a measure of operating efficiency. The return on the book value of the bank's equity.
Investment bank/broker liquidity ratios	
Current ratio (lines 4 + 10 + 17) ÷ 30	A measure of the extent to which there is a liquidity cushion if there was a run on the funding sources of the bank.

Figure 4.5

and commercial paper or long-term instruments such as fixed rate bonds, floating rate notes, medium-term notes.)

- Underwriting issuing and trading and broking equities.
- Research analysis: many investment houses provide research papers for existing investors or sell to interested parties their analysis of the future prospects of securities in the markets in which they operate. (See Box 4.5 re some of the conflicts of interest in this area.)
- Providing and trading derivative products.
- Trading in foreign exchange and commodities.
- Corporate advisory services; mergers and acquisitions and corporate restructuring.
- Bridge finance (loans to be taken out by a subsequent bond or equity issue).
- Investment management.

Box 4.5

BBC NEWS | Business | SEC tightens rules on analysts
Thursday 6 February, 2003, 21:29 GMT
SEC tightens rules on analysts

Wall Street analysts are facing new rules. Wall Street analysts will have to state that the opinions given in their research are their own under new rules passed by the US stock market watchdog, the Securities and Exchange Commission (SEC).

The move follows allegations that, during the 1990s tech stock boom, some analysts gave unreasonably favourable reports on companies to help their employer win investment banking business.

"Simply put, we want analysts to say what they mean, and mean what they say, and to sign their name to that," said SEC commissioner Cynthia Glassman.

Last December, the main banks and brokerages on Wall Street paid more than USD 1.4bn in order to settle stock-tipping allegations with US regulators.

Informing investors

Under Regulation Analyst Certification, or Reg AC, share analysts will have to certify that the research they publish is truly their own personal view.

They will also have to vouch that they received no payment that could influence their buy or sell recommendations on shares and bonds.

"It's . . . important that investors be fully informed of compensation arrangements and other conflicts that could influence an analyst's recommendations or views," said the outgoing SEC chairman Harvey Pitt.

Mr Pitt resigned from the SEC in November but is staying on until his nominated successor William Donaldson is cleared by Senate.

SEC commissioner Harvey Goldschmid said: "The modifications we have made . . . are sensible" within an analyst system that "is badly broken."

But some people said the new regulations would make little change.

"I'm not sure what it adds to the mix," said Saul Cohen, a partner at the law firm of Proskauer Rose. "But if it makes some people more comfortable, fine."

4.3.7.2   The key risks

The key risks relating to investment banks are different than commercial banks. Investment banks are transaction-driven organisations while commercial banks are loan-driven entities. The key risks are:

- **Where will next year's profits come from?** Investment banks do not have the regular income flow provided by a loan portfolio with staggered maturity schedules over time. Investment banks' income comes from fee income – from setting up deals. Obviously, deals are generated on a one-on-one basis. Investment banks therefore have to find their income every year.
- **Operational risks** – the trading environment in investment banks can be extremely complex and not understood by auditors or management, resulting in the problems encountered by Barings and Daiwa.
- **Proprietary trading risks** – much of the activities of investment banks is position taking in securities and other instruments which is inherently speculative and therefore highly risky. The losses suffered by several houses in 1994 were caused by an unexpected rise in dollar interest rates and a collapse in bond prices.
- **Conflicts of interest** – loss of confidence in investment bankers can result from selling investments which are complex and inappropriate. Recent scandals show that supposedly "impartial" research has been little more than "advertising" as a means of selling an investment bank's high inventory of securities (see press extracts, Box 4.5) Similarly the separation of corporate finance advisory work and trading activities is extremely sensitive. Indeed recent scandals have resulted in departures of analysts and their managers at brokerage houses such as Merrill Lynch, and scandals which have led to laws requiring analysts to sign off assuming responsibility on the "research" they produce.
- **Management risk** – the salaries and bonuses earned in the securities industry are extremely high and the need to ensure an open and team culture is paramount. Failure to manage this

well has led to mass defections of key players making investment banks vulnerable to sudden losses of business.

4.3.8   Risk profile of investment banks

The main activities, in ascending level area of risk, are:

- **Asset management** – this has typically targeted retail and wholesale investors, although the big firms, at least prior to the beating shares have taken during 2002–03, have tended to do best selling mutual funds to individuals. This business pays annual fees rather than generates one-off returns, which makes them very attractive to firms whose other businesses are inherently cyclical.
- **Broking** – a commission-generating activity: a business in which firms appeal to customers mainly on price.
- **Investment banking or corporate finance** – this includes underwriting new issues, advisory work, and mergers and acquisitions. Underwriting typically contributes around four-fifths of the fees earned in this area, although all elements of the business are highly cyclical, as they are deal driven. M&A activity, though cyclical, can be very profitable due to the lucrative underwriting fees.
- **Trading** –which thrives on volatility and has been growing in importance as firms have committed more capital and resources.

Bankscope and Comparative Techniques

5.1 BANKSCOPE SPREADSHEET ANALYSIS

Bankscope is a database produced by Bureau van Dijk in collaboration with Fitch (the Fimalac-Euronotation-ICBA-Fitch-Duff & Phelps-Thompson Bankwatch collective), and other providers of financial information including Moody's, Standard & Poor's, and Reuters.

The database was originally distributed on CDROM and DVD, but is now available online over the internet, considerably facilitating updates and logistics.

Bankscope is a rather rich and complete database on over 12 000 banks and contains:

- a database of financial statements
- shareholder information
- ratings from the major rating agencies and
- Reuters news database on 10 000+banks

all linked with a powerful search tool enabling searches by bank name, bank size, capitalisation, geographic coverage, specific words, etc.

Bankscope also enables detailing certain items in the financial statements and the extraction of data for compilation of peer group indicators for comparative purposes.

The financial element contains a database on the world banks' financial statements typically going back five years or more.

The typical format of a Bankscope bank report typically contains:

- A cover sheet with summary financial data and ratings
- An abbreviated (global) set of financial statements and ratios enabling international comparisons
- A complete set of financial statements with ratios (which can be further broken down by account category) by clicking on the relative item with a mouse
- A sheet with lists of shareholders and subsidiaries and
- A database of Reuters news articles going back two years relating to the bank in question

Figures 5.1 to 5.4 provide some Bankscope screencaps showing:

- List of banks in one country sorted by total assets
- Bank summary data page
- Bank summary financial data
- Bank income statement (with account breakdowns)

We shall now turn to examining financial spreadsheets generated by Bankscope.

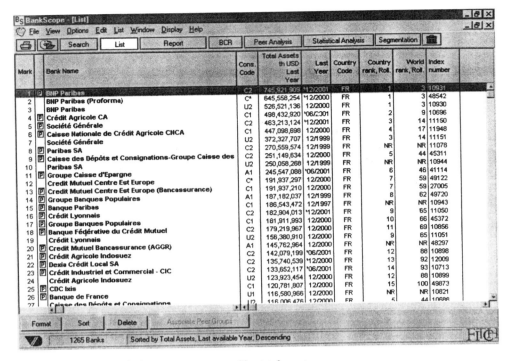

Figure 5.1 List of banks in one country sorted by total assets
Source: BANKSCOPE, Bureau van Dijk, http://www.bankscope.com

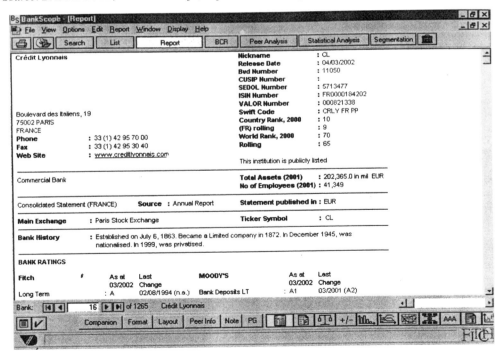

Figure 5.2 Bank summary data page
Source: BANKSCOPE, Bureau van Dijk, http://www.bankscope.com

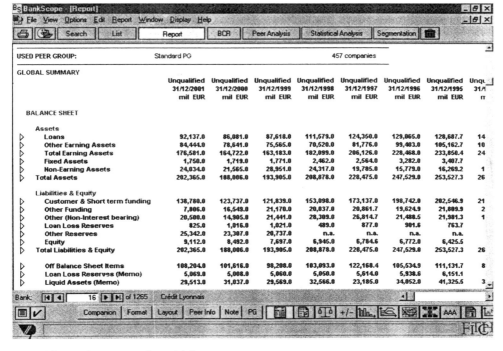

Figure 5.3 Bank summary financial data
Source: BANKSCOPE, Bureau van Dijk, http://www.bankscope.com

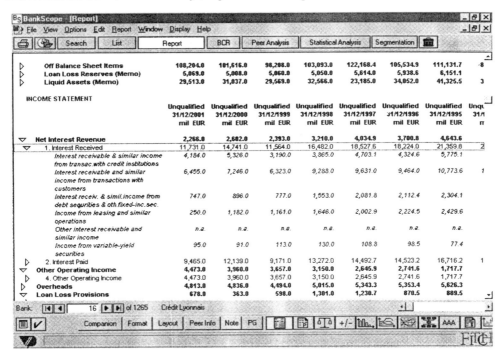

Figure 5.4 Bank income statement (with account breakdowns)
Source: BANKSCOPE, Bureau van Dijk, http://www.bankscope.com

5.2   BANKSCOPE RATIOS AND RATIO ANALYSIS

5.2.1   Lines of the bankscope global format

As we saw in our summary spreadsheets in the previous section, each item in the spreadsheet has a corresponding item number.

In the screencap of Figure 5.5 we see that in the Bankscope database, each item in the spreadsheet is also numbered. Numbering the individual accounts in a spreadsheet is necessary for three reasons:

- When spreading the financial statements, each item in the annual report provided by the bank is numbered and then ticked off so that the analyst spreading the statements in the following year's annual report can easily track the predecessor analyst's methodology in breaking down and reclassifying the bank's accounts and inserting them in the relevant account of the spreadsheet.
- When calculating ratios and cash flow statements, easy reference can be made as to which items of the spreadsheet are being included in the ratio or cash flow item.
- When compiling peer group analysis tables, the reference numbers ensure that the same figures are being extracted from the spreadsheets and being compiled into the peer group comparative table.

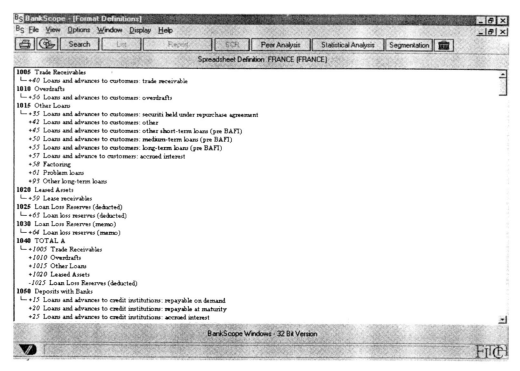

Figure 5.5
Source: BANKSCOPE, Bureau van Dijk, http://www.bankscope.com

Numbering the spreadsheet accounts therefore is an important tool in ensuring a consistent methodology and facilitating spreadsheet programming.

5.2.2   Financial ratio analysis

While certain financial trends are discernible in the balance sheet and income statement spreadsheets we examined in the previous section, a more thorough analysis needs to use a complete set of financial ratios. The value of ratios is that they allow you to compare different sizes of banks on a comparable basis. Ratio analysis enables you to identify positive or negative trends over time, compare a bank to a group of similar banks (peer group analysis), or even to a set of "average ratios" generated from the peer group ("peer group average") to see how any bank is doing relative to its peers.

Since some ratios are more appropriate than others depending on circumstances and requirements, Bankscope provides a complete set of ratios; analysts can therefore use and select the most pertinent ratios for their analytical requirements.

Bankscope enables the rapid visualisation of information which in the past was manually calculated into ratios.

In the screencaps of Figures 5.6 and 5.7:

* The first depicts a group of financial ratios in numerical presentation
* The second plots various ratios graphically over time to illustrate any major movements

These techniques are useful in undertaking historical trend analysis.

5.2.3   The Bankscope ratios

For sake of standardisation, we shall concern ourselves with the ratios generated by Bankscope, since this is a widely distributed generic tool.

The Global Format uses four digits to identify individual headings in the Bankscope spreadsheet.

The ratios generated by Bankscope are calculated using the Global Format. They use the adjacent item numbers which refer to the spreadsheet items in the Bankscope Global Format input spreads.

The ratios can be divided into four main categories and measure various aspects of:

* Asset quality
* Capital
* Operations (i.e. profitability and efficiency)
* Liquidity

The following section on Bankscope ratios comprise the official definition of the Bankscope ratios in the Bankscope database (BANKSCOPE, Bureau van Dijk, http://www.bankscope.com).

5.2.3.1   Asset quality

Before analysing provision and asset quality ratios, one should note that from country to country and indeed, within the same country, policies vary as to:

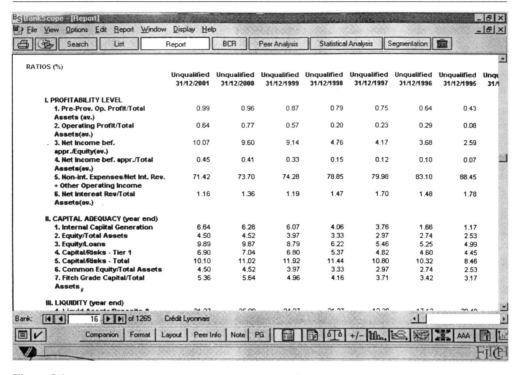

Figure 5.6
Source: BANKSCOPE, Bureau van Dijk, http://www.bankscope.com

- how aggressively or otherwise banks provide for loan losses,
- when they charge off a loan, and
- when they define loans as non-performing.

These differences obviously can distort ratios.

1 Loan loss reserves/Gross loans

2070/(2000 + 2070) * 100

This ratio indicates how much of the total portfolio has been provided for but not charged off. It is a reserve for losses expressed as a percentage of total loans. Given a similar charge-off policy, the higher the ratio the poorer the quality of the loan portfolio will be.

2 Loan loss provisions/Net interest revenue

2095/2080 * 100

This is the relationship between provisions in the profit and loss account and the interest income over the same period. Ideally this ratio should be as low as possible and in a well run bank if the lending book is higher risk this should be reflected by higher interest margins. If the ratio deteriorates this means that risk is not being properly remunerated by margins.

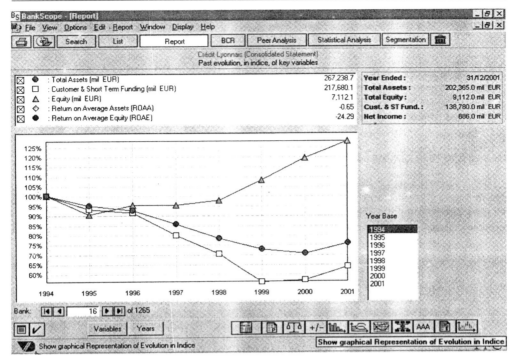

Figure 5.7
Source: BANKSCOPE, Bureau van Dijk, http://www.bankscope.com

3 Loan loss reserves/Non performing loans

2070/2170 * 100

This ratio relates loan loss reserves to non performing or impaired loans and the higher this ratio is the better provided the bank is and the more comfortable we will feel about the asset quality.

4 Non performing loans/Gross loans

2170/(2000 + 2070) * 100

This is a measure of the amount of total loans which are doubtful. The lower this figure is the better the asset quality.

5 NCO/Average gross loans

2150/(2000 + 2070) AVG * 100

Net charge-offs or the amount written-off from loan loss reserves less recoveries is measured at a percentage of the gross loans. It indicates what percentage of today's loans have been finally been written off the books. The lower this figure the better as long as the write off policy is consistent across comparable banks.

6 NCO/Net income before loan loss provision

$2150/(2115 + 2095)/100$

This ratio similarly measures charge-offs but against income generated in the year and again the lower this figure the better, other things being equal.

If Net Interest Revenue (2080) is negative, ratio 2 is meaningless and is noted ns. The same is true for ratio 6 if Net Income before Loan Loss Provision is negative.

It may happen that the institution is disclosing only the net value of Non Performing Loans. In such cases, NPL is underestimated. Nevertheless, ratios 3 and 4 are computed; ratio 3 is followed by the sign + indicating it is overestimated; ratio 4 is followed by the sign − indicating it is underestimated.

Conversely, some institutions might disclose the value of NPL including past due interest. In such cases, NPL is overestimated and the figures for the ratios 3 and 4 would be followed by the − and + signs.

5.2.3.2   Capital

7 Tier 1 ratio

2130

This measure of capital adequacy measures Tier 1 capital; that is, shareholders' funds plus perpetual non-cumulative preference shares as a percentage of risk-weighted assets and off-balance sheet risks measured under the Basle rules. This figure should be at least 4%.

8 Capital adequacy ratio

2125

This ratio is the total capital adequacy ratio under the Basle rules. It measures Tier 1 + Tier 2 capital which includes subordinated debt, hybrids, loan loss reserves and the valuation reserves as a percentage of risk-weighted assets and off-balance sheet risks. This ratio should be at least 8%. This ratio cannot be calculated simply by looking at the balance sheet of a bank but has to be calculated internally by the bank. At their option they may publish this number in their annual report.

Both figures for Ratios 7 and 8 are supplied by the concerned institutions.

9 Equity/Total assets

$2055/2060 * 100$

As equity is a cushion against asset malfunction, this ratio measures the amount of protection afforded to the bank by the equity invested in it; the higher this figure the more protection there is.

10 Equity/Loans

2055/2000 * 100

Similarly this ratio measures the equity cushion available to absorb losses on the loan book.

11 Equity/Customer and short term funding

2055/2030 * 100

This ratio measures the amount of permanent funding relative to short term potentially volatile funding and the higher this figure the better.

12 Equity/Liabilities

$2055/(2060 - 2055 - 2160 - 2165) * 100$

This leverage ratio is simply another way of looking at the equity funding of the balance sheet and is another way of looking at capital adequacy.

Ratios 13–16 are identical to 9–12 with the exception that in the denominator we have capital funds rather than equity. Capital funds include not only equity but also hybrid capital and subordinated debt which share the characteristics of equity namely that they are junior in liquidation to all other deposits and liabilities.

13 Capital funds/Total assets

$(2055 + 2160 + 2165)/2060 * 100$

14 Capital funds/Net loans

$(2055 + 2160 \sim 2165)/2000 * 100$

15 Capital funds/Customer ST funding

$(2055 + 2160 + 2165)/2030 * 100$

16 Capital funds/Liabilities

$(2055 + 2160 + 2165)/(2060 - 2055 - 2160 - 2165) * 100$

17 Subordinated debt/Capital funds

$2165/(2055 + 2160 + 2165) * 100$

This ratio indicates what percentage of total capital funds is provided in the form of subordinated debt and as this is the least permanent form of capital then the lower this figure is the better.

As an application of the general rule mentioned above, if no figure is available for Subordinated Debt (2165), ratios 13 to 17 are noted na.

5.2.3.3 Operations

18 Net interest margin

2080/2010 AVG * 100

This ratio is the net interest income expressed as a percentage of earning assets and the higher this figure the cheaper the funding or the higher the margin the bank is commanding. Higher margins and profitability are desirable as long as the asset quality is being maintained.

19 Net interest income/Average assets

2080/2025 AVG * 100

This ratio indicates the same but expresses it as a percentage of the total balance sheet.

20 Other operating income/Average assets

2085/2025 AVG * 100

When compared to the above ratio this indicates to what extent fees and other income represent a greater percentage of earnings of the bank and as long as this is not volatile trading income it can be seen as a lower risk form of income. The higher this figure is the better.

21 Non-interest expenses/Average assets

(2090 + 2095)/2025 AVG * 100

Non-interest expenses or overheads plus provisions give a measure of the cost side of the bank's performance relative to the assets invested.

22 Pre-tax operating income/Average assets

(2105 − 2100)/2025 AVG * 100

This is a measure of the operating performance of the bank before tax and unusual items. This is a good measure of profitability unaffected by one-off non-trading activities.

23 Non-operating items/Average assets

(2100 − 2110)/2025 AVG * 100

This ratio measures unusual items and tax as a percentage of assets.

24 Return on average assets (ROAA)

2115/2025 AVG * 100

This is perhaps the most important single ratio in comparing the efficiency and operational performance of banks as it looks at the returns generated from the assets financed by the bank.

25 Return on average equity (ROAE)

2115/2055 AVG * 100

The return on equity is a measure of the return on shareholders' funds. Obviously here the higher the figure the better but one should be careful in putting too much weight on this ratio as it may be at the expense of an over-leveraged balance sheet.

26 Dividend payout

2120/2115 * 100

This is a measure of the amount of post tax profits paid out to shareholders. In general the higher the ratio the better, but not if it is at the cost of restricting reinvestment in the bank and its ability to grow its business.

27 Income net of dividends/Average equity

(2115 − 2120)/2055 AVG * 100

This ratio is effectively the return on equity after deducting the dividend from the return and it shows by what percentage the equity has increased from internally generated funds. The higher the better.

28 Non-operating items/Net income

2100/2115 * 100

This denotes what percentage of total net income consists of unusual items.

29 Cost-to-income ratio

2090/(2080 + 2085) * 100

This is one of the most focused on ratios currently and measures the overheads or costs of running the bank, the major element of which is normally salaries, as a percentage of the income generated before provisions. It is a measure of efficiency, although, if the lending margins in a particular country are very high then the ratio will improve as a result. It can be distorted by high net income from associates or volatile trading income.

30 Recurring earning power

(2105 − 2100 + 2095)/2025 AVG * 100

This ratio is a measure of before tax profits adding back provisions for bad debts as a percentage of total assets. Effectively this is a return on assets performance measurement without deducting provisions or unusual items.

5.2.3.4   Liquidity

31 Interbank ratio

2180/2185 * 100

This is money lent to other banks divided by money borrowed from other banks. If this ratio is greater than 100 then it indicates the bank is a net placer rather than a borrower of funds in the market place, and therefore more liquid.

32 Net loans/Total assets

2000/2025 * 100

This liquidity ratio indicates what percentage of the assets of the bank are tied up in loans. The higher this ratio the less liquid the bank will be.

33 Net loans/Customer and ST funds

2000/2030 * 100

This loan to deposit ratio is a measure of liquidity in as much as a high figure denotes lower liquidity.

34 Net loans/Total deposits and borrowings

2000/(2030 + 2035 − 2160 − 2165) * 100

This similar ratio has as its denominator deposits and borrowings with the exception of "capital instruments".

35 Liquid assets/Customer and ST funds

2075/2030 * 100

This is a deposit run-off ratio and looks at what percentage of customer and short term funds could be met if they were withdrawn suddenly, the higher this percentage the more liquid the bank is and less vulnerable to a classic run on the bank.

36 Liquid assets/Total deposits and borrowings

2075/(2030 + 2035 − 2160 − 2165) * 100
This ratio is similar to 35 but looks at the amount of liquid assets available to borrowers as well as depositors.

5.2.3.5   In the Group Reports

AVG means that the item is averaged using the arithmetic mean of the value at the end of year t and $t-1$. In order not to lose information, when figures are available for one year only, ratios implying average figures are nevertheless calculated using the values of the only available year. The same is true for the values of such ratios relating to the oldest year available in the series shown. In these cases, the values displayed or printed are followed by the sign * showing that the denominator is not averaged.

If any one of the items included in the calculation of a ratio is not available, the ratio is noted na.

5.3   BANK PEER GROUP ANALYSIS

5.3.1   Analytical techniques

The financial analysis of banks can indicate how strong a bank is and how it is performing on three levels.

- The first method we looked at was trend analysis. Trend analysis basically looks at how a bank is performing over time, and whether its profitability or liquidity is improving or deteriorating. This will primarily be a function of the quality of management, but competition and business environment will also have an impact.
- The second method is to analyse a bank's performance against national regulatory requirements such as the BIS risk weighted asset ratio and see how it compares with those required prudential norms.
- The third method to evaluate banks is by comparing them to similar banks doing the same type of business in the same environment. This method is called peer group analysis and it is a particularly valuable analytical tool. Peer group analysis is useful, for example, in cases such as deciding one or two broadly based commercial banks in one country, for example, as a trading counterparty. At a glance we can see which institutions are the safest to deal with.

The first two analytical techniques are useful but tend to look at the bank in isolation.

Peer group analysis on the other hand may not say much about the bank's historical performance, but it can help situate that performance in an overall context, which can help clarify the factors affecting a bank's historical performance – factors which may be industry specific rather than specific to the bank being analysed. Peer group analysis therefore solves the problem of analysing a bank in isolation without any outside reference points.

It is important in peer group analysis to compare like with like. For example, comparing a commercial bank to an investment bank and a savings bank would be misleading because each of these banks is in a substantially different business.

Often, there may not be enough banks in a small country to warrant undertaking a peer group analysis and the analysis will therefore have to compare banks on a cross-border basis. In such cases, it is important to bear in mind that national accounting differences can accordingly impact the financial ratios.

The screencaps of Figures 5.8 and 5.9 illustrate peer group analysis.

- In the first screencap (Figure 5.8), the bank highlighted is compared against its peer group. Size, profitability, and key ratios are easily discerned.
- In the second screencap (Figure 5.9), the reference bank highlighted is compared against its peer group. In this case, the key account being compared is Operating Income.

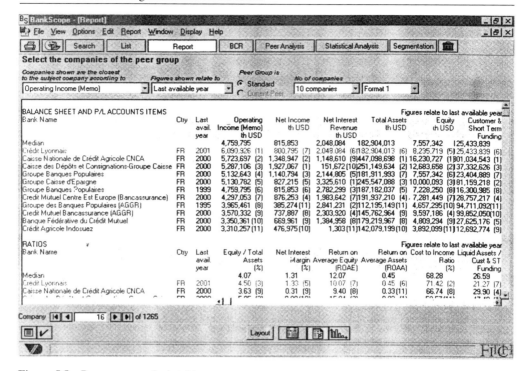

Figure 5.8 Peer group analysis table
Source: BANKSCOPE, Bureau van Dijk, http://www.bankscope.com

When undertaking a peer group analysis, it is helpful to arrange the data in a comparative table before considering the following points:

- How does the balance sheet structure of the banks affect their profitability?
- What is the proportion of short-vs long-term funding in financing the loan portfolio?
- How does the net profitability and equity figures of the various banks compare?
- How does asset quality affect provisions? What does the weight of loans in the balance sheet, ratios of problem loans to total loans, provisions to total loans, and provisions to operating or pretax profit tell you? How does provisioning compare across the peer group sample?
- Does the table tell you anything about liquidity, i.e. the ability of the banks to repay depositors if there were a sudden crisis in the banking sector or a "run" on deposits?
- How might you focus your inquiry into the bank's funding (customer vs interbank funding) vs the availability of liquid assets (cash, deposits with banks, marketable securities).
- How might cross-border comparisons help you to shed light on certain aspects of performance? What comparison factors might be distorted when undertaking a cross-border comparison?

Peer group analyses can highlight and put into perspective certain industry wide issues that affect all banks. The following press extract from *The Economist*, 29 May 1998, illustrates an adverse development which is affecting the industry as a banking industry as a whole (rather than a bank in isolation) in Japan.

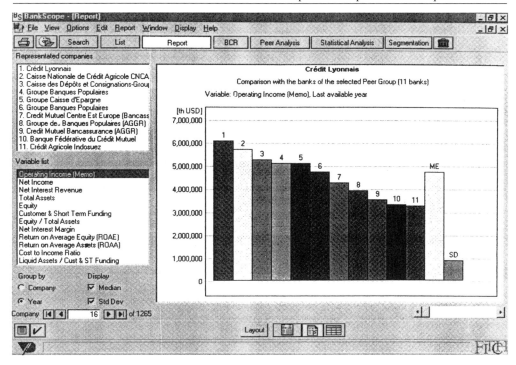

Figure 5.9   Peer group analysis graph
Source: BANKSCOPE, Bureau van Dijk, http://www.bankscope.com

Japan's banks continued the Augean task of clearing out their bad loans, declaring vast losses (and a few tiny profits) in the process. The country's top 18 banks declared a collective loss of Yen 4.35 trillion (USD 35.4 billion), with provisions totalling Yen 10 trillion. Bank of Tokyo-Mitsubishi, the world's biggest, announced a stunning pre-tax loss of Yen 918 billion – close to USD 7.5 billion. Moody's cut its ratings and those of four other banks, and put four more under review.

5.4   PROBLEMS WITH INTERCOUNTRY COMPARISONS

5.4.1   Local vs international accounting standards

When analysing the financial statements of foreign banks, it is essential to begin with the premise that the statements have been prepared in conformance with "local accounting standards". While these standards can differ from one country to another, in the OECD, for example, international accounting standards (IAS) are often in place and meaningful analyses and comparisons can be undertaken.

In emerging or transition economies, however, the problem becomes more difficult. In the Newly Independent States of the ex-USSR, for example, the move towards IAS has been lengthy. Legacy accounting standards reveal little about a bank's health, due to some extent to Russian accounting statements being prepared on a cash basis instead of an accrual basis.

For example, Russian accounting standards do not account for loan loss provisions – Russian accounting did not require loans to be declared as lost until they were overdue, and most banks have been in the habit of simply rescheduling dud loans to avoid this problem.

Investors wanting to invest in the Russian economy naturally want IAS accounts to be implemented. While Russian banks and regulators are responding and acknowledge the need to harmonise their accounting systems with IAS, full reform is still a way off, as there are many underlying issues affecting this agenda.

For example, *Pravda* notes that:

> The transfer of Russian banks to International Accounting Standards (IAS) starting in 2004 would activate their takeovers by foreign competitors, Alexander Mamut, head of the task group for the financial and stock market in the Russian Union of Industrialists and Entrepreneurs, forecasted at a meeting with a French delegation of businessmen, MEDEF, today. He explained that foreign banks would have goals for purchases after Russian banks became transparent.

For the analyst looking at a bank in another country, it is essential that local accounting standards' peculiarities be identified and understood, and that the impact on the subject bank be at least identified if quantification is not possible.

5.4.2   Inflation accounting

Brazil in the early 1980s was unique in developing accounting systems to cope with the country's hyperinflation. During this period, under Brazilian accounting rules, permanent assets and stockholders' equity were subject to monetary correction. The monetary correction was linked to the index for readjustable national treasury bonds (ORTN in Portuguese).

The readjustment process involved writing up the balance sheet carrying value of permanent assets and equity in line with the increases in inflation as measured by the ORTN index. The adjustment amounts were carried to the monetary correction line on the profit and loss statement: an increase in permanent assets as a credit, an increase in equity as a debit. The net entry on the monetary correction line of the profit and loss statement is included in calculating taxable income; the net monetary correction figure affects the amount of taxes paid.

Brazilian inflation accounting procedures had two further impacts which relate to changing monetary values and inflation and affect the stated profit position of banks.

First, assets and liabilities denominated in a foreign currency were adjusted on the balance sheet based on the exchange rate prevailing at the statement date. The adjusted amounts are carried to the profit and loss statement: an increase in foreign exchange assets as a credit, an increase in liabilities as a debit.

Second, because of the country's high inflation rate, loans and deposits are generally booked to compensate for the expected drop in the value of money. For example, a borrower taking out a loan of say Crs 1000 is obligated to repay a higher amount, say Crs 1800. Over the period of the loan, the difference of Crs 800 is taken by the bank as income. Conversely, in the case of a time deposit, the difference is taken by the bank as an expense on its profit and loss statement.

It is important for the analyst to be familiar with the accounting conventions in effect in the subject country and to understand how these special mechanisms impact the bank's financial statements so that they can be noted in the scope of the analysis.

5.4.3   Creative accounting and ratio manipulation

One problem in bank financial analysis is the varying quality of the financial information they are presented with by different banks in different countries. Regulatory authorities have different requirements as to what must go into the financial statements of banks. The result of this is that in some countries there is much information while in others there is scanty information. This makes the task of analysing the quality of earnings, the liquidity of the balance sheet and the quality of capital among other things, difficult.

It is therefore important to be aware of the different accounting rules if one is going to run peer group analyses among banks in different countries. In many countries, especially in Eastern Europe, there is a transition from legacy accounting systems to IAS. Until this transition is complete, analysts are obliged to deal with, in some instances, insufficient information and distortions.

Here are some of the ways banks can manipulate their financial statements:

5.4.3.1   Inflating the balance sheet

Many banks inflate their balance sheet to appear larger than they really are. The balance sheet can be artificially inflated by borrowing in the interbank market and placing the money with other institutions, or buying short-term participations in corporate loans from other banks that have excessively large balance sheets. Conversely the banks whose growth looks excessive can try to conceal this by "deflating" their balance sheet by buying back their own paper in the market if they have surplus funds.

5.4.3.2   Manipulating the profit and loss statement

The easiest way to manipulate profits is via movements in provisions. Two of the motivations for overstating or understating provisions is a desire to increase profit and thus share price, or understate profits to avoid tax.

In most jurisdictions specific provisions are tax deductible and general provisions may not be. It is therefore important to know what the tax rules in any country are and how banks may be influenced by them.

In many countries there are specific rules as to when one should make provisions and this is normally related to non-performing assets. Problems arise as to what constitutes a non-performing loan – in some cases, if a customer is unable to repay a loan then he may be given a new loan to replace the old one, and this would not show as an overdue account.

Other tricks are to classify only the partial repayment due 90 days previously as non-performing, rather than the whole loan. Since in many countries, classifying loans as non-performing is up to the discretion of the credit managers or board of directors, it is important to know what these criteria are, and how they can be motivated by various political, tax or self-preservation motives.

5.4.3.3   Realising profits from "trading securities"

Generally bonds or long-term securities held to maturity for income purposes are valued at cost so that gains and losses are not recorded on an annual basis. In the case of "trading assets" (i.e. securities held for trading purposes), these are usually marked to market showing a gain or a loss which is reflected through the profit and loss statement. In principle these two definitions and accounting treatments are reasonable. The only problem occurs when at the end of the year a bank decides to reclassify those assets which would either improve or reduce the profitability of the bank.

5.4.3.4 Currency mismatching "profits"

In some countries, banks may fund their domestic currency loans by taking out foreign currency borrowings in a low interest rate denominated currency. This can also be motivated by a shallow domestic market which simply does not have the depth to provide funding to the bank. This has the effect of improving their funding costs and therefore their profit margin on their lending. However, in such cases, the hard currency can appreciate; this would be shown as a loss movement in reserves.

5.4.3.5 Movements in hidden reserves

Some jurisdictions allow banks to declare their profits after "movement in inner reserves". This is a method of allowing banks to understate and keep high profits for leaner years in the future and thus smooth the income profile of the bank. The danger of this is that a bank may have high hidden reserves that diminish over two or three years hiding a very poor performance.

5.4.3.6 Improving the net worth of the bank

Some banks have significant property portfolio holdings, for example a nationwide branch network. These property holdings can be fast-appreciating assets. Some countries' banks are allowed to revalue assets on condition that this is done by professional valuers. The resultant increase in fixed assets is reflected on the liability side of the balance sheet by a corresponding increase in revaluation reserves which are in fact an increase in net worth.

The problem with this procedure is that often the timing is discretionary. For example, if there is later a fall in the property market this diminution of revaluation reserves is very seldom carried out. This has the effect of distorting the net worth and the capital asset ratio of banks.

Some banks are in fact very conservative and write down their fixed assets to a nominal or zero amount thus giving a conservative picture of the gearing or leverage of the bank.

5.4.3.7 Manipulating liquidity

One of the classic liquidity ratios or measures of liquidity of a bank is the liquid asset to deposit ratio. Traditionally cash due from banks and short-term deposits are considered to be liquid assets and deposits with central bank or government securities would be classified as liquid. The problem is that many of these deposits or securities may be in overseas countries where there is high risk of currency devaluation. Similarly, to get a good idea of the demand that may be made on the bank by depositors one has to look at the tenor of the deposits they are holding. Another factor that may reduce the likelihood of a run on deposits is the existence of a deposit insurance scheme organised by the central bank or a fund supported by all the banks in the country.

This is why it is important to distinguish between domestic and foreign government securities held, as the foreign holdings may be more "illiquid" than their nature suggests.

6

Country and Political Risk

6.1 COUNTRY RISK

6.1.1 Introduction to country risk

Banks traditionally operate as intermediaries, making and receiving payments and funds transfers and engaging in commercial lending and underwriting. This type of risk is called commercial risk. Commercial risks vary and so can be further sudivided into categories such as industry sector risk, credit risk, performance risk, documentation risk, etc. These risks all suggest the possibility of non-repayment.

In international banking, where you find cross-border lending situations in currencies other than the home currency of the debtor, you have further risk assessment factors to consider. In addition to an assessment of the creditworthiness of the particular debtor (or transaction), you have to assess the risk that the debtor country will be unable or unwilling to obtain or commit the necessary foreign exchange to enable cross-border loan repayments.

This is known as transfer risk, which is one of the elements comprising the larger category of country risk.

It is very important to see that the success of a bank has always depended on its judgement and foresight regarding the risk involved, not only in terms of commercial risk but also of country risk.

6.1.2 Definition of country risk

The first matter to deal with, of course, is to find a generally accepted definition on country risk. For example, is country risk the same as transfer risk, political risk or even sovereign risk?

Panras Nagy offered one definition of country risk in *Euromoney*:

> Country risk is the exposure to a loss in cross-border lending caused by events in a particular country which are, at least to some extent, under the control of the government but definitely not under the control of a private enterprise or individual.

When analysing this definition, one can find that country risk can arise through different paths. Indeed three types of event can cause country risk:

- Political events (war, ideology, neighbouring countries, political unrest, revolution, etc.). Political risk is the risk that a country is not willing or able, due to political reasons, to service/repay its foreign debt/obligations.
- Economic factors (internal and external debt levels, GDP growth, inflation, import dependency, etc.). Economic risk is the risk that a country is not willing or able, due to economic reasons, to service/repay its foreign debt/obligations.
- Social factors (religious, ethnic, or class conflict, inequitable income distribution, etc.). Social risk is the risk that a country is not willing or able, to repay its foreign debt/obligations due to social reasons.

Country risk therefore means the exposure to a loss in cross-border lending (of different types) due to events more or less under the control of the government.

6.1.3   Types of countries

While the above definition of country risk is generally accepted, we should bear in mind that the term "country" can be subject to various interpretations.

It is therefore useful for risk analysis purposes to group countries into specific categories, as companies are grouped into specific industries for peer group analysis.

It is clear that bankers are seeking to diversify risks and financial markets' operations also serve to diversify risk. Accordingly, banks (prudent ones) seek to structure their lending portfolio diversifying into different industries and then try to pick the best credit risks in each. A similar modus operandi exists vis à vis country risk.

The question then arises what kind of classification scheme should we look at when evaluating a heterogeneous group of countries.

One possible solution is to look at a geographical grouping and speak about the Latin American countries or the African countries. However, there are also other ways of looking at this matter.

There are six main types of countries, which follow broadly the World Bank classification. It is clear that a country can move from one type to another over time.

The six types of countries are:

- Main industrial nations
- Smaller industrialised countries
- Countries in transition (countries formerly with a state-planned economy)
- Newly industrialised countries
- Less developed countries
- Emerging markets

This method of grouping countries is more useful than the geographic model for assessing country risk. These different categories enable meaningful comparisons to be made among similar peer groups.

6.1.3.1   Main industrial countries

This group consists of the major industrialised countries of Europe, North America and Japan.

These countries are the main political and economic powers of the global economy. They have a well-diversified, mature, high quality industrial base, transport and infrastructure base, and a substantial home market.

Their exports are important, but in general not larger than 25% of GNP. Population generally exceeds 50 million inhabitants per country. Currencies are freely convertible and there is a liberal capital market.

Large differences occur when looking to the availability of natural resources.

6.1.3.2   Smaller industrialised countries

This group includes other Western European countries as well as Australia and New Zealand. In geographic size, they rank from Australia to Luxembourg, in population size from Spain to

Norway. What they have in common is a democratically based political system. Foreign trade is important for all of them in order to enable payment of vital imports. Infrastructure in these countries is generally well developed.

6.1.3.3 Countries in transition

This group is formed by the former Soviet bloc countries. At this moment, they are trying to transform their economies into free economies, and on the political level they are trying to become more democratic.

6.1.3.4 Newly industrialised countries

Since the 1960s, these countries are developing a patchy industrial base capable of competing in certain sectors of the international markets. They have different political systems and reached the stage of an industrialised country through substantial imports of capital goods and centralised planning. Due to these imports, these countries have to borrow heavily in the international markets. They are high up on the list of countries with foreign debts. The newly industrialised countries depend upon a buoyant world economy since home market demand is typically insufficient to support the production base. These countries are vulnerable to world recession (as was the case in the Asian meltdown).

6.1.3.5 Less developed countries

This group of countries is by far the largest in number, population and geographical extension. These countries represent a wide range of political and economic systems. It makes sense to make a distinction between the countries with oil and all the others.

Within the group of oil-producing countries, we have to distinguish between those countries that are depleting their oil revenues quickly due to their large and fast-growing populations (Iran), and the others (Saudi Arabia, Kuwait).

The non-oil-producing LCDs constitute a category that is easily defined. It is, however, the group which is the most heterogeneous of all in terms of size, population, political system, economic system, natural resources, etc.

This necessitates careful interpretation when comparing non-oil-producing LCDs with each other.

6.1.3.6 Emerging markets

Here we refer to that category of countries where there is a lot of incentive to invest. Classification is difficult because these countries may also belong to other categories like the less developed countries, countries in transition, or even the newly industrialised countries which are vulnerable to economic cyclicality.

6.1.4 Country risk assessment

When considering bank risk, the usual starting point is country risk analysis.

A country analysis must be completed before a meaningful analysis of a particular bank and its banking system can be undertaken.

While most risk rating systems have a tendency to generalise with the statement "a bank can never have a better risk rating than that of the country in which it is located", there are exceptions to the case (i.e. the majority of its assets can be located in another country).

While a bank can operate profitably in its home country, there can always be a risk if the country does not have sufficient foreign exchange revenues to enable the banks to convert locally denominated profits into foreign currencies in order to pay off foreign creditors.

A well-known case arose during the Latin American debt crisis of the 1980s in Brazil. The rescheduling and moratorium on the repayment of what were then called "Resolution 63 loans" were a case in point. It did not matter how profitable Brazilian banks were in local currency terms; the country did not have sufficient FX reserves to enable repayment on foreign currency loans. Country risk assessment can therefore be directly relevant to assessing an individual bank's performance.

Devaluation can also reduce the ability to freely convert into foreign currency. This can result in banks having mismatched local currency assets and foreign currency liabilities, and being subjected to huge FX losses. This can cause the bank either to go bankrupt or to reschedule its foreign liabilities.

Economic environment risks can also impact foreign banks. Problems in certain economic sectors such as shipping, energy, insurance, or real estate will affect banks which will have portfolio concentrations in those sectors.

Finally, the country's political system has an important effect on the economic and regulatory policies which shape its banking system. Political interests and social structure can determine the types of policies that are formulated and implemented. Understanding the political objectives and positions of special interest groups will enable an analyst to focus on particular risks such as the enactment of legislation which may be detrimental or beneficial to a country's banks. The nationalisation of banks in France following the election of the Socialist government of President Mitterrand is an example.

Given the importance of country risk assessment, most banks and rating agencies devise and implement a country risk assessment matrix and rating system. For banks that choose not to expend the resources to devise such systems, they can obtain such information from outside sources.

6.2 POLITICAL RISK

6.2.1 Introduction to political risk

Political risk (at least for bankers) can be defined as follows:

> The risk of change in a government or governing structure of a country which will affect, directly or indirectly, a country's ability or willingness to pay its debt.

Political risk is generally viewed as a non-business risk introduced strictly by political forces. Banks and other multinational corporations have identified political risk as a factor that could seriously affect the profitability of their international ventures. Political risk is analogous to sovereign risk and lies within the broader framework of country risk. Political risk emerges from events such as wars, internal and external conflicts, territorial disputes, revolutions leading to changes of government, and terrorist attacks around the world.

Social risks include civil unrests due to ideological differences, unequal income distribution, and religious clashes.

Even if a country has no difficulties with its financial position now we still need to judge what political events, stresses or structural features will make it a less (or more) favourable debtor. Here we are not just talking about an unwillingness to pay foreign debtors or the nationalisation of foreign assets, but also those features in a country's political position, whether internal or external, which may cause its economic position to deteriorate or improve and hence affect its ability to pay as well as its willingness to do so.

If we are to examine political risk in a logical, systematic way we must in some way categorise the large number of potential influences and then try to establish their importance.

There are three broad categories under which we should examine the potential for political change. These are:

- The political structure itself
- The leadership or controlling party
- The policies within the existing government

6.2.2   Time dimension

Political risk analysis needs to focus on the short, medium, and long term.

6.2.2.1   Short term

Key pointers to watch out for:

- Rising opposition – especially if taking a violent form
- Growing discontent with economic or social policies
- Overdependence on one group or person
- Vigorous external anti-government activity, perhaps linked to guerrilla activity
- War – especially if going to be lost

6.2.2.2   Medium term

Here we must deal with very many of the same factors as for the short term but it becomes more important to identify those features which may bring about shifts not just in political policies but in those controlling the state, and even more so to try to identify where pressures exist, and are growing, for a fundamental shift in the system.

6.2.2.3   Longer term

Longer-term analysis must focus more on the fundamental, underlying pressures upon the political life of a country rather than those that may lead to a change in a policy here and there. Indeed it is almost the art of thinking about the impossible.

6.2.3   Political risk analysis methodologies

6.2.3.1   "Wise men" systems

- "Old hands" or "external experts" – this means that you are dependent upon the advice of external experts for assessing the politico-economic situation. Needless to say, this is a very dangerous method since you are abdicating responsibility, quite possibly, to eccentric chaps who often "go native".

- "Grand tours" – making a tour in the country before investing. This is also a dangerous method since the local "tour guides" will put you up in the only air-conditioned five-star hotel in town and chauffeur you around in limousines showing you dams, highways, and shopping centres instead of the underlying reality of the country such as unelectrified slums teeming with revolutionary groups longing to overthrow the existing regime or "designated successors".

6.2.3.2   Consulting technique

This technique offers a more systematic approach to political risk analysis. For consultant assessments to be meaningful, the following is required:

- A comprehensive and accurate listing of the major determinants of political risk.
- Well-reasoned analysis by knowledgeable professionals.
- An appropriate mechanism for weighting and combining individual opinions.

This is a highly subjective approach. Often, one of these is missing and the technique begins to produce erroneous conclusions.

6.2.3.3   Quantitative systems

A variety of these have been put forward. A major problem has been to establish some underlying theoretical basis for such systems. Moreover, there has been a lack of reliability of validity in the results.

Because there is no generally accepted theory of political change, there is no agreement on which variables should be quantified and how those variables should be combined.

Given that the formal models lack theoretical foundations, are unreliable, and do not address the right questions anyway, the methodologists have in many cases had recourse to creating panels of experts and deriving various statistical summaries of their opinion.

6.2.3.4   Checklists

In essence in this approach you draw up a list of key features and assess them for risk. Yet given the vast number of potential topics for inclusion the choice of which to include becomes critical.

In drawing up a checklist, it is important that the object of the exercise is kept in mind. This where the long list, or short list, is unstructured, falls down, for the purpose of this approach is to provide a uniform list of factors that are likely to affect political stability across all countries. This ensures a prime aim of political risk analysis is met, namely that we judge all countries by the same criteria and standards. Checklists drawn up by the credit rating agencies feature in Appendix II.

6.2.4   World Bank list of countries

The World Bank has a similar classification scheme in Appendix III.

The table in Appendix III classifies all World Bank member economies, and all other economies with populations of more than 30 000. For operational and analytical purposes, economies are divided among income groups according to 2001 gross national income (GNI) per capita, calculated using the World Bank Atlas method. The groups are: low income, $745 or less; lower middle income, $746–2 975; upper middle income, $2976–9205; and high income, $9206 or more. Other analytical groups, based on geographic regions and levels of external debt, are also used.

Geographic classifications and data reported for geographic regions are for low-income and middle-income economies only. Low-income and middle-income economies are sometimes referred to as developing economies. The use of the term is convenient; it is not intended to imply that all economies in the group are experiencing similar development or that other economies have reached a preferred or final stage of development. Classification by income does not necessarily reflect development status.

Standard World Bank definitions of severe and moderate indebtedness are used to classify economies by levels of external debt. Severely indebted means either: present value of debt service to GNI exceeds 80% or present value of debt service to exports exceeds 220%. Moderately indebted means either of the two key ratios exceeds 60% of, but does not reach, the critical levels. For economies that do not report detailed debt statistics to the World Bank Debtor Reporting System (DRS), present-value calculation is not possible. Instead, the following methodology is used to classify the non-DRS economies. Severely indebted means three of four key ratios (averaged over 1999–2001) are above critical levels: debt to GNI (50%); debt to exports (275%); debt service to exports (30%); and interest to exports (20%).

Moderately indebted means three of the four key ratios exceed 60% of, but do not reach, the critical levels. All other classified low-income and middle-income economies are listed as less indebted.

Note: Region and income classifications are in effect until 1 July 2003. Indebtedness classifications were revised in April 2003. Taiwan, China is also included in high income.

6.3 TYPICAL SOVEREIGN RATINGS PROCESS

6.3.1 Introduction

The objective in assigning a credit rating to a debt instrument issued by a sovereign government, as in the rating of an obligation of any type of entity, is to determine the likelihood of timely repayment of interest and principal. The rating of a sovereign government's debt is an assessment of a country's overall creditworthiness, and is based on the willingness and ability of the government to meet its obligations in accordance with the terms of the debt issue.

The rating analysis for a sovereign government varies depending upon whether the debt issue is denominated in foreign or domestic currency. In the latter case, the general question of country risk, which is defined below, and the subsumed question of foreign exchange convertibility are not relevant, thus simplifying the analysis. A sovereign government's ability to raise the revenues necessary for repayment of debt denominated in local currency is virtually unlimited, given its substantial power to raise taxes and even issue the notes required to settle its obligations. It is also unlikely that a sovereign government would wilfully refuse to honour its internal obligations, especially in those instances where the obligations are held by its own citizens. Only in the event of a radical change in government or an occupation by a foreign power is a sovereign government likely to repudiate or willingly default on its internal obligations.

In the case of external obligations issued by a sovereign government, the rating process must address the question of country risk. Broadly defined, country risk is the probability of incurring a loss on a cross-country claim due to events which are to a certain extent under the control of the government. Consequently, it represents the minimum risk to an investor holding a claim on any entity within a foreign nation. Country risk is a function of a wide range of economic and political factors which determine a sovereign government's willingness and ability to provide the foreign exchange necessary to meet the country's external obligations.

In contrast to claims denominated in domestic currency, the economic ability of a sovereign government to repay its external obligations is constrained by its access to foreign exchange. The rigidity of this foreign exchange constraint varies depending upon the degree of convertibility of a country's currency, but the key distinction remains that a government cannot simply adjust taxes or issue notes to meet its external obligations. Instead, timely repayment depends upon a country's external payments position, which over the long term depends on its ability to export goods and services. The economic ability to generate foreign exchange earnings, in turn, reflects a broad array of factors, encompassing a country's economic structure, growth and management.

The assessment of a government's willingness to repay its debts assumes greater importance with external obligations because the enforceability of a legal claim against a sovereign government by a foreign investor is very limited. Although the assessment of willingness to repay is highly subjective, several factors can be examined in order to determine a government's economic and political self-interest in honouring its external obligations. As in the case of internal debts, the likelihood of a government refusing to repay its obligations is also a function of the country's internal political and social stability and the degree of harmony characterising its external relations.

Finally, it should be emphasised that Standard & Poor's ratings on sovereign government debt seek to determine the likelihood of timely repayment. Although the probability of outright default is quite low for sovereign governments, the possibility of other types of disruptions in the debt service schedule is somewhat greater. For example, the more likely occurrence of external debt restructurings and rescheduling involves at the very least an opportunity cost to investors, and in some cases actual losses due to repayment delays. The rating seeks to determine the probability of any such type of disruption in the debt service schedule.

6.3.2   Political risk

Standard & Poor's defines political risk as "political and social factors which affect the availability of foreign exchange and the willingness of authorities to meet foreign debt obligations".

Assessing political risk requires evaluating a country's underlying political and social stability, as well as its external relations. While such stability reflects indirectly the country's economic performance, several non-economic factors can also be included in the assessment of political risk.

6.3.2.1   Political system

Examining a country's political system is a logical starting point for assessing political risk. The stability of a political system is influenced by variables such as the form of government, executive leadership, government institutions, and social coalitions. The most common forms of government (i.e. democracy, military dictatorship, and totalitarian systems) have different advantages and disadvantages. The most important characteristics of a political system from the political risk standpoint are the degree of public participation, the orderliness of successions in government, the extent of government control, and the general flexibility and responsiveness of the system.

The assessment of government institutions, such as the military, government ministries, agencies and state enterprises, relates to their effectiveness in implementing programmes prescribed by executive leadership and their ability to provide quality inputs to the executive decision-making process. Finally, an analysis must be done of the strength of existing social coalitions (i.e. labour unions, landlords, industrial leadership, small business, civil service and religious and ethnic groups) and their relationship with the government. An examination of these various characteristics of a political system can only be accomplished by the careful study of a country's political track record over an extended period. Signals of high political risk include such events as periodic social disorder and rioting, military coups or radical ideological shifts in the government.

6.3.2.2 Social environment

Social conditions within a country are another determinant of the degree of political risk. Social stability reflects a combination of economic and non-economic factors. Among the non-economic factors, demographic variables such as the rate of population growth, the density and distribution of the population and the homogeneity of the populace, all serve as indicators of the potential for social tensions which could undermine a country's political stability. Rapid population growth and high population densities can result in pressure on a country's economy, leading to dissatisfaction with the government. Similarly, although a heterogeneous population need not heighten political risk, there are certainly numerous examples of racial, religious or cultural differences within a nation leading to widespread social disorder, often disrupting the political and economic process.

Certain economic factors also have an impact on a country's social environment and, in turn, influence the level of political risk. For example, social stability is influenced by such economic variables as average per capita income levels, the distribution of wealth and income, and the extent of unemployment and underemployment. Where these variables are unfavourable, the likelihood of social and political disorder during an economic downturn is much greater. Moreover, in a country with a low standard of living and high unemployment, the government is likely to be extremely hesitant to take austerity measures to solve an external payments problem, thus increasing the probability of debt servicing difficulties.

6.3.2.3 External relations

A nation's external relations play a major part in determining the political risk inherent in lending to a foreign government. The impact of external relations on the level of political risk may be divided into two broad areas:

- The country's economic and political self-interest in honouring its external obligations and
- The nation's international security

Self-interest can be assessed by such factors as the degree of economic integration of a country within the western economic system, the extent of participation in international organisations and the ideological orientation of the government. In general, the greater a country's involvement in the western economic system, the greater the cost of willingly repudiating its external debt, as such action would have extremely adverse implications for its trade relations and future ability to obtain external finance and investment. National security can be the overriding concern for investors in some nations, owing to strained relations with their neighbours or their geopolitical importance in terms of the balance of power between competing geographical areas.

6.3.3   Economic risk

Economic risk assessment involves the analysis of a country's capacity to support its current and anticipated level of external debt. A nation's debt servicing capacity is a function of those factors which affect its balance of payments. The initial step in evaluating external debt-bearing capacity is the determination of the existing debt burden. This debt burden is then compared with the country's international liquidity position and with its balance of payments flexibility. The assessment of balance of payments flexibility, in turn, involves the analysis of the country's economic structure, growth and management.

6.3.3.1   Debt burden

The determination of debt burden begins with a quantification of outstanding external debt, focusing initially on the most readily available and comparable figures – those for direct and guaranteed long-term (i.e. original maturity of over one year) external debt of the central government.

However, since this measurement of external debt excludes other public and private sector debt and all short-term debt, it may provide a misleading picture of a country's debt burden. In many countries, government agencies, regional authorities and state enterprises borrow abroad without the guarantee of the central government. Indeed, in some cases these public entities may be encouraged to borrow in foreign markets in order to finance balance of payments deficits without requiring the national government to be frequently in the market borrowing foreign currencies. Given that many of these public entities may be less than fully self-supporting and since the national government is likely to be called upon to meet their debt service obligations when the entities encounter financial difficulties, the external debt of such public entities should be added to the direct and guaranteed external debt of the central government. Unfortunately, for many industrialised countries it is difficult to obtain numbers for this measure of aggregate public sector external debt. For developing countries, however, this task has been simplified, as the World Bank regularly collects and publishes figures on the public and publicly guaranteed long-term debt of its borrowing member countries.

This more comprehensive estimate of total public sector external debt still understates the burden of external obligations on a country's balance of payments, as private sector external debt must be serviced from the same limited supply of foreign exchange earnings. For many developing countries, external claims on the private sector may be insignificant in size, and consequently their exclusion from debt burden calculations will involve very little error. However, for newly industrialising countries the private sector external debt can be relatively large, and for some advanced economies the private sector's external debt may well exceed that of the public sector's. In the case of many industrialised countries, the private sector's large external debt is offset by equally large private claims on other countries, and a determination of the private sector's net external debt is more meaningful.

Finally, the quantification of external debt must incorporate some estimate of short-term debt obligations of the public and private sector. This is perhaps the most difficult area in which to find reliable data, but it is also one of the most important areas, as rapid accumulation of short-term debt usually accompanies periods of debt servicing problems. Published figures are rarely available, but some limited coverage is provided in publications by the Bank for International Settlement (BIS), and in publications by several central banks which are members of the BIS. In addition, estimates of the changes in a country's short-term debt position can usually be derived from balance of payments data.

Once the country's external debt has been estimated, the burden posed by that debt can be crudely measured by several basic ratios comparing its level with total national output (i.e. GDP) and with total foreign exchange earnings (i.e. exports of goods and services). In addition, the external debt can be compared with the country's foreign assets, providing an estimate of the net external debt burden.

In addition to examining the stock of external debt outstanding, the level of debt service payments is analysed to gain a better understanding of the external debt's impact on the balance of payments. The terms and structure of the external debt are examined to determine the future schedule of debt services payments and isolate such potential problems as a bunching of maturities. Current and future debt service payments are compared with present and projected exports of goods and services. Of course, this traditional debt service ratio understates the future debt burden, as it fails to include the impact of future borrowing requirements. Consequently, balance of payments forecasts are used to approximate future external borrowing needs and, in turn, adjust the debt service schedule.

6.3.3.2   International liquidity

During a period of balance of payments difficulties, one option for a government is to draw down its international reserves. As a result, international reserves are an important aspect of economic risk assessment, as they provide a cushion during periods of temporary shortfalls in export earnings, unexpected jumps in import requirements or other cash flow problems. A starting point for analysis of reserve adequacy is a simple comparison of the level of gross international reserves to annual imports of goods and services. However, the adequacy of international reserves varies depending on the country's currency convertibility, its access to foreign credit and the sophistication of its financial system. Clearly, a major industrial economy whose currency is widely used as a means of payment in world trade doesn't need to hold as relatively large a level of reserves as a small developing country with persistent balance of payments problems. Membership in international organisations such as the International Monetary Fund and the BIS, as well as regional organisations such as the European Economic Community, may enhance liquidity. In addition, some countries have developed large secondary reserves through bilateral agreements with major trading partners, providing additional flexibility during periods of external stress. Finally, official reserve levels must be adjusted for the net shortterm external position of the banking system. Although official reserves may be quite modest, the net foreign asset position of the banking system may be sufficiently strong to warrant a lower level of official international reserves.

6.3.3.3   Balance of payments flexibility

The strength and stability of a country's external payments position is, perhaps, the focal point of the rating process for sovereign governments, as most instances of debt servicing problems occur in conjunction with large and/or persistent deficits in the balance of payments. Balance of payments flexibility reflects two interrelated factors: the responsiveness of a country's external economy to changes in domestic and world economic activity, and the ability of the authorities to implement policies designed to prevent or adjust an imbalance in the external sector.

The responsiveness of a country's balance of payments to internal and external developments is a function of the composition of its exports and imports, as well as the geographic distribution of its external trade. In the case of exports, the key concepts are growth, stability and diversity. Steady growth in exports is required to meet external debt service commitments if the country is to be able to at least maintain its current level of imports. Stability and growth of exports are influenced by the variability of the supply and demand for those products which the country sells abroad. On the supply side, the susceptibility of major export items to sharp declines in production is examined. For example, climatic factors tend to cause the supply of agricultural products to fluctuate more than the output of manufactured goods. On the demand side, the price and income elasticity of the demand for major export products is analysed in order to determine the potential volatility of foreign exchange earnings. For instance, economic downturns in foreign markets are likely to have a more adverse impact on exports of capital goods and industrial raw materials than they have on exports of basic consumer goods. Conversely, the price sensitivity of demand may be greater for non-essential consumer goods than it is for vital intermediate imports, such as petroleum. In general, the more diversified a country's export products and markets, the more likely are export earnings to remain stable. Clearly, a developing country dependent on a few primary commodities for its export earnings is more susceptible to a sudden short fall in exports than an industrialised economy with a wide variety of exports of manufactured goods. Similarly, an economy whose trade is highly concentrated with a few countries is more vulnerable to economic cycles abroad than a country with varied export markets.

With imports, the analysis focuses on the responsiveness of imports to changes in prices and the level of domestic economic activity, as well as the related concepts of import dependency and compressibility. Generally, the more open an economy, the greater will be the import response to changes in the rate of growth of domestic demand. The structure of imports is also a valuable indicator of the responsiveness of imports to changes in domestic output. For example, a country which imports most of its capital goods will tend to experience a surge in imports in conjunction with an acceleration in investment activity. The sensitivity of imports to external price developments is measured by the price elasticity of demand for imports, which provides an estimate of the extent to which the volume of imports can be expected to change in response to price movements.

The concepts of import dependency and compressibility involve a determination of the extent to which imports are essential to the local economy, and consequently the degree to which imports could be reduced during a period of external imbalance without imposing severe hardship on the populace. Import dependency and compressibility are a function of both the size of imports relative to GDP and the composition of imports. For example, a country whose imports are largely composed of basic foodstuffs and energy products would be in a position of heavy import dependence, and would have little flexibility in compressing imports to adjust for an external payments deficit. Conversely, if a fairly high proportion of imports are of non-essential consumer goods, the compressibility of imports would be quite high.

In addition to the structure of imports and exports, the analysis of balance of payments flexibility must consider the country's ability to attract external capital. Some countries, through favourable foreign investment regulations, strong internal growth prospects, and stable political environments, are able to attract steady inflows of long-term capital. In such cases, persistently large current account deficits can often be financed without drawing down international reserves and jeopardising debt service payments.

Related to these structural aspects of balance of payments flexibility is the ability of the government to take measures to avoid or correct for a deterioration in the country's external payments position. This requires an assessment of the appropriateness, effectiveness and timeliness of government policies which affect the balance of payments. Although the policy instruments at the disposal of the authorities may be adequate to adjust for an external imbalance, the social and economic costs of implementing such measures may be so high as to preclude their use at a given time, or at least postpone their implementation until a financial crisis has developed. The level of economic development is often a useful measure of the extent to which a government may impose austerity measures to correct for an external payments problem. An industrialised economy with a high standard of living is generally better able to maintain a stabilisation programme than is a developing country with low income levels and a rapidly expanding population. However, measures of wealth and income may tend to indicate that there is room for adjustment, but the government's ability to take action may be impaired by conflicting policy objectives and institutional rigidities which slow the formation and implementation of appropriate policies. For example, the desire to maintain a low rate of domestic inflation may result in the government's failure to adjust the exchange rate, even though export competitiveness is being adversely affected. Likewise, a legislative commitment to maintain certain expenditure programmes or reduce tax rates may impede the economic policymakers' ability to take swift corrective action.

In evaluating the structural and policy aspects of balance of payments flexibility, an historical analysis of major external payments variables is extremely instructive. In particular, the experience of a country during periods of major exogenous shocks, such as the OPEC price-hikes and the subsequent recessions in the industrial world, serve as indicators of the vulnerability of the balance of payments and the ability of the authorities to cope with imbalances. Moreover, an examination of the options available to policymakers and measures taken during such periods of stress provide insights into the economic policy process and the skill of government institutions.

6.3.3.4 Economic structure

In analysing a country's economic structure, two factors are especially important for its debt servicing capacity:

* The level of economic development and
* The degree of diversification in output

With regard to the level of development, the higher standard of living enjoyed by residents of an industrialised nation provides the government with greater flexibility when confronted with an external payments imbalance. Adjustment policies can be more easily implemented without the dire consequences similar measures could have in a low income, developing country. Similarly the extensive and modern physical and social infrastructure available in more advanced economies serves to enhance their international competitiveness, thereby placing them at an advantage relative to developing countries in terms of generating foreign exchange earnings.

With regard to diversification of output, an economy with widely varied productive activities, other things being equal, is more likely to avoid external payments difficulties than an economy with highly concentrated production. Generally, diversification lessens the economy's susceptibility to large cyclical swings in the level of total output and exports, thus reducing the likelihood of a temporary shortfall in foreign exchange earnings.

The analysis of economic structure also focuses on the energy sector. Special emphasis is placed on a nation's current and prospective external energy balance, given that adequate energy supplies are essential for economic prosperity and that imported energy is subject to sudden, large swings in prices under current world market conditions.

6.3.3.5   Growth performance

Closely related to economic structure, the rate of growth of an economy is another key indicator of its future debt service capacity. Other things being equal, a higher rate of growth in total output and especially exports suggests a better ability to meet future debt obligations. Particularly important in this regard is the level and rate of growth in investment, as traditionally there is a strong correlation between the current level of fixed capital formation and the subsequent rate of expansion of production. In general, the growth of economic output relative to investment is a rough approximation of the return on capital employed in the economy. The extent to which investment serves to boost exports or replace imports enhances the country's balance of payments flexibility and, in turn, its debt service capacity.

Another important aspect of a country's growth performance, and one closely related to investment, is the level and rate of expansion of domestic savings. Generally, the higher the marginal savings rate, the greater the flow of domestic resources into capital accumulation and, other things being equal, the higher the rate of economic growth. If domestic savings are insufficient to meet a country's demand for investment, then the resulting savings–investment gap must be covered by external savings, which are difficult to sustain over the long term.

The analysis of trends in aggregate savings, investment and output is supplemented by an examination of sectorial growth trends to identify growth sectors and their potential, as well as declining sectors and their long-term viability.

6.3.3.6   Economic management

Economic management is related to all of the previous areas of analysis, and as a result is a critical consideration in the rating process. The assessment of economic management focuses on the government's ability to maintain internal and external balance. Economic growth, as previously mentioned, is an important determinant of a country's future debt-bearing capacity, but if such growth is achieved at the cost of high inflation and large balance of payments deficits, then it may not be sustainable. Under such a scenario, the government may need to induce a slowdown in growth in order to avoid severe external payments problems. The ability and willingness of the authorities to implement effective adjustment measures in such circumstances is an important aspect of the evaluation of economic management and, in turn, economic risk.

The analysis of economic management begins with an examination of the policy instruments available, their level of sophistication, the extent of their use, and their effectiveness in various situations. This involves the study of income, monetary, fiscal and exchange rate policies, and their impact on such economic variables as wages, prices, employment and output. Policy tradeoffs are identified and examined in light of long-term economic plans, where such plans exist.

In the case of incomes policy, the government's efforts to influence the distribution of value added between labour and business are analysed in conjunction with the role of major labour unions and business organisations. Special attention is paid to the wage settlement process and the relationship between trends in wages, prices and productivity. The degree to which wages are explicitly or implicitly indexed to the cost of living is assessed to determine the potential flexibility of incomes policy.

With monetary policy, the focus of policy is identified and its consistency with fiscal objectives is analysed. The flexibility of monetary policy is evaluated in light of external constraints, such as exchange rate considerations and the extent to which monetary authorities are independent of the political process. The effectiveness of monetary policy is also influenced by the sophistication and depth of a country's financial system.

The analysis of fiscal policy concentrates on budgetary factors, such as the extent to which expenditures may be considered discretionary, the breakdown of expenditures between current and capital items, the use of subsidies and transfer payments, the composition and income elasticity of revenues, and the extent and types of deficit financing employed. A key consideration is the government's ability to quickly adjust the budget, with or without legislative approval. In addition to analysing the central government's fiscal performance, Standard & Poor's examines the role of the overall public sector, including government agencies, state enterprises and local governments. These decentralised components of the public sector are evaluated in terms of their economic impact, their financial performance, and the degree to which they are effectively controlled by the central government.

Exchange rate policy is examined considering several factors, including:

- The relationship between exchange rate changes and movements in relative prices
- External trade policy objectives and
- The level of international reserves

The use of other external policy instruments such as tariffs, quotas and capital controls is also assessed.

6.3.3.7   Economic outlook

Given that ratings are indicators of future debt service capacity, sovereign risk assessment involves a determination of a country's economic prospects. The economic outlook is largely a function of the rating criteria outlined above, specifically the structure and management of the economy. Emphasis is placed on the prospects for the export sector since expanding foreign exchange earnings is a critical aspect of a country's future ability to meet its external debt service requirements. Where they are available, the government's medium- and long-term economic plans are reviewed to gain a better understanding of the rate and direction of economic development. These plans are evaluated in terms of internal and external resource constraints, with special emphasis on the impact of such plans on a country's future external borrowing requirements.

6.3.4   S&P's sovereign ratings profiles

The checklists in Appendix II (political, economic, and sovereign) have been used by Standard & Poor's for rating sovereign entities. Other credit rating agencies have similar checklists, which they mistakenly call "methodologies".

The rating agencies claim that these checklists attempt to evaluate the general characteristics of a country's economy in broad brushstrokes in order to assess overall risk.

It is interesting to note that while these checklists give the appearance of detailed complexity, no specific information is offered regarding what data exactly is obtained from the questions in the checklist, and in what format, and how these elements are assessed, quantified, weighted, and converted into a credit risk rating.

A cynic might suggest that these checklists feature in the rating agencies' promotional literature to give the impression of authoritative completeness and complexity, but that no underlying methodology to assess the data and transform it into a credit rating exists since the details of such a methodology have never been communicated to the public.

After all, a checklist of all the raw materials required to build an atomic bomb is not the same thing as the methodology that explains how to build it and do so optimally.

While transaction and country risk assessment is not the same as issuing a country risk rating, the systematic treatment of a wide range of indices can help you to focus your inquiry. Accordingly, the S&P checklists feature for reference purpose.

6.3.5   Behind the sovereign ratings exercise

Some agencies such as Standard & Poor's admit that their analytical processes rely on quantitative as well as subjective criteria. The quantitative aspects incorporate a number of measures of economic and financial performance such as ratios. The analysis is subjective, however, because Standard & Poor's ratings rely on subjective data and indicate an opinion as to future debt service capacity.

One agency similarly concedes that the sovereign risk rating exercise is:

> far less certain than our ability to analyse either bank or corporate risks of default. The essential problem is that the world of sovereign borrowers is far smaller than the world of large banks or corporations, and that the number of instances of default in the modern period when we have reasonable national accounts is tinier still . . . So the rating of sovereigns depends more on the art of political economy than on the science of econometrics. The assessment of sovereign risk inevitably requires more judgement because we have fewer examples of success and failure.

None of the agencies, however, will admit that the exercise in guesswork should be treated as such in their promotional literature.

Some agencies use a "top-down" as well as "bottom-up" analysis to determine sovereign ratings.

- "Top-down" considers global systemic factors, which past experience suggests influence both the timing and magnitude of sovereign defaults such as quarterly analysis of default trends throughout the sector as well as examination of global financial sector risks.
- "Bottom-up" analyses focus on the credit fundamentals affecting each government. S&P divides its analytical framework into eight categories. Each category relates to both economic and political risk, the key determinants of credit risk. Economic risk addresses the government's ability to repay its obligations on time and is a function of both quantitative

and qualitative factors. Political risk addresses the sovereign's willingness to repay debt.

While the above appears clear enough, the specifics of these techniques are never clearly described, reminding one of the old adage that "it does not pay a prophet to be too specific".

An example of a qualitative issue is assessing a sovereign's "willingness to pay". This issue is one that distinguishes sovereigns from most other types of issuers. Because creditors have only limited legal redress, governments can (and sometimes do) default selectively on its obligations, even when they possess the financial capacity for timely debt service. A rating agency would be hard pressed to come up with an exact formula to quantify the likelihood of such selective defaults, meaning that the process is highly subjective.

Moreover, while political, social, and economic factors affect the government's ability and willingness to honour local and foreign currency debt, they do so in varying degrees. A government's ability and willingness to service local currency debt is supported by its taxation power and ability to control the domestic financial system by printing money. To service foreign currency debt, however, the sovereign must obtain foreign exchange, usually by purchasing it in the currency markets. This can be a binding constraint, as reflected in the higher frequency of foreign as opposed to local currency debt defaults.

While rating agencies look at the fiscal, monetary, and inflation outcomes of government policies that support or erode incentives for timely debt service, the specific methodologies and formulae in use (if any) remain arcane and little understood.

Standard & Poor's, for example, state in their promotional literature that their foreign currency debt analysis "places more weight on the interaction between fiscal and monetary policies, the balance of payments and its impact on the growth of external debt, and the degree of each country's integration in the global financial system" without exactly stipulating what this means, how it is defined, or how it is quantified. Indeed, it would be a challenge for anyone to understand what the preceding sentence actually means.

The fact of the matter is, no one really believes in such pronouncements or really cares. They merely enable bank managers to rationalise their operational decisions by saying "Oh, our exposure levels are based on a matrix of credit ratings compiled from the three major agencies", thereby exonerating oneself from the chain of responsibility.

The value attached to such pronouncements then is basically an act of faith in the rating agency – a dangerous position to be in when things go wrong as in the East Asian meltdown – because while the rating agencies play with words to refocus past ambiguous pronouncements and continue conducting business under the US SEC sponsored protected NRSRO status, investors are left counting their losses.

7

The World of E-finance

E-finance is the next major frontier for banks in developed markets. As banks compete more and more in mature markets with a fixed size population base, growth will come at the expense of other players.

To win this growth, banks will need to invest in systems which increase the bank's competitively. It is crucial to understand the importance and role of IT in banking, which tends to be overlooked in classic bank financial analysis.

We discussed at length bank capitalisation requirements and effective ALM policy in generating an appropriately sized retail depositor base to fund banking activist, as well as the MIS systems able to compile data from diverse operations in order to produce management information enabling bank managers to reach informed and effective decisions in running the bank.

E-finance technology offers the means of achieving these goals.

It is important to realise that effective bank management is somewhat broader than simply relying on CAMEL analysis. E-finance and information technology is effectively the distillation of a bank's internal strategy to equip itself with the tools required to survive and thrive in the future. Assessing the effectiveness of these techniques is difficult in that the technology has not yet reached a plateau and the analytical methods to assess these technologies is nascent.

More responsive systems, lowered operational costs, and more accurate and reliable systems all impact the quality of service offered to clients, which translates into competitive advantage.

Very little is actually said in classic bank risk analysis literature about the characteristics and mechanics of e-finance. It is, however, increasingly becoming a crucial means of distinguishing oneself from the competition and achieving competitive advantage.[1]

Accordingly, we look in this chapter at some of the key areas of e-finance and see how it impacts banking operations and provides a more complete view of banking operations and competitivity.

7.1 A QUICK DEFINITION OF E-FINANCE

E-finance can be defined as:

> All which relates to the linking of business, finance, and banking via electronic means, encompassing information gathering, processing, retrieval, and transmission of data as well as the transmission, purchase, and selling of goods and services.

But the definition broadens when we look at the new possibilities offered by technology. Computers and the use of one time data entry and relational databases mean that online real-time data about a company's business and accounts can be generated, enabling managers to manage their companies in new and more proactive ways.

A case in point is the use of Customer Relationship Management techniques arising from the use of client-driven (as opposed to accounting-driven) relational databases. CRM can assist in

---

[1] Material adapted from *E-Finance*, by Andrew Fight, Wiley Capstone Publishing.

providing a more bespoke and personalised service to clients which in turn impacts on issues of marketing strategy and branding of products and services.

The field of e-finance, however, is broader when we consider other factors such as the use of encryption and security at the service of "digital finance" – a broad term we define to include any type of electronic financial service or product. While digital finance has been in existence for many years, and certainly predates the commercial version of the internet (e.g. the international bank's payment network SWIFT), the use of new technologies and encryption is enabling a wider propagation of the concept.

The phenomenon of "e-finance", just as "new economy", "e-commerce" or "e-business", is at present in a nascent state, only hinting at the future networks and services that will be on offer.

One of the first obstacles in considering e-finance is a definition dilemma and, consequently, the lack of an explicit definition of what it encompasses.

The current surge of globalisation in the financial sector, considered to be an irreversible and universal trend, has been sparked off by a combination of factors led by the Americanisation of the world system. Globalisation and internationalisation are accompanied by new opportunities and challenges, as well as costs, risks and threats.

The process of e-finance is not a panacea in itself: it is necessary for development and growth, but it is not enough. From the perspective of developing or transition economies, the "new economy", e-commerce, e-business, e-finance, etc., could pose a "deadly threat" which might make these countries secondary or even marginal. However, under certain circumstances, the above-mentioned phenomena may also stand for extraordinary opportunities and the internet may become the engine of economic growth and development.

The subject is vast but can be divided into several areas that we consider in the following headings:

- CRM – Customer Relationship Management
- STP/CLS
- SWIFT
- Electronic funds transfer
- Online banking
- Day trading
- Smart cards

7.2 CRM – CUSTOMER RELATIONSHIP MANAGEMENT

What exactly is Customer Relationship Management (CRM)?

CRM is the seamless coordination between sales, customer service, marketing, field support and other customer-touching functions. Simply put, CRM integrates people, process and technology to maximise relationships with customers and partners, e-customers, traditional customers, distribution channel members, internal customers and suppliers.

What comprises the critical areas of Customer Relationship Management? Some of them are:

- Strategic masterplan – this comprises developing a clear and decisive plan to address the complex people, process and technology issues of CRM.
- Customer Relationship Management enabling technologies – developing best practices for designing flexible infrastructures and leveraging existing technologies.

- Integrated marketing applications – harnessing the latest technologies, internet solutions and integrated marketing strategies in order to market more effectively.
- Customer-centric e-business platform – designing and implementing a customer-facing solution that is integrated with your traditional channels by attending this how-to, step-by-step programme.
- Customer Contact Centre (CCC) customer-centric business strategy – integrating customer contact centre technology with existing CRM initiatives.
- Contact centre technology – communicating with your customers via their preferred channel (web-based communication, e-mail, interactive voice response, phone and fax).
- Mobile and wireless technologies – identifying those technologies holding the greatest promise for CRM, understanding how they fit together, and implementing them.
- Winning mobile strategies – set goals and develop strategies for deploying wireless solutions with minimum cost and maximum payoff.
- Data warehousing – build a better data warehouse to enable leveraging your data warehouse for improved strategic decision making.

CRM enables the automatic capture, route and qualification of leads. It enables

- The company to understand which marketing programme performme the best
- The measurement of the effectiveness of lead generation activities with detailed reporting and analysis
- Increased awareness, communication and productivity with a shared, global view of all relevant customer information, and having an instant snapshot of your company's performance
- To automatically track the sales pipeline and opportunities and easily generate forecasts on demand

Executives can track forecasts at any organisational level including individual representative, and view monthly breakout of deals and performances sorted to various criteria.

7.3   STP/CLS

Straight Through Processing (STP) and/or Continuous Linked Settlement (CLS) is another area of e-finance which is revolutionising the traditional ways in which banks conduct their business: reshaping global FX trading cycles is becoming an area of key interest as technology becomes available.

7.3.1   STP – Straight Through Processing

Straight Through Processing is a concept being championed by the Global Straight Through Processing Association (GSTPA), an organisation set up by key players in the industry. STP relates to the concept of one time deal capture as follows.

The basic idea is that the transaction data is entered once upon deal capture and that all subsequent transaction processes are effected using the data keyed in at source, and the data flows through all the required steps of the electronic trade processing procedure. The reduction in data capture and automated processing aims to accelerate the settlement cycle, reduce the possibility of error and settlement risk, and enable the extraction of data for Management Information Reporting purposes.

7.3.2   CLS – Continuous Linked Settlement

Continuous Linked Settlement is closely related to STP. CLS was founded with the objective of eliminating settlement risk, which is inherent in all foreign exchange transactions using current settlement methods.

The Bank of International Settlements, in its report on Settlement Risk in Foreign Exchange Transactions of March 1996, defines settlement risk as:

> Settlement of a foreign exchange (FX) trade requires the payment of one currency and the receipt of another. In the absence of a settlement arrangement that ensures that the final transfer of one currency will occur if and only if the final transfer of the other currency also occurs, one party to an FX trade could pay out the currency it sold but not receive the currency it bought. This principal risk in the settlement of foreign exchange transactions is variously called foreign exchange settlement risk or cross-currency settlement risk.

- A risk associated with settlement risk is liquidity risk. It can be differentiated into two forms:
  – market liquidity risk, which arises when a firm is unable to conclude a large transaction in a particular instrument at anything near the current market price and
  – funding liquidity risk, which is defined as the inability to obtain funds to meet cash flow obligations
- The second dimension to settlement risk is the associated credit risk. If a transaction cannot be settled, the party which paid out first faces the risk of fully losing the principal amount of the transaction. The party's exposure equals the full amount.

Awareness of settlement risk and its potential effects on global markets was highlighted in 1974, through the failure of Bankhaus Herstatt, a small foreign exchange trading bank in Germany. At that time, some of Herstatt Bank's counterparties had irrevocably paid DM to the bank during the day but before the banking licence was withdrawn. They had done so in good faith, anticipating the receipt of US dollars later in the same day in New York. Herstatt's New York correspondent bank suspended all outgoing US dollar payments from Herstatt's account. The counterparties were therefore fully exposed to the value of traded Deutschmarks.

The term "Herstatt-risk" was coined to describe this kind of settlement risk. It occurs when one party pays out the currency it sold but does not receive the currency it bought. During the banking day, the bank's banking licence was withdrawn and it was ordered into liquidation by the German authorities. This happened after the close of the German interbank payments system.

As trading volumes rose (daily global FX volumes reached USD 3 trillion in the 1990s), central banks became more and more interested and concerned about the potential disruptive consequences on financial markets due to settlement risk.

7.3.3   Establishment of Continuous Linked Settlement services

In 1995, a group of major FX trading banks (known as the Group of 20 or G20, with UBS as major participant) got together to consider how the private sector might develop a solution to the problem of settlement risk. The result of this study was the CLS concept. In July 1997, the G20 banks formed a company, CLS Services Ltd (CLSS), to develop and build the CLS system.

The initial shareholders of CLSS were the G20 banks. CLS differentiates between settlement members and user members.

settlement members maintain accounts with CLS Bank in the eligible CLS currencies and can submit trades directly to CLS. Members are responsible for the net funding obligations of all transactions submitted.

User members have no direct accounting relationship with CLS Bank. They are able to submit trades directly to CLS but they have to rely on a settlement member to settle their transactions over CLS.

Both memberships enable direct submission of trades for non-members, which are also known as third parties. CLS members can carry out settlements on behalf of third parties. These transactions are the direct responsibility of the particular CLS member which submitted the transactions.

E-finance technology is at the heart of CLS since the data capture and deal flows will all be processed electronically. The main winners will be reduced settlement risk but also reduced settlement periods, resulting in increased efficiency in the management of the FX "float" – the period of time prior to clearance when the funds are "in limbo" and not generating a return. This reduction in settlement from three days to one day offers the possibility of substantial revenues due to more proactive management of these liquid funds.

The impact of CLS will be the elimination of settlement risk of foreign exchange deals in the eligible CLS currencies. As a consequence, provisions taken to cover losses through settlement risk can be lowered. Settlement risk still exists for non-CLS banks. It is therefore expected that banks which do not want to invest in or cannot become CLS members will look for means and services to have access to CLS and perform foreign exchange transactions settlement risk free.

As deals are settled across CLS's books and only net positions are relevant, it follows that thousands of deals can be settled with a very limited number of payment orders issued by settlement members. This will lower transaction costs for banks considerably.

Indirectly, operational risk is lowered because fewer payments will be generated and therefore fewer errors can occur in processing them.

CLS over time will be expected to reduce the volume of transactions cleared through the relevant national RTGS system; this will affect the profitability of the 'vanilla' currency clearing business and cause banks to expand the range of services offered. Current estimates project a 30% decrease in the number of transactions.

As the technology matures, these new developments will not be confined to the foreign exchange market but could possibly extend to other cash-based products and must be extended to the securities world in order to support an intra-day securities market.

7.4 SWIFT

7.4.1 Background

SWIFT, the Society for Worldwide Interbank Financial Telecommunications, is the worldwide banking telecommunications network founded by international banks in 1973 and in direct competition with the telex and private networks. SWIFT's business is to support the financial data communication and processing needs of financial institutions. SWIFT's markets are financial institutions conducting business in payments, foreign exchange, money markets, securities trading, and trade finance.

SWIFT provides financial data communications and exchanges which are secure, and reliable. SWIFT's products and services are supported by an organisation of 1200 professionals based in key financial centres around the world.

SWIFT has been at the forefront of automating the financial services industry for years. SWIFT's customer benefits are:

- Replacement of paper-based processing through automated procedures using SWIFT standards
- Increased productivity, cost reductions, control of financial risk and exposure through integrated end to end transaction processing between financial institutions and their own customers

SWIFT originally began operations with the SWIFT I service, which was designed in the early 1970s. As transaction volumes grew, the original network was upgraded and new services were added.

SWIFT II was the second generation of network services. The main feature of the SWIFT II system and the SWIFT transport network is the ability to handle the ever growing volume of users' messages quickly, effectively, and securely.

SWIFT II was eventually replaced by SWIFTAlliance, a series of terminals operating on UNIX open systems, hereby enabling banks to enjoy hardware independence and not be tied into the proprietary systems conundrum.

At about the time SWIFTAlliance was implemented (early to mid-1990s), the internet began to exhibit its phenomenal growth.

Implementation of the internet and formation of cross-industry initiatives such as GSTPA (setting up effectively parallel networks threatening the monopoly) led SWIFT to take a more extroverted look at industry developments. The result was SWIFT leveraging on its skills set of providing secure financial payment and messaging systems and international networks to enter the arena of the internet and offer credible services and a larger range of offerings to its clientele.

SWIFTNet is an effort to develop a secure network that can be used for CLS or any other market infrastructure, thereby enlarging the scope of SWIFT offerings.

- Release 1 of SWIFTNet was delivered in March 2000 and met all the deliverables for CLS, one of the first early adopter market infrastructures. It included the deployment of the secure IP network (SIPN), an initial version of SWIFTNet InterAct, the interactive messaging service, and the SWIFTNet Link and SWIFTNet PKI security software. This first release has already processed more than 11 million messages as part of the ongoing CLS trials.
- Release 2, including an interactive service that can be used for CLS or any other financial market infrastructure, moved into pilot phase in September. This will allow other early adopters such as GSTPA and central banking institutions to begin tailoring their own applications. This second release also includes a range of connectivity options including SWIFTAlliance WebStation and the SWIFTAlliance Gateway interface for application to application messaging and connectivity with host platforms.
- Release 3 is due to be operationally live in March 2001 and will add SWIFTNet FileAct bulk messaging capability.

SWIFT is betting on the fact that SWIFTNet will replace the existing FIN messaging service.

SWIFT is well aware of the potential of the internet despite current drawbacks – and has begun research into how it can harness the power of the internet to extend the SWIFTNet offering.

7.5   ELECTRONIC FUNDS TRANSFER

Electronic fund transfers, automatic teller machines, debit and smart cards, point-of-sale mechanisms, home PC banking/trading services and digital securities transfers have been a part of the financial landscape for decades. For instance, consumers and businesses have been accustomed to transferring funds digitally, rather than physically, for many years, debiting and crediting accounts via computers rather than physically withdrawing and redepositing currency. The electronic fund transfer (EFT) – a mechanism used to send "digital money" across the wire, from one account to another – has been in widespread use for decades and forms the core of electronic payments between companies, governments and other institutions. More than USD 5T in electronic payments occurs every day – including USD 2T which is transferred between banks; large value electronic payment systems and clearinghouses such as SWIFT, CHIPS, ACH, CHAPS, BACS, and others are a fundamental component of the electronic payment network.

Other electronic mechanisms for obtaining cash, moving funds, and completing purchases have been in use for years and are well entrenched in today's society. Consumers have actively used automatic teller machines (ATMs) since the 1980s, accessing cash, depositing funds, and transferring balances with their ATM cards. Though ATMs took more than 15 years to become firmly established in consumer banking, they are now an indispensable part of retail finance; ATMs currently account for 50% of all cash-based banking transactions and have replaced many of the functions previously handled by branch-based tellers.

7.6   ONLINE BANKING

The history of phone banking and PC dial-up services dates back some 20 years. Through basic technology, customers have been able to manage funds and payments using phone keypads and computers. This variant of e-finance, however, is primitive compared to the future promises of this technology, which will enable a far more proactive involvement and richer functionality to the end user than has hitherto been possible.

PC-based online banking started in the late 1970s and early 1980s with proprietary dial-up services. Banks such as Chemical and Citibank offered, for a monthly fee, a basic home-based PC banking service which included balance lookup, fund transfers, and bill payment.

The efforts to promote these services, however, never really took off due to high user fees and cumbersome interfaces which were further handicapped by slow response times, complicated access procedures, and uncertain security.

In the mid-1980s software companies such as Intuit introduced third-party software solutions (Quicken) to act as an interface linking customers and banks. Customers could use the platform to access account information, transfer funds and pay bills. Customers could also authorise the payment of funds to a given merchant. Quicken would then process the customer approval and determine (via Intuit Services Corporation (ISC)) if the merchant was part of the Federal Reserve's Automated Clearing House (ACH). If it was, ISC would effect an electronic payment through the ACH and, if not, would mail a check to the merchant.

7.7   DAY TRADING

Securities transactions including stock and bond trading have also been driven by technology for the past few decades.

While it has been common for many years to pass stock/bond orders through brokers, who then transmit verbal or electronic information to an exchange and then revert with appropriate debits and credits to cash and securities accounts, actual physical possession of the securities is practically non-existent.

Instead, many securities now exist only in a "dematerialised" electronic form and are transferred between seller and buyer by computer.

Discount brokerage companies, such as Schwab, started offering basic PC trading capabilities via proprietary software accessing services via a dial-up connection with an ISP (AOL, Compuserve) in the mid- to late 1980s. The increasing complexity of software and the need for augmented data feeds now mean that an ISDN connection ideally is needed to engage in online day trading.

Day trading is the buying and selling of stock in such a way that at the end of each day you have no holdings. In other words, you "close your position" and sell whatever securities you bought before the close of the day.

This is the pure definition and may not always be either possible or feasible. There may be times when you may either accidentally or on purpose find yourself holding over night. If you do this more often than not you then become a "short time trader" and if you hold even longer, you become an "investor".

The uniqueness of day trading is that you are simply playing against other day traders and could it care less about the company, what brokers think about the stock or corporate performance, or even what it does. The day trader is merely concerned with the movement of the stock during the day and profiting from that movement.

What do you need to be a day trader?

- A brokerage account – their are numerous e-brokerage accounts willing to take your money for trading. Many of these websites can be accessed over the internet.
- Computer with web access – some may say this is not needed and they would technically be right but it is very hard to play this game without one. Day trading relies on speed, speed of getting information and speed on reacting to information, and a computer just makes it faster. The facilities you will be accessing include
  – news, stock quotes, charts, etc.
  – your broker – you can get in and out of stocks quicker online than you can by phone.
- Proprietary software – many of the e-brokerages will provide you with specialised software to be able to execute the trades directly on your PC screen. Some e-brokerages even provide specialised training services to familiarise novices with the mechanics of day trading and the features of the software. Some software may require special graphics cards in the PC in order to have a two-monitor display which can contain the several user screens required for the trading activity.

7.8 SMART CARDS

Smart cards and stored value cards (monetary and token based), embedded with ICs and capable of holding identities, authorisations, certificates, records and monetary value are another significant feature of e-finance.

These smart cards were originally invented by Roland Moreno in France, and were developed by Bull Computers in France. Developed in the late 1960s, they began to appear in "workable" form in the late 1970s. They have gradually increased in popularity since that time – particularly in Europe, where more than 100 million were in circulation at the end of the 1990s. Their use ranges from simple phone cards to credit cards and now even cards to access medical services, embedded with key data about the card holder.

The smart card is one of the developments from the world of information technology that will have a significant impact on e-finance. Similar in size to today's plastic credit card, the smart card has a microprocessor or memory chip embedded in it. The chip stores electronic data and programs that are protected by advanced security features.

When coupled with a reader, the smart card has the processing power to serve many different applications such as secure transactions over electronic networks (e.g. SWIFT). Smart cards can also act as an access-control device, to ensure that personal and business data, or indeed secure offices or facilities are available only to authorised users.

Smart cards can also store "digital cash" or "electronic money" to enable users to effect purchases or exchange value over electronic networks. Smart cards provide data portability, security and convenience.

Smart cards come in two varieties: memory cards and microprocessor cards. Memory cards simply store data and can be viewed as a data storage device with optional security, while microprocessor cards can add, delete and manipulate information in their memory on the card.

There are different types of security mechanisms used in smart cards. Those necessary for a memory-only card are less sophisticated than those for a microprocessor card. Access to the information contained in a smart card is controlled two ways:

- Who can access the information (everybody, the card holder or a specific third party).
- How the information can be accessed (read only, added to, modified or erased).

One form of protection is ciphering, which is like translating the information into some unknown foreign language. Some smart cards are capable of ciphering and deciphering (translating back to an easily understood form) so the stored information can be transmitted without compromising confidentiality.

The important thing about smart cards is that they are everyday objects that people can carry in their pockets, yet they have the capacity to retain and protect critical information stored in electronic form.

The proliferation of this technology is evident when one considers that the same electronic function can be performed by embedding similar circuits in other everyday objects, such as keyrings, watches, glasses, rings or earrings (e.g. smart cards can be used for pay-TV subscriptions).

Contactless card technology also offers significant potential in that it can enable the manipulation of "tags". Tags function like contactless smart cards but are in the form of a ring, sticker, or baggage label. They can be attached to objects such as gas bottles, cars or animals and can hold and protect information concerning that object. This allows the object to be managed by an information system or customer relationship management system without any manual data handling. The possibilities of such systems in areas as inventory control and trade finance are limitless.

The current state of development of smart cards is relatively new and has already made a significant impact in increasing the security of transactions and dramatically limiting the incidence of fraudulent transactions. For example, in France, which has adopted the smart card as the standard payment mechanism of choice for credit cards, the rate of fraudulent use plummeted from several per cent (3–5% unofficially) to under 0.5%, radically reducing the cost of fraud to banks. Other countries such as the US and the UK have yet to adopt this French-developed technology, no doubt for reasons of national preference.

The smart card is in its infancy and it promises ultimately to influence the way business, data processing, and e-finance is conducted.

7.9   EVOLUTION OF E-FINANCE

85	Classic electronic proprietary networks
	SWIFT installs a high volume satellite link between US and European operations
86	Internet Engineering Task Force established
87	
88	First internet worm virus
89	
90	
91	WWW released by CERN
92	SWIFT introduces Interbank File Transfer
	World bank comes online
	Term "surfing the internet" is coined by Jean Armour Polly
93	InterNIC is created by NSF to provide internet services (domain name)
	UN goes online
	Mosaic is the first browser
	Extension of MIME
94	In 1994, Marc Andreessen, one of the developers of Mosaic, left NCSA, co-founded Netscape Communications Corp., released the Netscape Navigator, a graphical web browser
	House/Senate provide information servers
	Shopping malls arrive on the internet
	SWIFT introduces SWIFTAlliance UNIX-based terminals
95	In 1995, Microsoft stepped in the web browser market, released the Internet Explorer version 1.0. Traditional online dial-up systems (Compuserve, America Online, Prodigy) begin to provide internet access
	A number of Net related companies go public, with Netscape leading the pack with the third largest ever NASDAQ IPO share value (9 August)
	Two of the biggest names in e-commerce are launched: Amazon.com and eBay.com.
	Technologies of the year: WWW, search engines
	Emerging technologies: mobile code (JAVA, JAVAscript), virtual environments (VRML), collaborative tools
	Hacks of the year: The Spot (June 12), Hackers Movie Page (12 August)
96	SWIFT gears up for STP with a dedicated team
	Technologies of the year: search engines, JAVA, internet phone
	Emerging technologies: virtual environments (VRML), collaborative tools, internet appliance (network computer)
	Technologies of the year: e-commerce, e-auctions, portals
	Emerging technologies: e-trade, XML, intrusion detection
97	June 1997–35 million internet users
98	June, 1998–60 million internet users
	Companies flock to the Turkmenistan NIC in order to register their name under the .tm domain, the English abbreviation for trademark
99	June, 1999–130 million internet users
	First Internet Bank of Indiana, the first full-service bank available only on the Net, opens for business on 22 February
	First large-scale cyberwar takes place simultaneously with the war in Serbia/Kosovo
	Retail spending over the internet reaches USD 20 billion, according to Business.com
	.ps is registered to Palestine (11 October)
	Emerging technologies: net-cell phones, thin computing, embedded computing
	Viruses of the year: Melissa (March), ExploreZip (June)

00	A massive denial of service attack is launched against major websites, including Yahoo!, Amazon, and eBay in early February

00 A massive denial of service attack is launched against major websites, including Yahoo!, Amazon, and eBay in early February
After months of legal proceedings, the French court rules Yahoo! must block French users from accessing hate memorabilia in its auction site (November). Given its inability to provide such a block on the internet, Yahoo! removes those auctions entirely (January 2001)
SWIFT announces plans for two services for trust and payments into the business-to-business domain: TrustAct, which assures the identity of corporates trading over the internet and e-paymentsPlus, which provides corporates with web-based payment initiation and assurance services
Technologies of the year: ASP, Napster
Emerging technologies: wireless devices, IPv6
Viruses of the year: Love Letter (May)
01 Afghanistan's Taliban bans internet access country-wide, including from government offices, in an attempt to control content (13 July)
Code Red worm and Sircam virus infiltrate thousands of web servers and email accounts, respectively, causing a spike in internet bandwidth usage and security breaches (July)
A fire in a train tunnel running through Baltimore, Maryland, seriously damages various fibre-optic cable bundles used by backbone providers, disrupting internet traffic in the Mid-Atlantic states and creating a ripple effect across the US (18 July)

7.10   ORIGIN OF E-FINANCE AND INTERNET COMMERCE

E-finance, as we have seen, began with the development of several disparate elements, many of which were developed in isolation. As these individual elements progressed, they began to be tied together in networks.

The true era of *internet enabled* e-finance began in the mid-1990s when the internet became the network of networks. This enabled businesses to communicate in hitherto unforeseen ways, in transmitting information and payments, but also in conducting business.

Businesses then began to develop web-based platforms to deliver financial services. The process started in the B2C sector and has gradually moved into the B2B arena as systems became more robust and secure.

As different groups began developing business models for the banking industry, several clear advantages have become evident.

- Using the internet, companies can use standard internet communications protocols (TCP/IP) meta-languages (XML, extensible markup language) and OFX (open financial exchange) to conduct electronic business flexibly and dynamically.
- E-finance platforms enable internet payments systems to be linked together and process customer payments more efficiently, while technology enables the creation of user-friendly GUIs, which help promote interest and activity among consumers.
- Smart cards promise to add additional security to the development of electronic purchases and transactions.
- Increased volume usage moreover leads to a lowering of unit transaction costs and the development of secure payment mechanisms such as firewalls, encryption, and digital signatures.

Not surprisingly, it was the smaller players and institutions which adopted these technologies as they saw them as a means of bypassing traditional costly entry barriers to the business rather than the large Wall Street institutions which were quite content to operate in the status quo and protect their turf. Such pioneers include companies like Charles Schwab, the online broker, and Ameritrade. Other smaller players also began as startups, obtaining capital from venture capitalists or incubator funds.

While many companies have since evolved into broader and more sophisticated platforms, all of them began life as corporate storefronts, promoting proprietary products and services through their own company-specific websites.

7.10.1 Rise of e-finance and electronic trading

Discount broker Schwab began providing its customers with a rudimentary PC trading access in 1984. The service was basic and cumbersome and routed through relatively slow dial-up access.

True online trading began in the USA in 1995 when the first (IPO) initial public offering of a company was placed via the internet. Over 3500 investors purchased shares, marking this the first time securities had been sold via the web.

The Securities and Exchange Commission (SEC) was concerned about this new activity and the potential precedent it might establish; it therefore investigated the initial offering and the ongoing secondary trading. The SEC subsequently issued a "no-action letter" sanctioning the transaction, effectively giving the green light to true internet-based trading.

The SEC's green light led to other players beginning trading. Some of these include:

* Web Street Securities, E*Trade, Schwab, Ameritrade and Datek, who altered their existing discount brokerage operations in the same year and migrated to the internet.
* Web Street Securities, a "pure play" (e.g. one which exists only in a computerised state with no traditional "bricks and mortar" offices or infrastructure), commenced its operations in 1996 by offering customers a full-service information and execution platform.
* Schwab, who also began operations in 1996 by building its web-based platform and offering innovative online services and competitive pricing.

Full service brokers, such as Merrill Lynch, Morgan Stanley Dean Witter, and Paine Webber, in contrast, preferred to wait and see the results. By 2000 Schwab had 3.5 million active online accounts (equal to 50% of its total client base) and was executing nearly 250 000 trades per day.

Discount brokers, which had already embraced technology such as phone banking and PC banking during the 1980s, took advantage of these crumbling entry barriers and were particularly successful in adapting to the internet.

Internet banking also came to the fore: the first true internet bank was Security First Network Bank (SFNB), created in Atlanta in 1995. In 1995 the Office of Thrift Supervision approved the proposal to change First Federal's business focus from that of a savings institution to a pure play electronic bank. Cardinal received approval in mid-1995, changed the bank's name to SFNB and commenced operations by offering web-based balance lookup, unlimited third-party bill paying, funds transfers, loans, and Federal Deposit Insurance Corporation (FDIC) insured deposits.

As is typical in the field of banking information technology, software and e-finance infrastructure systems developed for in-house uses have applications in other industry sectors and can, in turn, be sold to defray development costs and generate profits. Hence, players who have developed web platforms can in turn forge links combining its proprietary technology solutions with other solutions providers in the IT sphere. Hence, new entities arise which can offer financial institutions an internet turnkey product for online banking.

With very few exceptions, the world's largest financial institutions have generally failed to act as innovators and movers in web-based finance and delayed their offerings until new innovative startups had built considerable market shares and brand identification.

The initial lack of interest or foresight of major players meant that many of them found themselves chasing the upstarts during the late 1990s. Once it became clear that internet-based commerce was a new force that was here to stay, the major players, with deep pockets, began to change their tune and pay attention to the developments and issues being raised by e-commerce and e-finance.

In other words, institutions moved from denying the need to have an internet presence and using the internet as a medium to diffuse "brochureware" to employing it as an aggressive, transaction-enabled business-gathering tool. These institutions also realised that the internet allowed them to create a new "high tech" image, offer new products/services, and enlarge reach/presence without having to spend additional capital on physical expansion.

Full service brokers such as Merrill Lynch and Morgan Stanley Dean Witter hence rushed to redefine their business models and provide customers with services that more internet-aggressive firms such as Schwab and Ameritrade were already supplying.

Merrill Lynch moreover had to back out of the corner it had painted itself into in late 1998 when it declared that "the do-it-yourself model of investing, cantered on Internet trading, should be considered as a serious threat to Americans' financial lives". It is particularly ironic that large Wall Street securities firms – which pride themselves on being adept, dynamic and responsive as, in fact, they are – were unable to adapt to the new business paradigm with the same agility.

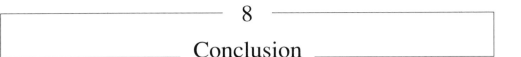

8
Conclusion

Looking back, what broad conclusions can we make about understanding international bank risk? Well, the subject of bank analysis is somewhat larger and more interesting than initial impressions imply. It is a tale not only of finance but of people, with management goals and ambitions, often at odds.

The main importance of understanding international bank risk in its larger context is that it enables effective risk management when dealing with banks, and extending credit to them, and to understand the regulatory and business pressures that they are subject to.

Predicting bank risk is an ambiguous exercise but that is what makes it interesting. The various pronouncements and classic analytical techniques offered to bank trainees by their training organisations or rating agencies provide an idealistic framework of the subject. While this is fine in itself, as it enables a proper mastery, use, and understanding of financial analysis fundamentals, it often leads to a straitjacket approach which can be misleading in that it ignores underlying fundamentals and realities, for two basic reasons – many of the elements cannot be quantified, and many of the elements are unacceptable to address head on because it is akin to washing one's dirty laundry in public – it is excessively revelatory of the basic human characteristics motivating the people in the business and the business itself. Formalising acknowledgement of these elements in classic analytical literature formalises certain unacceptable assumptions about the nature of the business. Indeed, so unacceptable that it is ignored.

Ignoring them, however, does not mean that they do not exist and accordingly, no analysis of bank risk would be complete without them. Fine tuning financial analysis techniques with corrupted financial data, when there is a rotten captain at the helm, is akin to fiddling with the thermostat when the house is burning down. Those who ignore this do so at their own peril.

The recent spate of financial and accounting scandals is indeed fascinating, not in that it reveals corrupt practices (which admittedly have always existed), but in that it reveals the extent of them, and suggests that they are becoming the unspoken norm of doing business. It is the banality of corruption that is shocking, as it threatens to turn established financial models and systems on their head. In the long run, this can only be damaging to the system as a whole, and foster an ideological backlash.

Unfortunately, these elements are rarely taught in classic financial analysis or are alluded to in rating agency literature. They become apparent after specialising in the financial and risk analysis of banks over a number of years, and accumulating information that is not immediately apparent in either bank financial statements or financial analysis and training literature. Over time, one begins to discern patterns in bank growth, activity, and management behaviour. The techniques change but human nature remains constant over time.

Many of these elements are indeed reliable indicators of bank failure, or indicators about what sort of problems a bank may be experiencing, enabling financial analysis to focus accordingly. Business pressures and management behaviour can provide an indicator of which areas of the bank is experiencing problems and help to focus a more detailed financial analysis. These elements also make analysis interesting because paradoxically, they add a human face to the anonymity of the business. Acting upon that knowledge, however, is a different story.

It is hoped that this book helps provide interest and stimulation into a most interesting subject.

Glossary

Acceleration	Occurs after an event of default (q.v.) where the whole loan is declared immediately due and payable even though the agreed repayment date has not been reached.
Acceptance	A type of bill of exchange. By accepting (or adding acceptance to) a bill of exchange, the drawee undertakes to pay it on the maturity date. Accepted bills are often called acceptances. Acceptance can also be by endorsement. Bankers' acceptances are those where a bank has endorsed the bill and thus guarantees payment.
Accepting house	(UK) A bank or financial organisation whose speciality is adding its acceptance to its customer's bills of exchange so that they can be discounted in the discount market at favourable rates. They are members of the Accepting Houses Committee.
Accounting period	Period of time from one balance sheet to the next. Period of the income statement, usually one year.
Accounts payable (payables or creditors)	Amounts owed to suppliers for goods or services received.
Accounts receivable (receivables or debtors)	Amounts owed by customers or buyers as a result of a sale of goods, or the performance of a service.
Accounts receivable financing	Procedure whereby a specialised financial institution or bank makes loans against the pledge of accounts receivable.
Accrual basis	Accounting for income or expenses when earned or incurred irrespective of whether they have been received or paid. The rationale is to match expenses incurred with the revenues that result.
Accrual liability	Creditor, accounts payable, current liability. Accounting concept: income and expense for the accounting period must be included whether for cash or credit.
Accrued interest	The interest earned since the latest interest payment due but not yet paid.

Accrued interest payable	Interest owing on loans or other financial assets and thereby passed through the income statement but which has not yet been remitted by the bank.
Accrued interest receivable	Interest accrued on loans or other financial assets and thereby passed through the income statement but which has not been received by the bank.
Accumulated depreciation	Extent to which the fixed asset cost has been allocated to depreciate expense, since the asset was originally acquired. "Reserve" for depreciation. "Provision" for depreciation. Deducted from fixed assets.
Acquisition	The purchase of assets or a controlling interest in a company by another company. It is generally used to describe cash transactions as opposed to equity transactions.
ADB	Asian Development Bank, headquartered in Manila, Philippines.
Administrative agent	The US term for the arranger of a syndicated transaction.
Advance	A generic term for the ways in which a bank lends money, whether loan, overdraft, or discount.
Advance payment guarantee	A guarantee issued by a bank on behalf of, say, a contractor to protect the buyer and which provides for repayment of the advance payments in the event of the contractor's failure to carry out the contract terms.
After-market	The period (synonymous with the secondary market) when securities are traded after the initial issuing process is over.
AIBD	Association of International Bond Dealers.
ALCO	Asset Liability Management Committee.
American option	Option that can be exercised any time before the final exercise date (cf. European option).
AMEX	American Stock Exchange.
Amortisation (1)	The expending of an intangible asset in a company's income statement over a period of time judged to be the economic life of the asset. Like depreciation, amortisation is a non-cash expense.
Amortisation (2)	The paying off of a loan in staged payments (repayment instalments).
Arbitrage	Simultaneous purchase and sale of the same or equivalent items, to take advantage of a price discrepancy. The purchase of a security traded on two or more markets at the same time; also, occurs in the foreign exchange, commodity and money markets. The two deals can be in the same market (e.g. FX) or different markets. Arbitrage relies on the continuous movement of sections of markets at different speeds to create "opportunities".
Arrangement fees	For their efforts in arranging a deal, banks collect arrangement fees. These fees are attractive for the bank because they represent revenues that do not have to be generated by the balance sheet, which are subject to capital adequacy (Cooke) ratios.
Arranging banks	The banks which arrange the financing on behalf of a corporate borrower. Usually, the banks commit to underwrite the whole amount only if they are unable to place the deal fully. Typically, however, they place the bulk of the facility and retain a portion on their books for themselves.
Asset bubble	A boom period marked by speculative excess and investor euphoria that tends to occur during an economic upsizing just prior to its peak,

during which the prices of real or financial assets rise to an unprecedented level.

Asset liability management (ALM) — A technique to match cash flows, and maturities of assets and liabilities to maximise return and minimise the interest rate risk from mismatching.

Asset quality — Asset quality refers to the ability of a bank's assets, especially its loans, to continue to perform according to their terms and generate net interest income for the bank. An evaluation of a bank's asset quality includes not only quantitative measures of the bank's problem loans but also qualitative elements such as the bank's policy for allocating loan loss provisions, lending strategies, credit review policies and procedures, loan portfolio composition, and general credit culture.

Asset trading — In banking, this refers to buying and selling loans on the secondary markets. Although loans are generally viewed as illiquid assets, banks may be able to trade loans (usually blue chip although trading in distressed debt also exists). Typically this depended on having no prohibition in the loan agreement but typically clauses permitting asset trading are now included as standard clauses in the loan agreements due to the initiatives of industry groups such as the Loan Marketing Association in London. The reason for trading in this market may be that a bank desires to re-configure its loan portfolio. Asset trading is the logical continuation of syndicated lending.

Asset-backed — Securities whose value is linked to (and securities usually supported by) a pledged quantity of another asset.

Asset-backed loans — A loan which is supported by assets owned by the issuer of the debt and usually placed with a trustee.

Assets — Resources or legal rights owned by the business. These may be physical (e.g. a building) or contractual (e.g. a receivable).

Assignment — An agreement to transfer all of the rights (but not the obligations) under the contract to a new lender via an assignment agreement. In the USA the term can also denote the transfer of obligations.

Audit — A process of examination of financial statements and the underlying accounting. An independent audit will provide a systematic investigation of the accounting systems and controls to ensure compliance with prescribed accounting and auditing standards.

Authorised but unissued shares — Shares that are authorised by a bank's charter but are unissued.

Availability period — Time period after the signing of the loan agreement during which the borrower, having satisfied conditions precedent, is permitted to draw down advances.

Average assets — Average assets are calculated as Assets $(Y1 + Y2)/2$. Average assets are used in financial ratios such as the Bankscope ratios to avoid distortions arising from one year to the next.

Average Life — The total of the amounts outstanding at the end of each year of the loan for its entire life, divided by the total principal sum borrowed to give the average life of the loan in years.

Back to back loan — Companies with surplus liquidity in one currency may wish to obtain funds in another, for investment or expansion, by employing their own

	surplus resources without conversion or incurring exchange exposure, or without incurring increased interest costs by borrowing unmatched funds; this may be arranged by means of a parallel, or back to back loan.
Bad Loan	A loan which is not expected to be collectible in full. This term is often used to describe non-performing loans, or impaired loans.
Balance sheet	A statement reflecting the financial position at a specific moment in time.
Balloon payment	Large final payment (e.g. when a loan is repaid in instalments).
Bank	A financial institution licensed to accept money deposits and make loans (often called a "commercial bank" to differentiate it from a securities house or investment bank).
Bank of International Settlements	The BIS was established in 1930 and is known as the "Central Banks' Central Bank". It accepts deposits and makes loans to its member banks, and acts as a source of information for issues related to international capital movements. The BIS is based in Basle, Switzerland, and has provided a forum for the Basle Committee on Banking Supervision, a group of regulators from the Group of 10 (G10) countries which has been involved in promoting uniform rules on bank capital adequacy, risk management, and bank supervision.
Banker's acceptance (BA)	Written demand that has been accepted by a bank to pay a given sum at a future date (cf. trade acceptance). US equivalent of UK sterling bills of exchange, i.e. a draft or bill of exchange accepted by a bank. The accepting institution guarantees payment on the bill.
Banking crisis	A loss of confidence which threatens the breakdown or collapse of a banking system's ability to function as a supplier of credit and payment system. A banking crisis typically features capital flight (withdrawal of assets and transfer of these assets abroad or conversion into foreign currency) and a liquidity crunch (insufficient funds to enable banks to act as a provider of capital). Such a crisis can result in corporate failures and a fall in overall economic activity.
Banking environment	The business, regulatory and competitive environment in which a bank operates. The banking environment includes elements such as country and sovereign risk, macroeconomic factors, political factors, competition, consolidation, interest rate environment, entry of new players, changes in banking regulation and legislation, changes in capitalisation requirements, etc., all basically macroeconomic elements exterior to the bank.
Basis (or reference) rate	The bench mark cost of funds to which the margin will be added or deducted to determine the total rate payable by the borrower (e.g. LIBOR, LIBID, and Prime are basis rates).
Basis point	One 100th of one cent.
Basle Accord	The Basle Capital Accord of 1988, formally known as "International Convergence of Capital Measurement and Capital Standards". The Basle Accord attempts to apply uniform measures in a heterogeneous international environment. The Basle Accord is in the process of being revised under the "Basle 2" arrangements – in which a first consultative

	document was issued in 1999, and a final consultative document in 2001, with approval in 2001 and final implementation in 2004.
Basle Committee	The Basle Committee on Banking Supervision comprises a panel of regulators from the Group of 10 (G10) countries that convenes at the Bank of International Settlements (BIS) in Basle, Switzerland. It should be noted that these two organisations are separate organisations. The committee established the first standards for international capital adequacy of banks.
Bear market	Widespread decline in security prices (cf. bull market).
Bearer negotiable security	Security for which primary evidence of ownership is possession of the certificate (cf. registered securities).
Bearer securities	They are in bearer form when the certificate itself is the instrument of value.
Bid rate	The lower side of interest rate quotations. It is the rate of interest a bank is prepared to pay for deposits or to acquire securities.
Bank run	A bank run is a panic in which depositors, fearing that a bank is experiencing financial difficulty, queue up at a bank's offices demanding the return of their deposits (usually by then far too late). This vulnerability to panic underscores the importance of public confidence in the banking system.
Boilerplate	Clauses found regularly in loan documentation which are standard and vary little from agreement to agreement.
Bond	A debt instrument, i.e. an obligation to pay, which is negotiable (that is to say it can be traded). It is one of the basic forms of securities, also can be considered as long-term debt.
Book debts	The item in the balance sheet of a company representing the amount owing for goods sold as shown by the books.
Borrower risk	Risks pertaining to the company, including management, profitably, non-performance, and bankruptcy: all factors relating to the borrower.
Break-even analysis	Analysis of the level of sales at which a project would just break even (e.g. project revenues cover project costs).
Bretton Woods	A conference held in 1944, where fixed exchange rates were agreed upon as the basis for FX trading.
Bull market	Widespread rise in security prices (cf. bear market).
Bull–bear bonds	Bonds whose principal repayment is linked to the price of another security. The bonds are issued in two tranches: in the first the repayment increases with the price of the other security; in the second the repayment decreases with the price of the other security.
Bullet loans	A loan whose interest is payable at intervals agreed in the loan agreement, and whose principal is repayable in a lump sum (bullet repayment) at final maturity. There are no principal repayments along the way. The source of repayment is usually a new facility which is put into place.
Call deposits	Deposits which are repayable on the demand either of the bank or of the depositor.
Call money	Interest bearing bank deposits that can be withdrawn on 24 hours' notice. Thus, money can be placed on deposit "on call".

Cap	An option strategy that sets a ceiling on the holder's interest rate exposure.
Capital and reserves (shareholders' funds/net worth)	The value the owners have invested in the business. This is represented by share capital and reserves.
Capital markets	The market for debt and equity instruments.
Capitalisation	Long-term debt, preferred stock, plus net worth.
Capitalised interest	Accrued interest (and margin) which is not paid but added ("rolled up") at the end of each interest period to the principal amount lent (e.g. in relation to balloon repayment).
Cash	Money assets of a business. Includes both cash in hand and cash at bank. Balance sheet current assets.
Cash flow lending	Lending whose repayment is to come from the borrower's future cash flow.
CEDEL	A clearing system for notes based in Luxembourg with representative depositories in all major financial centres, where notes are physically exchanged and stored: in safe custody.
Certificate of deposit (CD)	Interest bearing negotiable bearer certificate which evidences a time deposit with the bank.
Cheque	An unconditional order in writing, drawn on a bank, signed by the drawer, requiring the bank to pay on demand a sum certain in money to or to the order of a specified person or the bearer, also a bill of exchange.
CHIPS	The New York Clearing House's computerised Clearing House Interbank Payments System through which most large US dollar transactions are settled.
COB	Commission des Opérations de Bourse. The French stock exchange supervisory and regulatory agency.
Collar	A premium-reducing option strategy in which the holder has bought a cap at one level and, to recoup some or all of its cost, has sold a floor at a much lower level.
Collateral	See security.
Commercial Paper	Short-term promissory notes which are listed in the secondary markets. For high quality borrowers, this can be a source of low cost albeit uncommitted funding.
Common stock	Ordinary shares.
Company (corporation)	A legal entity with perpetual succession.
Contingent liabilities	Items which do not represent a liability on the balance sheet at the time of statement date but which could do so in the future. Such items include guarantees issued in favour of third parties, and lawsuits currently in progress whose outcome is uncertain.
Contingent liability	A potential liability which may in time have a greater or lesser likelihood of becoming an actual liability.
Convertible bonds	Bonds issued by a corporation which may be converted by the holder into stock of the corporation within a specified time period and a specified price.

Convertible security	Bond or preferred stock that may be converted into another security at the holder's option.
Cooke ratio	The capital adequacy or risk weighted asset ratios prescribed by the Basle Committee on Banking Supervision.
Corporate lending	Lending to large and multinational corporations. Smaller and medium sized companies are referred to as "SME" lending.
Correspondent banks	Banks which have an agency relationship with each other and act for each other in their respective parts of the world. Very important for the financing of world trade.
Cost of funds	A term sometimes used as the basis for a loan pricing, particularly when the source of funding is uncertain or includes reserve asset costs. A precise definition of what is meant by this term should be established if it is to be of any practical value; it should be noted that the normal funding cost of a commercial loan is the offered rate, being the rate which the bank has to pay to another bank in the market for the funds obtained for the purpose.
Cost of goods sold	The direct cost of acquiring or producing goods which have been sold.
Country exposure	Country exposure is the amount of an institution's total investment and/or claims on borrowers in a specific country, direct as well as indirect.
Country limit	Country limits are the numerical amounts up to which an institution such as a bank or company is willing to take an exposure to in a particular country.
Country rating	Country ratings are the result of the individual appraisal of a particular country in view of its standing to honour its foreign debts in relation to other countries or groups of countries.
Country risk	"Country risk is the exposure to a loss in cross-border lending caused by events in a particular country which are, at least to some extent, under the control of the government but definitely not under the control of a private enterprise or individual." (P J Nagy 1984)

Three types of events can cause country risk:

- Political events such as war, ideology, neighbouring countries, political unrest, revolution, etc. comprise political risk. Political risk is the risk that a country is not willing or able, due to political reasons, to service/repay its foreign debt/obligations.
- Economic factors such as internal and external debt levels, GDP growth, inflation, import dependency, etc. comprise economic risk. Economic risk is the risk that a country is not willing or able, due to economic reasons, to service/repay its foreign debt/obligations.
- Social factors such as religious, ethnic, or class conflict, trade unions, inequitable income distribution, etc. comprise social risk. Social risk is the risk that a country is not able, or is unwilling, to repay its foreign debt/obligations due to social reasons.

Covenant	An agreement by a borrower to perform certain acts (such as the provision of financial statements or the respecting of a financial ratio) or

	to refrain from certain acts (such as incurring further indebtedness beyond an agreed level).
Credit	The process of taking a risk for the settlement of an obligation in the future.
Credit approval process	The loan approval procedure within a lending institution.
Credit limit/credit lines	The limits up to which a bank is prepared to lend money or grant credit to a customer. Credit limits/credit lines are usually used for internal management purposes and guidelines are not normally a legal commitment, only a willingness to do business.
Credit risk	The risk of losses arising from defaults by the counterparty.
Credit scoring	Technique used to evaluate a potential borrower according to a predefined matrix procedure (e.g. matrix such as the Altman Bankruptcy Predictor using Multiple Discriminant Analysis to generate a Z-score). Usually used in retail banking and credit card processing, also used in evaluating corporates.
Creditor	Payable, account payable, liability. Money owed to other parties. Current or long-term liability.
Crony capitalism	Refers to packing management boards of corporations or banks with persons pushed by the current regime in power. Also refers to banks lending to insiders or family groups or companies managed by friends or families.
Cross-default	One of the events of default which leads to the loan becoming immediately repayable. Triggered if the borrower defaults under any other indebtedness to other lenders (under a separate facility).
Currency swap	A contract between two parties to convert currencies from one currency to another, and then to convert back again into the original currencies at an agreed forward exchange rate.
Current assets	Assets owned which by their nature are likely to be transformed (sold, used in production, increased or decreased) within one year. These include stocks, cash, debtors and prepayments.
Current liabilities	Liabilities which will have to be met by the business within the next year. These include short-term bank debt, creditors, taxes due.
Current ratio	The relationship between current assets and current liabilities.
Debenture	A formal acknowledgement of a debt, usually incorporating a charge over the unencumbered assets of the company issuing it; the rights of debenture holders rank before those of shareholders and unsecured creditors in the event of the issuer's liquidation. Often also used to refer to a document creating a charge, mortgage, or other security interest.
Debt equity ratio	The ratio of a company's ordinary share capital to its fixed interest capital, including debentures, loan stock, and preference shares; calculations are often simply based on the ratio of ordinary shares plus retained reserves to prior charge capital.
Debt ratings	The classification of a company's financial (credit) standing by specialist agencies such as Moody's and Standard & Poor's (e.g. A+, A, A−, B+, B, B−, C).

Debt securities	An instrument denoting an obligation by the issuer to pay the current and/or future holder(s) the due interest and principal.
Debt service	The payment of interest, fees and principal in accordance with the loan agreement.
Deed poll	A deed to which there is only one party or one set of parties and that party makes "unilateral promise" to members of any identifiable class which although they have no privity of contract can enforce against the promisor.
Default	The debtor notifies the creditor that he will definitely cease making any further service payments because he cannot, or does not want to, pay.
Default interest clause	A clause providing for interest to continue to accrue on an overdue debt, usually at an enhanced rate. The clause may be void as a penalty under English law if the rate of interest imposed does not represent a genuine estimate of the loss being suffered by the lender.
Default, event of	Failure to fulfil the conditions of a contract (see event of default, and cross-default).
Deposits	Current liabilities of the bank in the form of current account funds or monies at call, notice or fixed term.
Derivative instrument	A security or contract whose value is dependent on or derived from the value of an underlying asset. The main classes of derivative instruments are forward speeches, options, their securitised equivalents and warrants and swaps. Derivative contracts can be on currencies, commodities, equities, equity indices, and interest rates. Derivatives can be exchanged, traded or over-the-counter (OTC) traded. The latter are between counter parties and are telephone and screen traded by banks, outside the regulated exchanges.
Direct country risk	Direct country risk in cross-border lending and/or investment is the country risk of the country where the borrower takes up his liabilities and/or the investment is made.
Disclaimer	Statement made by the arranger and contained in documents such as information memoranda which asserts that certain information provided in the prospectus was supplied by the borrower, and is therefore not the responsibility of the arranger.
Discount basis	In relation to notes, this means the way in which the interest over the life of the note is calculated when the note is issued and deducted from the amount paid by the purchaser to the issuer so that the interest is paid "up front".
Disintermediation	Withdrawal of funds from a financial institution in order to invest them directly.
Dividend	The payment or distribution by a business to its shareholders.
Documentary credit	A method of financing overseas trade by bank's payment of goods by issuer of a letter of credit. Usually coupled with a pledge of documents of title and sometimes a trust receipt.
Documentation risk	The risk of non-repayment due to defect in the loan agreement or security arrangements. This can arise due to faulty drafting, mitigating circumstances, juridically non-enforceable and faulty collateral, or guarantees

	which have expired and not been renewed. Analysts are not expected to assess legal issues, but are expected to obtain legal opinions when necessary and note them accordingly.
Domestic issue	Loans, notes, or equity raised in the indigenous capital market and currency of the country of issue. USD raised in the US, FrF raised in France, etc.
Drawdown	The actual borrowing of money (advance) under the terms of a facility.
DTI	Department of Trade and Industry (UK). The DTI is a valuable source of information on companies and many business matters in the UK and abroad.
EBIT	Earnings before interest and taxes.
EBITDA	Earnings before interest, taxes, depreciation and amortisation (normally excludes extraordinary items).
EBRD	European Bank for Reconstruction and Development. The EBRD's London head office is noteworthy for its lavish premises and lobby: its new marble surfacing has been recently replaced with exquisite Italian marble. As a minor sideline, the EBRD is involved in financing the economic development of Eastern Europe.
ECU	European Currency Unit. The bête noire of Euro sceptics, nationalists, and xenophobes (imagine the USA with 50 different currencies). The ECU is a monetary unit whose value is defined by a basket of currencies of the member states of the European Community. The ECU is the core of the European Monetary System (EMS).
Efficient market	Market in which security prices reflect information instantaneously.
Efficient portfolio	Portfolio that offers the lowest risk (standard deviation) for its expected return and the highest expected return for its level of risk.
EIB	European Investment Bank.
Equity	An ownership interest in a company. Usually this is in the form of ordinary shares (European English) or common stock (American). Equities and bonds are the main basic types of "securities".
EURIBOR	Euro interbank offered rate.
Eurobond	Bond denominated in a currency and issued outside the currency's issuing country.
Euroclear	A computerised clearing house for Eurobonds located in Brussells.
Eurocurrency	Currency held and traded outside its country of origin.
Eurodollar deposit	Dollar deposit with a bank outside the USA.
Eurodollars	US dollars held by a non-resident of the USA in an account outside the USA.
Euroloan	A loan denominated in a Eurocurrency.
European option	Option that can be exercised only on the final exercise date (cf. American option).
Event of default	An event listed in the loan documentation which enables the lender to cancel the credit facility and declare all amounts owing by the debtor in the subject credit facility to be immediately due and payable. Events of default typically include non-payment of amounts due to the lender, breach of covenant, cross-default, insolvency and material adverse change.

Evergreen facility	A facility which is renewable from year to year.
Exchange rate	The price of one currency in terms of another.
Exposure	The extent to which a bank or institution is reliant on one or more counterparties as a result of trading transactions
Facility	The grant of availability of money at some future date in return for a fee.
Facility agent	The agent of the banks in the syndicate who provides the committed facility, who fixes LIBOR, LIBID, and other reference rates and coordinates the banks.
Facility fee	An annual percentage fee payable on a pro rata basis to banks providing a credit facility on the full amount of the facility, whether or not it is used.
FASB	Financial Accounting Standards Board.
Fed	Federal Reserve System. US central regulatory banking authority.
Fee letter	A very important document – sets out the fees to be paid to the arranging bank and/or agent. This is very confidential as often not all fees paid are shared with the syndicate members.
Final maturity date	The date for payment of the last repayment instalment.
Fixed assets	Assets owned which by their nature are not likely to be transformed (sold, used in production, increased or decreased) within one year. These include land and buildings, plant and machinery fixtures and fittings.
Fixed charge	A charge usually contained in a debenture over a company's assets which prevents the company from dealing in any way with the property covered by the fixed charge without the consent of the chargee.
Fixed rate loan	A term loan for which the interest rate for the whole period is determined at the outset.
Floating charge	A charge usually contained in a debenture as well as fixed charge over stock, book debts, and the general undertaking of a company. The company can deal with the charged assets in the ordinary course of business. They become crystallised when security documents terms are breached. Automatic ability of the chargee to appoint a receiver upon crystallisation.
Floating rate note	Notes bearing interest that will be determined at regular intervals by a formula based upon prevailing short-term money market rates.
Floor	An option strategy that sets a floor on the holder's exposure to the underlying stock.
FOREX	Foreign exchange market from spot or forward exchange dealings.
Forfaiting	The discounting of medium-term bank guaranteed trade bills without recourse.
Forward contracts	A contract to buy or sell a currency for future delivery fixing the future exchange rate today.
Forward market	A market where a rate is agreed for a transaction due to occur at a defined future time.
FRA	Forward rate agreement. A transaction designed to lock in a future fixed interest rate.

FRN floating rate note	A bond which pays a rate of interest pegged to a certain benchmark interest rate and with whose level it varies every six months.
Front-end costs	Commission, fees, or other payments that are taken at the "outset" of a loan, such as, for example, discounting; the front-end charges for capital issues are very considerable and in calculating the total cost, a borrower should be aware of the additional cost of being short of such disbursements at the outset when compared with the cost of interest payments that are payable after the loan period and not before.
Funding	Acquisition of liabilities to match, cover, or balance the particular asset or assets for which they are required.
Funds	Value used in a business (includes cash, credit, capital).
Futures	These are formal agreements to purchase a given item in the future at a price agreed today. The purpose is to hedge against price changes. The practice began in Chicago in the nineteenth century and centred on the agricultural market, but records show that it was common in Holland and Japan in the sixteenth century.
Futures contract	An agreement to buy or sell a given quantity of a particular asset at a specified future date at a pre-agreed price. Like forwards, futures differ from options in that they represent an obligation to buy or sell the underlying stock. Unlike forwards, they have standardised delivery dates, trading units and terms and conditions. They are available on a wide range of financial and commodity assets, generally expire quarterly and can be cash or physically settled. They are traded on exchanges, which act as counterparties to all transactions that run margining systems.
Futures market	Centrally organised market where contracts for future commodity deliveries are transacted in a formalised way.
FX	Aka Forex. Foreign exchange.
Gearing	The relationship between total financial debt and shareholders' funds (or net worth).
Glass-Steagall	1933 US Act which forbids banks to deal in securities.
Governing law	The legal system to which the terms and conditions of a transaction are subject.
Grace period	A period of days within which the borrower is allowed to remedy a breach or failure of payment before that breach or failure becomes an event of default; confusingly, can also mean the period before the first repayment instalment is due (e.g. repayment by five semi-annual instalments, two years' grace, which means that the loan is repaid at six monthly intervals starting after two years).
Gross margin	Sales revenue minus cost of goods sold.
Grossing up	The provision in the facility agreements whereby the borrower agrees that in the event of an imposition of any withholding or similar taxes in its country of incorporation, it will pay such additional amount as will ensure that the banks are effectively free of such taxes.
Guarantee	An undertaking in writing by one person (the guarantor) given to another, usually a bank (the creditor) to be answerable for the debt of a third person (the debtor) to the creditor, upon default of the debtor. Different from but usually coupled with an indemnity.

Hedge	An action taken to reduce liability to market price fluctuations of an asset including money.
Horizontal integration	A diversification strategy that calls for the acquisition of similar businesses or businesses that could benefit directly from existing operational capacity.
Horizontal merger	Merger between two companies that manufacture similar products (cf. vertical merger).
IBRD	International Bank for Reconstruction and Development (aka the World Bank), based in Washington DC.
IMM	International Monetary Market. The financial futures market within the Chicago Mercantile Exchange (cf. LIFFE (London), MATIF (France)).
Indemnity	An undertaking to hold harmless by one person to another, distinguished from a guarantee as it need not be in writing and is a primary liability rather than a collateral liability.
Indirect country risk	Indirect country risk in cross-border lending and/or investment is the country risk of the guarantor or of the main security if guarantor or security is in a different country than the one where the borrower has taken up his primary liabilities or where the investment has been made. The lender qualifies this risk as his ultimate country risk.
Intangible assets	Assets which are not tangible and do not have an easily ascertainable value, e.g. goodwill, patents, trademarks.
Interest	The cost of money; money paid for the use of money.
Interest period	The period by reference to which interest is paid, typically one, three, or six months as this tracks the interbank funding market. Interest is paid at a fixed rate during each period but is refixed at the start of the next period thus reflecting the change in market conditions.
Interest rate risk	The change in capital values of the investment introduces a serious risk into what may be a safe investment. Due to increased capital risk, long-term investments provide higher returns than short-term indicated by a positive yield term. Where long-term rates do not offer enhanced yields over short-term rates, a flat or inverted yield curve is seen.
Inventory	Finished goods, raw materials or work in progress.
Investment bank	A financial institution which (normally) underwrites and trades securities and offers related advisory services. It may be part of, or affiliated with, a "bank" (as defined above) – but not necessarily.
Issuance	The process of creating and distributing securities (also known as a new issue). By definition they can only be issued once: but other securities of the same class may be issued at different times. Also, once issued, they might at some point be traded in bulk.
Lead manager	A lead bank which syndicates or subparticipates a loan to various "takers" (subparticipants) in the market.
Letter of credit, L/C	A document issued by a bank authorising the bank to whom it is addressed to honour the cheques of the person named to the extent of a fixed amount. A non-negotiable instrument.
Letter of pledge	A document setting out the terms of a pledge, but an effective pledge can only be created when the documents are delivered to the possession of the bank taking the pledge.

Leverage	The ability to control a large nominal amount of an underlying asset with a relatively small amount of capital.
LIBID	The London Interbank Bid Rate: the rate at which banks buy deposits in the market.
LIBOR	London Interbank Offer Rate. The interest rate at which major international banks in London lend to each other. (LIBID is London Interbank Bid Rate; LIMEAN is mean of bid and offered rate.)
Lien	The right to retain chattels belonging to another until a debt due from the latter is paid. A "banker's lien" is a special form of lien which, as well as being the right to retain, can include a right to sell property after reasonable notice, and is more in the nature of an implied pledge.
LIFFE	London International Financial Futures Exchange.
LIMEAN	The arithmetic mean of LIBID and LIBOR.
Limit	Maximum exposure allowed in a currency, or to a counterparty, as set down internally by management.
Liquidity	The ability to service debt and redeem or reschedule liabilities when they mature, and the ability to exchange other assets for cash.
Liquidity ratios	The acid test and current ratios used to measure changes in liquidity between various accounting periods.
Liquidity risk	The risk of losses arising from a derivative market becoming a liquid or where the difficulty or cost issues arise when closing the position.
Listing	Obtaining a quotation on a stock market for bonds or equity instruments which may then be traded on the stock exchanges.
Long	A person who has bought futures or options, or other derivatives or other securities in the expectation that they will increase in value. Being long in futures is the commitment to buy the futures at a future date.
Long-term liabilities	Liabilities of the business which will fall due in a period more than 12 months from the balance sheet date.
Management accounting	Part of the accounting system used to provide information for managing the business in a form required for internal use compared to financial accounting which is for external use and must reflect prescribed formats and content.
Management buy out (MBO)	The purchase of a business by its managers, usually part financed by a syndicate of banks; may be several layers of debt, including mezzanine finance.
Margin	The rate taken by the lender over the cost of funds, which effectively represents his profit and remuneration for taking the risk of the loan; also known as "spread".
Market risk	The risk of losses arising from adverse market rate movements, e.g. foreign exchange (transaction, translation or economic), interest rates, commodity and equity prices.
Market value	The price at which an asset may be bought or sold.
Marketability	The degree of investment demand for a particular asset offered at a given price.
MATIF	Marché a Terme d'Instruments Financiers. French equivalent of the London International Financial Futures Exchange (LIFFE).
Maturity	The end date for a bond or loan. At maturity the issuer pays the then holder ("redemption").

Memorandum of deposit/letter of deposit	A document with the terms under which a deposit of security is made. It can be the written evidence of a pledge.
Mezzanine finance/debt	A second level of debt, below the "senior" debt, which ranks behind in priority to the senior debt, generally secured by second ranking charges and governed by a priorities deed.
Mismatched maturity	When the maturities of the funding cover and the loan or other asset do not coincide.
MOF	Multiple option facility – usually consisting of two or more options for the borrower to take loans (committed or through a tender panel procedure), swing line advances, bills of exchange, or notes.
Money markets	The trading of money. Money markets are largely unrelated to the securities markets.
Moratorium	A moratorium is the unilateral declaration of the borrower that he is unable and/or unwilling to honour all or part of his obligations and thereby stops the servicing of his debts.
Mortgage	A security a borrower gives to a lender usually over a specific property.
Multi-currency loan	A loan where the borrower has the option to draw down funds in more than one currency.
NASD	National Association of Security Dealers (USA).
NASDAQ	National Association of Securities Dealers Automatic Quotation System.
Negative pledge	A covenant in a facility agreement by the borrower not to grant security over its assets to other creditors (since this would put those other creditors in a preferential position).
Net worth (owners' equity)	The value owed by a business to its owners reflecting the difference between the total value of all assets and total of all liabilities. It is the value attributable to the owners in respect of the net financial position of the business.
NIF	Note issuance facility.
Nostro account	Account held at a foreign bank, used for the receipt and delivery of funds in settlement of trades.
Note	The promise or obligation to pay; promissory notes, bank notes, and floating rate notes all contain the issuer's primary responsibility for payment. In the context of euro notes, it generally means a maturity of less than one year of bonds which is generally used to describe instruments of more than seven years.
Novation	The transfer of rights and obligations from one entity to another, for example following the substitution of a new debtor for an old debtor or of one bank for another under a loan facility by way of substitution (transfer) certificate.
Novation agreement	A document which formally concludes the sale and transfer (by novation) of all rights and obligations from an existing lender to a new lender.
NRSRO	"NRSRO" is the acronym used in SEC rule 2a-7 to stand for a "nationally recognised statistical rating organisation" as per paragraph (a)(17) of rule 2a-7, as amended.

NRSROs are designated as such by the US Securities and Exchange Commission's Division of Market Regulation through the no-action letter process for purposes of the Commission's net capital rule (17 CFR 240.15c3-1)

In more mundane terms, NRSRO status confers upon a credit rating agency a quasi official role as one of the "official rites of passage" players for any entity accessing the capital markets in the USA. The mere fact there is a mere handful of NRSROs means that they are all practically guaranteed a slice of the economic pie. Since most issuers avail themselves of multiple ratings in order to avoid the accusation of "rating shopping" (getting rated by an entity willing to issue favourable ratings in order to get the business) they are in a virtually unassailable oligopoly.

NRSROs are in effect de-facto market regulators but not agencies of the US government nor are they subject to any particular regulatory control of aspects, for example such as the qualifications and knowledge of their analysts, either by educational qualifications or some sort of examination such as a bar examination that a lawyer is required to pass.

The clear inadequacies of the NRSRO nomination and control process has led to debate and controversy in the US financial markets.

NYSE   New York Stock Exchange, aka "the Big Board".

Off-shore   Outside the jurisdiction of a particular country.

Option   The opportunity to purchase a commodity at a given price at some time in the future. The option is paid even if never exercised.

OTC   Over the counter. Securities traded direct between traders, not on a central exchange floor.

Paper   Usually means a documented obligation such as bills of exchange or promissory notes, but may refer to any securities.

Pari passu   Literally "at the same rate" – usually with reference to a borrower's or guarantor's obligations ranking equally with each other in an insolvency.

Pledge   A delivery of chattels or a chose in action by a debtor to a creditor as security for his debt, the legal ownership remaining with the pledgor.

Political risk   The exposure to a loss in cross-border lending, caused by political factors in a certain country, political factors which are, at least to some extent under the control of the government but not under the control of a private enterprise or individual.

Portfolio   A bank's or investor's loan and investment assets.

Position   The relative status of a trader's dealings in various currencies or commodities.

Power of attorney An instrument by which one person is empowered to act for another. Banks often sign loan documentation by giving power of attorney to the facility agent.

Preference shares Shares which have priority, as far as dividend payments are concerned, over ordinary shares: but which have correspondingly junior voting rights.

Primary market   The new issue market (see issuance).

Principal trading	Trading by banks and investment banks/securities houses in securities which they own. It is also called "own account trading" or "proprietary trading". It has become much more favoured and practised by certain large firms in recent years.
Priorities deed	A document governing enforcement of security when there is more than one secured lender. Often found in management buyouts.
Profit and loss account	A record of income and expenses in the business in a specific period of time.
Project finance	The financing of a specific project on terms such that the banks will receive repayment out of cash flows generated by the project as opposed to the assets of the project sponsoring company.
Rating	A letter grade signifying a debt's investment quality. Two widely known rating agencies are Moody's Investors Service and Standard & Poor's.
Ratio analysis	Calculation of financial ratios as an aid to interpretation.
Redemption	The cancellation of a security by payment; redemption may be mandatory on a certain date, optional by the borrower after a certain date or conditional upon certain described and defined events having taken place (such as a change in tax laws which might jeopardise the borrower's position).
Reference banks	A group of banks (usually three) selected by the agent to quote their LIBOR (or other basis rate) on each rollover the average of which is taken as the rate applicable to the transaction.
Registered securities	Their value is acknowledged by the owner's/holder's name being logged on a central register (now normally computer based). Registered form is the antithesis of bearer form (defined above).
Regulatory actions	Legal requirements on a company. If the government passes a law obliging chemical companies to process carcinogenic waste instead of dumping it in our drinking water or the air we breathe, this is known as a regulatory action. Regulatory actions can adversely impact a company's profitability although positively impact the taxpayer's environment and quality of life.
Repos	(Repurchase agreements.) A cheap and easy method of borrowing money. The process is a sale and repurchase agreement. An investor sells his security to another party, simultaneously agreeing to buy it back at a later date. The sale and purchase price is agreed ahead of time. Investors find repos advantageous because they provide an inexpensive way of financing their long positions, if they are short and they find it convenient to be able to borrow bonds from dealers to meet their delivery obligations in spot markets. This is because most repos have overnight maturities.
Repudiation	The debtor notifies the creditor that he will definitely cease making any further service payment because he does not recognise the debt.
Rescheduling	Rescheduling is a process by which the lender and the borrower agree to arrange new conditions for an existing loan agreement.
Retail investors	Investors who own and trade securities on their own account.
Return on assets (ROA)	A measure of a syndicated loan's profitability to the lenders. ROA includes the margin, fees, and interest generated over the life of the facility.

	Since fees are allocated based on participation status, ROA varies from bank to bank.
Revolver/evergreen facility	A bank line of credit on which the customer (normally) pays a commitment fee and can draw down and repay funds according to his needs. Normally, the line involves a firm commitment from the bank for a period of several years.
Rights issue	A financing operation directed by a company at its shareholders who have the right (known as the "pre-emptive" right) to subscribe in priority to others.
Risk asset weighting	The weighting of individual assets on or off the balance sheets of commercial banks for purposes of calculating compliance with capitalisation adequacy ratios.
Rollover	The time when the interest rate of a floating rate loan is periodically reviewed at an agreed spread over, at, or under the currently prevailing LIBOR rate. In "true/classic" revolving facilities, the loans are repaid and redrawn on each rollover so that each loan is a separate and discrete borrowing.
Sales (sales turnover)	The value of goods sold or services provided in a specific accounting period. Sometimes described as "revenues".
SEC	Securities and Exchange Commission. The US regulatory agency which oversees the US securities markets and stock exchange.
Secondary market	A market in which securities, bonds, or debt is traded after issue, with profits accruing to the trader rather than to the original issuer.
Secured debt	Debt backed by specified assets or revenues of the borrower. Banks can call on these assets if the borrower is unable to repay the loan.
Securities	Notes, equity, loan stocks, bonds, or other debt instruments.
Securities house	Virtually synonymous with "investment bank" – a financial company underwriting, selling and trading securities.
Security	An asset which has been charged, whether formally or informally, to secure the repayment of a debt.
Senior debt	Debt which has priority of repayment in a liquidation.
Set-off	The total or partial merging of a claim of one person against another in a counterclaim by the latter against the former.
Settlement	The transfer of securities in exchange for payment.
SIB	Securities Investment Board (UK).
Sovereign risk	Is the risk of lending to the government or government controlled agency of a sovereign nation.
Special purpose vehicle	A legal entity created for the completion of a specific project such as a hotel, airport, or fund. SPVs are used to isolate the entity legally and financially from other participants such as the shareholders.
Spot	Price for immediate delivery (in foreign exchange two days from date of trade).
Spot rate	In currency markets it is today's market exchange rate for a transaction now. In interest rate markets, it is the rate at which the single future payment is discounted back to the present.
Spot rate of exchange	This is the rate obtained in the spot market for immediate as opposed to future delivery. In the spot market for FX, settlement (i.e. delivery/value)

is normally two business days ahead of the day on which the "deal" is struck.

Spread   The difference between the yields on two financial assets.

SSAP   Statement of Standard Accounting Practices (UK). A set of standardised guidelines and procedures which have become mandatory upon auditors in the UK for all company accounts.

Standby credit The arrangement to lend money in case of need, usually at market rates and sometimes with a commitment fee (see underwriters). Overdraft facilities are sometimes used as standbys by corporate borrowers.

Statement of cash flow   A statement which reconciles movements in cash between two accounting periods.

Subordinated loan   A loan whose seniority in a liquidation scenario is lower than classic bank debt but higher than equity. Subordinated loans will usually be made for long periods and will usually not be callable. Bankers therefore consider subordinated loans as quasi equity since their ranking order of priority is superior.

Subordination   A clause sometimes inserted in facilities whereby the rights of the lenders rank after the rights of some or all unsecured creditors of the borrower in the event of his liquidation.

Subparticipation   The sale of an asset where the subparticipant agrees to fund the loan and assume the credit risk but does not obtain any rights and obligations against the borrower. Subparticipations can either be public (acknowledged) or silent (unacknowledged).

Subrogation   The acquiring of another person's rights, usually as a result of assuming or discharging that person's liabilities, particularly in connection with guarantees.

Surety   Similar to a guarantor, but with a wider connotation; there need not be a contract of guarantee for there to be a surety.

Swap   A general term used to describe an interest exchange agreement or a currency and interest rate exchange agreement.

SWIFT   Society for Worldwide Interbank Financial Telecommunications. An organisation owned by several banks based in Brussels whose activities are well described by its name. SWIFT have recently exhibited Byzantine management changes.

Swing line   A facility enabling the borrower to draw substantial funds at very short, usually same day notice. Used to provide emergency funds if the borrower is unable to issue or roll over commercial paper for some reason.

Syndicate   A group of banks participating in a single credit facility. The level of commitment (underwriting or final take) and related title offered to banks invited into a syndicated transaction are defined by the following titles:

- arranger – a mandated bank responsible for originating, executing and in some cases underwriting a transaction
- joint arrangers – a group of mandated banks, sharing roles and underwriting commitments, if any
- lead manager – a bank committing to the highest level of participation

- co-arranger – a second-level mandated or underwriting bank
- lead manager – a bank committing to the highest level of participation
- manager – a bank committing to the second level of participation
- co-manager – a bank committing to a third level of participation and
- participant – a bank committing to the most junior level of participation

Not all of these titles are available on all transactions.

Syndicate list	The list of banks to be approached in the general syndication, following agreement between the arranger, the underwriter, if any, and the borrower.
Syndicated loan	A loan made available by a group of banks in predefined proportions under the same credit facility.
Syndication	The process of putting together the group of banks who will participate in the facility.
Tacking	The advancement of further sums by a mortgagee on the same security which are added to the first advance in priority to any second mortgage prevented by section 94 LPA unless by the terms of the mortgage he is bound to make further advances.
Tangible assets	Assets which have a tangible, real or ascertainable value.
Tangible net worth	The value attributable to shareholders when realistic (tangible) values are applied to the calculation of net worth.
Tap	Security such as a certificate of deposit issued on an "as required" basis by the borrower; it is not a "managed issue".
Term loan	A loan with a fixed drawdown period and a repayment schedule, where the principal is normally repaid in equal instalments (usually six monthly).
Tombstone	An advertisement which lists the managers and underwriters and sometimes the providers of a recently completed facility or issue.
Transfer risk	The impossibility of transferring payments abroad (in foreign currency) because the government imposed exchange restrictions.
Trust receipt	Aka "trust letter". These are used only in conjunction with a letter of pledge of documents or title to goods whereby the documents are released to the pledgor to enable him to sell the goods while they are still pledged to the bank.
Ultra vires	Literally "beyond the powers" – relating to the capacity of a company to enter into a transaction as authorised by its articles of association. Ultra vires transactions are void from the outset.
Units of account	Composite currency units designed to reduce exchange rate exposures of both borrower and investor (e.g. ECUs and SDRs).
Value at risk	A single number that identifies a statistically probable maximum change in profit or loss within a given time interval and a stated confidence interval.
Vertical integration	A diversification strategy that calls for the acquisition of businesses related to the production or distribution of the acquirer's product. Classic example is the oil refiner which acquires oil wells and gas stations.

Vertical merger	Merger between a supplier and its customer (cf. horizontal merger).
Volatility	The measure of a variable tendency to vary over time. This is crucially important in option prices since, the more volatile the price, rate or return on an asset, the more likely it is to reach the option strike price and so the more valuable the option.
Warrant	A securitised, generally medium-to long-term option issued by a company, usually to buy its stock.
Warrants	Securities which entitle the holder to exercise the right, on predetermined conditions, to buy "mainstream" securities, usually equity.
Working capital	The difference between current assets and current liabilities.
Z-score	The Z-score analytical technique was developed by Professor Edward Altman. The Z-score takes five financial ratios, expresses them in decimal format, and then sums them up to yield the "Z-score". This is also known as the "Altman Bankruptcy Predictor". The five ratios are:

- Working Capital/Total Assets * 1.2 = a
- Retained Earnings/Total Assets * 1.4 = b
- EBIT/Total Assets * 3.3 = c
- Market Value Equity/Book Value Debt * 0.6 = d
- Sales/Total Assets * 1.0 = e

$$a + b + c + d + e = \text{Z-score}$$

A Z-score over 2.99 places a firm in the safe sector. A Z-score below 1.81 places a firm in the bankrupt sector.

It should be noted that these averages can change from one country to another due to different regulations and accounting practice and that the Altman model should be interpreted accordingly.

Zero coupon bond	Discount bond making no coupon payments.

Suggested Readings

The following list of books on banking and banking regulation can provide further assistance on key areas of banking analysis:

Atkin, J M, Citibank, "Country Risk: What the Central Bank's Figures may be Signalling", *The Banker*, 1984

Austin, J E and Yoffie J C, "Political Forecasting as a Management Tool", *Journal of Forecasting*, Vol. 3, 1984

Avramovic, D A, *Long-run Growth and External Debt*, The Johns Hopkins Press, 1964

Balassa, B, "The Purchasing Power Parity Doctrine: A Reappraisal", *Journal of Political Economy*, Vol. 72, 1964

Basle Committee on Banking Supervision, "International Convergence of Capital Measurement and Capital Standards", 1988, http://www.bis.org/publ/bcbsc111.pdf

Basle Committee on Banking Supervision, "Core Principles for Effective Banking Supervision", Basle, September 1997, http://www.bis.org/publ/bcbs30a.pdf

Bessis, Joel, *Risk Management in Banking*, John Wiley & Sons, 1998

Bird, G, "New Approaches to Country Risk", *Lloyds Bank Review*, 1986

Brealey, Richard A and Myers, Stewart C, *Principles of Corporate Finance*, 5th ed, McGraw-Hill, 1996

Bureau Van Dijk Electronic Publishing, "Bankscope CD/Online database", Bankscope is a financial database on 11 000 World Banks, http://www.bvdep.com/

Cataquet, H, "Country Risk Analysis: Art, Science, and Sorcery?" *Kredit und Kapital*, Heft 8, 1985

Coplin, W D and O'Leary, M K, *Introduction to Political Risk Analysis*, Policy Studies Associates, Syracuse University, New York, 1983

Dornbusch, R, *Open Economy Macroeconomics*, Basic Books, New York, 1980 *Economist Magazine*, London

Ensor, R, *Assessing Country Risk*, Euromoney Publications, London, 1981

Feder, G, "On Exports and Economic Growth", World Bank Staff Working Papers, Number 508, 1982

Fight, A, *E-Finance*, Wiley-Capstone Publications, London, 2002

Fight, A, *Syndicated Lending*, Euromoney Publications, London, 2000

Fight, A, *The Ratings Game*, Wiley and Sons, 2001

Fitch IBCA, *Bank Rating Methodology*, 1988

Friedman, B M, "Targets, Instruments and Indicators of Monetary Policy", *Journal of Monetary Economics*, Vol. 1, No. 4, 1975

Genberg, H and Svoboda A K, "The Medium-Term Relationship between Performance Indicators and Policy: A Cross-Section Approach", The World Bank, Report No. EPD-01, 1987

Grosse, R E, "Political Risk Evaluation Procedures Used in US Based Banks", in T Brewer, *Political Risks in International Business*, Preager, 1985

Grosse, R E and Stack, U, "Noneconomic Risk Evaluation in Multinational Banks", *Management International Review*, 24(1), 1984

Group of Thirty, *Risk in International Lending*, New York, 1982

Hale, Roger H, *Credit Analysis: A Complete Guide*, John Wiley & Sons (1983, 1989)

Haner, F T and Ewing, J S, *Country Risk Assessment, Theory and Worldwide Practice*, Praeger Special Studies, New York, 1985

Hoti, Suhejla and McAleer, Michael, *Country Risk Ratings – An International Comparison*, University of Western Australia, 2002

Janjoeri, K, Union Bank of Switzerland, *Assessing Country Risk*, International Banking Publication, 1980

Kerry, Senator John and Brown, Senator Hank, "The BCCI Affair – A Report to the Committee on Foreign Relations United States Senate", 1992, http://fas.org/irp/congress/1992_rpt/bcci/

Kharas, H, "On Structural Change and Debt Servicing Capacity", *World Bank, Domestic Finance Studies*, No. 74, 1981

Krayenbuehl, T, *Country Risk Assessment and Monitoring*, Cambridge, 1985

Kuhner, Christoph, "Rating Agencies, Are they Credible? Insights into the Reporting Incentives of Rating Agencies in Times of Enhanced Systematic Risk", November 1998

Moody's Investor Service, "Rating Methodology Bank Credit Risk (an analytical framework for banks in developed markets)", 1999

Moody's Investor Service, "Rating Methodology Bank Credit Risk in Emerging Markets (an analytical framework), 1999

Morgan, Donald P, *Judging the Risk of Banks – What Makes Banks Opaque*, Federal Reserve Bank of New York, 1997

Nagy, P J, *Country Risk*, Euromoney Publications Limited, London, 1984

Overholt, W H, *Political Risk*, Euromoney Publications, London, 1983

Partnoy, Frank, "The Siskel and Ebert of Financial Markets? Two Thumbs Down for the Credit Rating Agencies", *Washington University Law Quarterly*, Vol. 77, No. 3 1999

Philipp, B C, "Swiss Bank Corporation's Approach to Country Risk Assessment", *Prospects* 2/1983

Robinson, J D, "Chase Manhattan: Country Risk Analyses", *The Banker*, 1981

Shine, E, "Detecting Country Risk: Corporate America on Its Own", *Corporate Finance*, Sept. 1987

Singer, Mark, *Funny Money* – May 1985, ISBN: 0394532368 Knopf, Alfred A. Incorporated. All about the spectacular saga of the Penn Square bankruptcy, high flying account officers, rubber stamp credit committees, and how Continental Illinois and Chase Manhattan ended up with dud loans on their books.

Smith, Terry, *Accounting for Growth: Stripping the Camouflage from Company Accounts, Century Business*, 1992

Standard & Poor's, "Sovereign Credit Ratings – A Primer", 1998

Standard & Poor's, "Financial Institutions Criteria Handbook", January 1999

World Resources Institute, "A Guide to the Private Financial Services Industry", 1998

Appendix I

Search engines

Alta Vista	http://www.altavista.com
Ask Jeeves	http://www.ask.com
Excite	http://www.excite.com
Google	http://www.google.com
Lycos	http://www.lycos.com
PROMT Online Website Translator	http://www.translate.ru
Web Crawler	http://www.webcrawler.com
Yahoo	http://www.yahoo.com

Financial press

BBC	http://www.bbc.co.uk
Daily Telegraph	http://www.telegraph.co.uk
Dealogic	http://www.dealogic.com
eFinancialNews	http://www.efinancialnews.com
El País	http://www.elpais.es
Euromoney	http://www.euromoney.com
Euroweek	http://www.euroweek.com
Financial Times	http://www.ft.com
Finanza Italiana	http://www.finanzaitaliana.it
Frankfurt Allgeimeine Zeitung	http://www.faz.de
Handelsblatt	http://www.handelsblatt.de
IFR Loans	http://www.ifrloans.com
IFR Magazine	http://www.ifrmagazine.com
Il Mondo	http://www.ilmondo.rcs.it
Il Sole 24 Ore	http://www.ilsole24ore.it
Independent	http://www.independent.co.uk
Investor Access	http://www.investoraccess.com
La Repubblicca	http://www.repubblica.it
La Stampa	http://www.lastampa.it
La Tribune	http://www.latribune.fr

Le Figaro	http://www.lefigaro.fr
Le Journal des Finances	http://www.journaldesfinances.com
Le Monde	http://www.lemonde.fr
Le Revenu Francais	http://www.lerevenu.com
Les Echos	http://www.lesechos.fr
London Evening Standard	http://www.thisislondon.co.uk
LPC/Intralinks	http://www.loaninvestor.com
Manchester Evening News	http://www.manchesteronline.co.uk/
Milano Finanza	http://www.milanofinanza.it
News Now	http://www.newsnow.co.uk
PR News Wire (US)	http://www.prnewswire.com
PR Newswire	http://www.prnewswire.com
Reuters	http://www.reuters.com
Scotland on Sunday	http://www.scotlandonsunday.com
Sunday Herald	http://www.sundayherald.com
The Economist	http://www.economist.com
The Guardian	http://www.guardian.co.uk
The Herald	http://www.theherald.co.uk
The Scotsman	http://www.scotsman.com
The Times	http://www.the-times.co.uk
Time Magazine	http://www.time.com
Wall Street Journal	http://www.wsj.com

Financial information

Bloomberg	http://www.bloomberg.com
Bridge	http://www.bridge.com
Business Information Library	http://www.biz-lib.com
Business and Law	http://www.businessandlaw.com
CAROL (link to company reports)	http://www.carol.co.uk
Centre Strategic Int'l Studies	http://www.csis.org
Competitive Enterprise Institute	http://www.cei.org
Country Comm Guides US State Dept	http://www.state.gov/e/eb/rls/rpts/ccg
Country/Industry Market Research (US Gov't)	http://www.export.gov/cntryind.html
EIA - Energy Information Administration	http://www.eia.doe.gov
Emerging Markets Online	http://www.emerging-markets.com
Energy Renewable Energy Network	http://www.eren.doe.gov
Euromoney Bank Register	http://www.euromoney.com
Ex-Im Bank – Project Finance	http://www.exim.gov/mpfprogs.htm
GRI Gas Research Institute	http://www.gri.org
Hemscott	http://www.hemscott.net
Hoovers	http://www.hoovers.com
IAEA International Atomic Energy Agency	http://www.iaea.or.at
IEA International Energy Agency	http://www.iea.org
IHS Energy Group Consultants	http://www.petroconsultants.com
International Business Magazine	http://www.International business.com
International Telecoms Union	http://www.itu.ch

IQ Financial Systems	http://www.iqfinancial.com
KMV	http://www.kmv.com
London Economics	http://www.londecon.co.uk
Market Tracking Int'l	http://www.marketfile.co.uk
National Information Services Corp.	http://www.nisc.com
Northcote (Link to Company Reports)	http://www.northcote.co.uk
Nuclear Energy Institute	http://www.nei.org
OECD	http://www.oecd.org
Pennwell (Oil) Publications	http://www.pennwell.com
Pennwell – Oil and Gas Journal Online	http://ogj.pennnet.com
Platts Global Energy	http://www.platts.com
Powermarketers	http://www.powermarketers.com
Securities Class Action Suits	http://securities.stanford.edu
Universal Library	http://www.ul.cs.cmu.edu
Wood Mackenzie Energy Consultants	http://www.woodmac.com

General information

Business traveler	http://www.btonline.com
Centre for Management Buyout Research	http://www.ccc.nottingham.ac.uk
Companies House	http://www.companieshouse.gov.uk
Currency converter	http://www.xe.net/currency/full
Dealogic	http://www.dealogic.com
Euromoney Directory	http://www.euromoneydirectory.com
Europages	http://www.europages.com/home-en.html
European Telephone Directories	http://www.phesk.demon.co.uk/internat.htm
Eurostat	http://www.europa.eu.int/comm/eurostat
Holiday festivals	http://www.holidayfestival.com
International petroleum	http://www.ipe.uk.com
London Int'l Financial Future Exchange	http://www.liffe.com
London Metal Exchange	http://www.metalprices.com
Metal prices	http://www.metalprices.com
Qualisteam	http://www.qualisteam.com.
Reuters Moneynet	http://www.moneynet.com
UK street maps	http://www.streetmap.co.uk
World maps	http://www.sitesatlas.com
World street maps	http://www.streetmap.com
Yellow Pages	http://www.yell.co.uk

Rating agencies

A M Best	http://www.ambest.com
Andrew Fight Consulting	http://www.andrewfight.com
Atlantic Ratings (Brazil)	http://www.atlanticrating.com
Bulgarian Rating Agency	http://ilyan.com/bra/web/main.html
Cantwell Rating Consultants	http://www.askcantwell.com

Capital Intelligence Ratings	http://www.ciratings.com
ComRatings (Switzerland)	http://www.comrating.ch
Cosapi Data SA	http://www.cosapidata.com.pe
Czech Ratings	http://www.crarating.com
Dominion Bond Ratings Service	http://www.dbrs.com
Everling Rating Advisory Services	http://www.everling.de
Fitch IBCA	http://www.fitchibca.com
Information Credit Rating Agency (India)	http://www.icraindia.com
Moody's	http://www.moodys.com
Rating and Investment Info Inc. (Japan)	http://www.r-i.co.jp/eng
Ratings Agentur (Germany)	http://www.ura.de
Red Stars (Russia)	http://www.rsf.ru/
Standard & Poor's	http://www.standardandpoors.com
Thailand Ratings and Information Service	http://www.tris.tnet.co.th
Weiss Ratings	http://www.weissratings.com

Professional organizations

Asia-Pacific Loan Market Association	http://www.aplma.com
Association of Corporate Treasurers	http://www.corporate-treasurers.co.uk
British Bankers Association	http://www.bankfacts.org.uk
British Chambers of Commerce	http://www.chamber.co.uk
Chartered Institute of Bankers	http://www.cib.org.uk
International Federation of Accountants	http://www.ifac.org
International Swaps & Derivatives Association	http://www.isda.org
Loan Syndications & Trading Association	http://www.lsta.org

Governmental agencies

BIS	http://www.bis.org
Competition Commission	http://www.competition-commission.org.uk
European Bank Reconstruction	http://www.ebrd.com
European Central Bank	http://www.ecb.int
European Union	http://www.europa.eu.int
Federal Trade Commission	http://www.ftc.gov
FSA	http://www.fsa.gov.uk
IMF	http://www.imf.org
Official Statistics Dept Worldwide	http://www.stats.gla.ac.uk/cti/linksdata.html
OECD	http://www.oecd.org
OFTEL Securities & Futures Author	http://www.sfa.org.uk
Press Release of EU	http://www.europa.eu.int/news-en.htm
RAPID – Search EU documents	http://www.europa.eu.int/rapid
SEC	http://www.sec.gov
SEC – Edgar	http://www.sec.gov/edgarhp.htm

UK Double Taxation Treaty Digest	http://www.inlandrevenue.gov.uk/cnr
UK Government Information Services	http://www.open.gov.uk
UK Government Statistical Service	http://www.statistics.gov.uk
United Nations	http://www.un.org/Pubs
US Dept of Justice	http://www.usdoj.gov
World Bank	http://www.worldbank.org
Worldwide governments on the WWW	http://www.gksoft.com/govt/en/world.html

Central banks

Austria	http://www.oenb.co.at/oenb
Belgium	http://www.bnb.be
Canada	http://www.bank-banque-canada.ca
Denmark	http://www.nationalbanken.dk
EIB	http://www.eib.org
European Central Bank	http://www.ecb.int
Finland	http://www.bof.fi
France	http://www.banque-france.fr
Germany	http://www.bundesbank.de
Greece	http://www.bankofgreece.gr
Ireland	http://www.centralbank.ie
Italy	http://www.bancaditalia.it
Japan	http://www.boj.or.jp
Luxembourg	http://www.bcl.lu
Netherlands	http://www.dnb.nl
Portugal	http://www.bportugal.pt
Spain	http://www.bde.es
Sweden	http://www.riksbank.se
Switzerland	http://www.snb.ch
United Kingdom	http://www.bankofengland.co.uk/
USA	http://www.federalreserve.gov

International stock exchanges

Athens Stock Exchange	http://www.ase.gr
Bolsa de Barcelona	http://www.borsabcn.es
Bolsa de Madrid	http://www.bolsamadrid.es
Bolsa de Valores de Lisboa	http://www.bvl.pt
Brussels Stock Exchange	http://www.tijd.be
Budapest Stock Exchange	http://www.fornax.hu
Charles Schwab	http://www.schwab.com
Copenhagen Stock Exchange	http://www.xcse.dk
Deutsche Borse	http://www.exchange.de
Easdaq	http://www.easdaq.fr
Le Nouveau Marche	http://www.nouveau-marche.fr
London Stock Exchange	http://www.londonstockexchange.com
Nasdaq	http://www.nasdaq.com

NCB Stockbroker, Dublin	http://www.ncb.ie
OM Group, Sweden	http://www.omgroup.com
Paris Bourse	http://www.bourse-de-paris.fr
Prague Stock Exchange	http://www.pse.cz
Stoxx	http://www.stoxx.com
Swiss Stock Exchange	http://www.swx.ch
Tel Aviv Stock Exchange	http://www.tase.co.il
Vienna Stock Exchange	http://www.wienerboerse.at
Warsaw London Stock Exchange	http://www.gpw.com.pl
Worldwide Stock Exchanges	http://www.tdd.lt/snews/stock exchanges

Appendix II

Checklist of soverign risk criteria

Political risk profile

1) **Characteristics of political system**
   a) Type of government
   b) Process and frequency of political succession
   c) Degree of public participation
   d) Degree of centralisation in decision-making process
2) **Executive leadership**
   a) Relationship with supporting government institutions
   b) Relationship with supporting political coalitions
3) **Government institutions**
   a) Responsiveness and access to executive leadership
   b) Effectiveness and efficiency
   c) Policy responsibilities
4) **Social coalitions**
   a) Major socio-economic and cultural groups (i.e., church, military, landowners, manage-ment, labour, ethnic groups, etc.)
   b) Political parties and their constituencies
5) **Social indicators**
   a) Level and growth of per capita income, and other measures of the standard of living
   b) Distribution of wealth and income
   c) Regional disparities
   d) Homogeneity of the populace
6) **External relations**
   a) Relationship with major trading partners
   b) Relationship with neighbouring countries
   c) Participation in international organisations

Economic risk profile

1) **Demographic characteristics**
   a) Level and growth of population
   b) Age distribution
   c) Urbanisation trends

2) Structure of the economy
  a) Extent and quality of infrastructure
    i) Transportation and communications
    ii) Utilities
    iii) Housing
    iv) Education
    v) Health services
  b) Natural resource endowment
    i) Agriculture, forestry, fishing
    ii) Non-energy minerals
    iii) Energy resources
  c) Distribution of productive activities
    i) Agriculture and livestock
      (1) Land tenure system
      (2) Degree of mechanisation
      (3) Principal crops
      (4) Markets
    ii) Forestry and fishing
    iii) Mining
    iv) Construction
      (1) Residential
      (2) Non-residential
    v) Manufacturing
      (1) Concentration and size of manufacturers
      (2) Product types (i.e., consumer, intermediate and
          capital goods)
      (3) Markets
    vi) Services – financial/non-financial, public/private
  d) Public sector participation in productive activities
3) Recent economic trends
  a) Composition and growth of aggregate demand
    (nominal and real terms)
    i) Consumption
      (1) Private sector
      (2) Public sector
    ii) Investment
      (1) Private sector
      (2) Public sector
    iii) External savings (i.e., exports/imports)
  b) Domestic economy
    i) Total production (i.e., GDP)
    ii) Production by sector
      (1) Agriculture, forestry and fishing
      (2) Mining
      (3) Construction
      (4) Manufacturing

     (5) Utilities

     (6) Services

   iii) Price movements and major determinants

     (1) External factors

     (2) Wages

     (3) Public sector deficit financing

     (4) Private sector credit expansion

     (5) Supply bottlenecks

   iv) Employment trends

     (1) Level of growth of employment and labour force

     (2) Labour participation rates

     (3) Unemployment rate and structure

     (4) Sectorial trends

     (5) Regional trends

     (6) Composition of employment: public vs. private

c) External sector

   i) Current account balance

     (1) Export growth and composition

       (a) Agricultural commodities

       (b) Minerals

       (c) Manufactured goods

     (2) Destination of exports (i.e., markets)

     (3) Price and income elasticity of exports

     (4) Import growth and composition

       (a) Food

       (b) Other consumer goods

       (c) Energy

       (d) Other intermediate goods

       (e) Capital goods

     (5) Price and income elasticity of imports

     (6) Geographic origin of imports

     (7) Terms of trade

     (8) Services account

       (a) Interest payments and receipts

       (b) Transportation

       (c) Other

     (9) Transfers

   ii) Capital account balance

     (1) Direct investment

     (2) Long-term capital flows

       (a) Private sector

       (b) Public sector

     (3) Short-term capital flows

     (4) Access to capital markets

       (a) Types of instruments used

       (b) Types of borrowers and lenders

iii) International reserves
    (1) Level
    (2) Composition (i.e., gold, foreign exchange)
    (3) Secondary reserves
iv) External debt
    (1) Amount outstanding
    (2) Composition by borrower
        (a) Central government
        (b) Other public sector
        (c) Publicly guaranteed
        (d) Private
    (3) Composition by lender
        (a) Bilateral
        (b) Multilateral
        (c) Private financial institutions
        (d) Suppliers' credits
    (4) Maturity structure
    (5) Currency composition
    (6) Growth rate
    (7) Comparison with export earnings and GDP
    (8) Debt service payments
        (a) Amortisation
        (b) Interest
        (c) Comparison with export earnings
        (d) Future debt service schedule

4) Economic policy
  a) Price and wage policies
    i) Wage settlement process
      (1) Trade union activity
      (2) Management groups
      (3) Role and influence of government
    ii) Degree of wage indexation
    iii) Productivity trends
    iv) Non-wage benefits and unemployment insurance
    v) Direct price controls
      (1) Public sector tariffs
      (2) Private sector pricing
    vi) Price subsidies (agricultural, industrial, etc.)
  b) Monetary policy
    i) Level of development of financial system
      (1) Types of financial institutions
      (2) Types of financial instruments
      (3) Role of government in credit allocation
      (4) Foreign participation
    ii) Trends for monetary aggregates
      (1) Money supply growth targets and actual experience
      (2) Domestic credit expansion

(a) Public sector
(b) Private sector
(3) Velocity (national income/money supply)
(4) Changes in international reserves
iii) Monetary policy instruments
(1) Reserve requirements
(2) Open market operations
(3) Credit controls
(4) Interest rate regulations
(5) Ability to sterilise international reserve flows
(6) Controls on foreign borrowing and
(7) Rediscount facilities
c) Fiscal policy
i) Structure of the public sector
(1) Central government
(2) Social security system
(3) State agencies and enterprises
(4) Regional and local governments
ii) Budgetary process
(1) Executive branch
(2) Legislative branch
(3) Major constituencies (business, labour, etc.)
iii) Revenues
(1) Composition
(a) Direct taxes – personal income, corporate income, property, others
(b) Indirect taxes – value added, sales, export & import duties, others
(c) Service charges and public sector tariffs
(2) Income elasticity of revenues
(3) Distribution of tax burden by income groups
(4) Overall tax burden (% of GDP)
(5) Tax collection and evasion
(6) Tax incentives (i.e., investment, export, employment)
iv) Expenditures
(1) Current expenditures
(a) Distribution by expenditure category
(b) Transfers to households
(c) Transfers to other levels of government
(2) Capital expenditures
v) Current operating balance (absolute level and relative to GDP)
vi) Gross financing requirements (operating balance plus net capital expenditures)
(1) Trend relative to GDP
(2) Means of financing
(a) Domestic money creation
(b) Domestic borrowing
(c) External borrowing
vii) Public sector debt: domestic and external
(1) Size (direct and guaranteed)

   (2) Debt service requirement
   (3) Debt management
  d) External policies
   i) Exchange rate policy
   ii) International reserve management
   iii) Export promotion measures
   iv) Import substitution/trade protectionist
    measures
  e) Long-term planning and special programmes
   i) Energy
   ii) Industrial development/restructuring
   iii) Employment creation
   iv) Others

S&P's sovereign rating profile

In order to evaluate the elements in the preceding political and economic risk profile, the most recent five years of the following information should be incorporated.

1) Demographic characteristics
 a) Total population (millions)
 b) Age structure (% of total)
  i) 0–14
  ii) 15–64
  iii) 66–over
 c) Urban population (% of total)
 d) Total labour force (millions)
  i) % Employment agriculture
  ii) % Employment industry
2) Economic structure & growth
 a) GDP, current prices
 b) GDP, constant prices
 c) GDP per capita, current prices
 d) Composition of real GDP (%)
  i) Agriculture
  ii) Mining
  iii) Manufacturing
  iv) Construction
  v) Electricity, gas & water
  vi) Transportation & communication
  vii) Trade & finance
  viii) Public administration
  ix) Other services
 e) Investment, constant prices
 f) Investment, current prices
 g) Investment/GDP
 h) Net energy imports/total energy consumption (%)

3) Economic management
   a) Consumer price index
   b) Money supply–M1
   c) Money supply–M2
   d) Domestic credit
   e) Wage index
   f) Unemployment rate
   g) Budget deficit/GDP (%)
   h) Public expenditures/GDP (%)
4) Government finance
   a) Current revenues
   b) Current expenditures
   c) Operating balance
   d) Net capital expenditures
   e) Budgetary balance
   f) Non-budgetary balance
   g) Domestic financing
   h) Foreign financing
5) External payments
   a) Exchange rate
     i) Local currency/USD
     ii) Local currency/GSD
   b) Imports/GDP (%)
   c) Composition of imports (%)
     i) Food
     ii) Nonfood agricultural
     iii) Nonfuel mining & metals
     iv) Fuels
     v) Machinery & equipment
     vi) Other manufactured goods
   d) Composition of exports (%)
     i) Food
     ii) Nonfood agricultural
     iii) Nonfuel mining & metals
     iv) Fuels
     v) Machinery & equipment
     vi) Other manufactured goods
   e) Balance of payments
     i) Exports
     ii) Imports
     iii) Trade balance
     iv) Net factor services (interest payments)
     v) Net transfers
     vi) Current account balance
     vii) Long-term capital flows
       (1) Public
       (2) Private

   viii) Short-term capital flows
      (1) Public
      (2) Private
    ix) Errors and omissions
     x) Reserves movements
    xi) Current account balance/GDP (%)
   xii) Current account balance/exports (%)
  f) International reserves
     i) Central bank reserves, minus gold
    ii) Central bank gold reserves (millions of troy ounces)
   iii) Reserves, rest of banking system
   iv) Reserves/imports (%)
    v) Net foreign assets of banking system
   vi) Imports (%)
  g) External debt
     i) Long-term debt
      (1) Public
      (2) Private
    ii) Short-term debt
      (1) Public
      (2) Private
   iii) External debt/GDP (%)
   iv) Debt service payments a. Public b. Private
    v) Debt service payments/exports (%)
   vi) Debt service schedule

Appendix III

World Bank list of economies (April 2003) (http://www.worldbank.org)

	Economy	Region	Income group	Indebtedness
1	Afghanistan	South Asia	Low	Severely indebted
2	Albania	Europe & Cent Asia	Lower Mid	Less indebted
3	Algeria	Mid East & N Africa	Lower Mid	Less indebted
4	American Samoa	East Asia & Pacific	Upper Mid	Debt not classified
5	Andorra	..	High: nonOECD	Debt not classified
6	Angola	Sub-Saharan Africa	Low	Severely indebted
7	Antigua and Barbuda	Latin America & Carib	Upper Mid	Less indebted
8	Argentina	Latin America & Carib	Upper Mid	Severely indebted
9	Armenia	Europe & Cent Asia	Low	Less indebted
10	Aruba	..	High: nonOECD	Debt not classified
11	Australia	..	High: OECD	Debt not classified
12	Austria	..	High: OECD	Debt not classified
13	Azerbaijan	Europe & Cent Asia	Low	Less indebted
14	Bahamas, The	..	High: nonOECD	Debt not classified
15	Bahrain	..	High: nonOECD	Debt not classified
16	Bangladesh	South Asia	Low	Less indebted
17	Barbados	Latin America & Carib	Upper Mid	Less indebted
18	Belarus	Europe & Cent Asia	Lower Mid	Less indebted
19	Belgium	..	High: OECD	Debt not classified
20	Belize	Latin America & Carib	Lower Mid	Severely indebted
21	Benin	Sub-Saharan Africa	Low	Severely indebted
22	Bermuda	..	High: nonOECD	Debt not classified
23	Bhutan	South Asia	Low	Moderately indebted
24	Bolivia	Latin America & Carib	Lower Mid	Moderately indebted
25	Bosnia and Herzegovina	Europe & Cent Asia	Lower Mid	Less indebted
26	Botswana	Sub-Saharan Africa	Upper Mid	Less indebted
27	Brazil	Latin America & Carib	Upper Mid	Severely indebted
28	Brunei	..	High: nonOECD	Debt not classified
29	Bulgaria	Europe & Cent Asia	Lower Mid	Moderately indebted
30	Burkina Faso	Sub-Saharan Africa	Low	Severely indebted
31	Burundi	Sub-Saharan Africa	Low	Severely indebted
32	Cambodia	East Asia & Pacific	Low	Moderately indebted
33	Cameroon	Sub-Saharan Africa	Low	Moderately indebted
34	Canada	..	High: OECD	Debt not classified

(*Cont.*)

World Bank list of economies (*Cont.*)

	Economy	Region	Income group	Indebtedness
35	Cape Verde	Sub-Saharan Africa	Lower Mid	Less indebted
36	Cayman Islands	..	High: nonOECD	Debt not classified
37	Cent African Republic	Sub-Saharan Africa	Low	Severely indebted
38	Chad	Sub-Saharan Africa	Low	Severely indebted
39	Channel Islands	..	High: nonOECD	Debt not classified
40	Chile	Latin America & Carib	Upper Mid	Moderately indebted
41	China	East Asia & Pacific	Lower Mid	Less indebted
42	Colombia	Latin America & Carib	Lower Mid	Moderately indebted
43	Comoros	Sub-Saharan Africa	Low	Severely indebted
44	Congo, Dem. Rep.	Sub-Saharan Africa	Low	Severely indebted
45	Congo, Rep.	Sub-Saharan Africa	Low	Severely indebted
46	Costa Rica	Latin America & Carib	Upper Mid	Less indebted
47	Côte d'Ivoire	Sub-Saharan Africa	Low	Severely indebted
48	Croatia	Europe & Cent Asia	Upper Mid	Moderately indebted
49	Cuba	Latin America & Carib	Lower Mid	Severely indebted
50	Cyprus	..	High: nonOECD	Debt not classified
51	Czech Republic	Europe & Cent Asia	Upper Mid	Less indebted
52	Denmark	..	High: OECD	Debt not classified
53	Djibouti	Mid East & N Africa	Lower Mid	Less indebted
54	Dominica	Latin America & Carib	Upper Mid	Moderately indebted
55	Dominican Republic	Latin America & Carib	Lower Mid	Less indebted
56	Ecuador	Latin America & Carib	Lower Mid	Severely indebted
57	Egypt, Arab Rep.	Mid East & N Africa	Lower Mid	Less indebted
58	El Salvador	Latin America & Carib	Lower Mid	Less indebted
59	Equatorial Guinea	Sub-Saharan Africa	Low	Less indebted
60	Eritrea	Sub-Saharan Africa	Low	Less indebted
61	Estonia	Europe & Cent Asia	Upper Mid	Moderately indebted
62	Ethiopia	Sub-Saharan Africa	Low	Severely indebted
63	Faeroe Islands	..	High: nonOECD	Debt not classified
64	Fiji	East Asia & Pacific	Lower Mid	Less indebted
65	Finland	..	High: OECD	Debt not classified
66	France	..	High: OECD	Debt not classified
67	French Polynesia	..	High: nonOECD	Debt not classified
68	Gabon	Sub-Saharan Africa	Upper Mid	Severely indebted
69	Gambia, The	Sub-Saharan Africa	Low	Severely indebted
70	Georgia	Europe & Cent Asia	Low	Less indebted
71	Germany	..	High: OECD	Debt not classified
72	Ghana	Sub-Saharan Africa	Low	Moderately indebted
73	Greece	..	High: OECD	Debt not classified
74	Greenland	..	High: nonOECD	Debt not classified
75	Grenada	Latin America & Carib	Upper Mid	Moderately indebted
76	Guam	..	High: nonOECD	Debt not classified
77	Guatemala	Latin America & Carib	Lower Mid	Less indebted
78	Guinea	Sub-Saharan Africa	Low	Severely indebted
79	Guinea-Bissau	Sub-Saharan Africa	Low	Severely indebted
80	Guyana	Latin America & Carib	Lower Mid	Severely indebted
81	Haiti	Latin America & Carib	Low	Moderately indebted
82	Honduras	Latin America & Carib	Lower Mid	Moderately indebted
83	Hong Kong, China	..	High: nonOECD	Debt not classified
84	Hungary	Europe & Cent Asia	Upper Mid	Moderately indebted
85	Iceland	..	High: OECD	Debt not classified

(*Cont.*)

World Bank list of economies (*Cont.*)

	Economy	Region	Income group	Indebtedness
86	India	South Asia	Low	Less indebted
87	Indonesia	East Asia & Pacific	Low	Severely indebted
88	Iran, Islamic Rep.	Mid East & N Africa	Lower Mid	Less indebted
89	Iraq	Mid East & N Africa	Lower Mid	Severely indebted
90	Ireland	..	High: OECD	Debt not classified
91	Isle of Man	Europe & Cent Asia	Upper Mid	Debt not classified
92	Israel	..	High: nonOECD	Debt not classified
93	Italy	..	High: OECD	Debt not classified
94	Jamaica	Latin America & Carib	Lower Mid	Moderately indebted
95	Japan	..	High: OECD	Debt not classified
96	Jordan	Mid East & N Africa	Lower Mid	Severely indebted
97	Kazakhstan	Europe & Cent Asia	Lower Mid	Moderately indebted
98	Kenya	Sub-Saharan Africa	Low	Moderately indebted
99	Kiribati	East Asia & Pacific	Lower Mid	Less indebted
100	Korea, Dem. Rep.	East Asia & Pacific	Low	Less indebted
101	Korea, Rep.	..	High: OECD	Debt not classified
102	Kuwait	..	High: nonOECD	Debt not classified
103	Kyrgyz Republic	Europe & Cent Asia	Low	Severely indebted
104	Lao PDR	East Asia & Pacific	Low	Severely indebted
105	Latvia	Europe & Cent Asia	Upper Mid	Moderately indebted
106	Lebanon	Mid East & N Africa	Upper Mid	Severely indebted
107	Lesotho	Sub-Saharan Africa	Low	Less indebted
108	Liberia	Sub-Saharan Africa	Low	Severely indebted
109	Libya	Mid East & N Africa	Upper Mid	Less indebted
110	Liechtenstein	..	High: nonOECD	Debt not classified
111	Lithuania	Europe & Cent Asia	Upper Mid	Less indebted
112	Luxembourg	..	High: OECD	Debt not classified
113	Macao, China	..	High: nonOECD	Debt not classified
114	Macedonia, FYR	Europe & Cent Asia	Lower Mid	Less indebted
115	Madagascar	Sub-Saharan Africa	Low	Severely indebted
116	Malawi	Sub-Saharan Africa	Low	Severely indebted
117	Malaysia	East Asia & Pacific	Upper Mid	Moderately indebted
118	Maldives	South Asia	Lower Mid	Less indebted
119	Mali	Sub-Saharan Africa	Low	Moderately indebted
120	Malta	Mid East & N Africa	Upper Mid	Less indebted
121	Marshall Islands	East Asia & Pacific	Lower Mid	Debt not classified
122	Mauritania	Sub-Saharan Africa	Low	Severely indebted
123	Mauritius	Sub-Saharan Africa	Upper Mid	Less indebted
124	Mayotte	Sub-Saharan Africa	Upper Mid	Debt not classified
125	Mexico	Latin America & Carib	Upper Mid	Less indebted
126	Micronesia, Fed. Sts.	East Asia & Pacific	Lower Mid	Debt not classified
127	Moldova	Europe & Cent Asia	Low	Severely indebted
128	Monaco	..	High: nonOECD	Debt not classified
129	Mongolia	East Asia & Pacific	Low	Moderately indebted
130	Morocco	Mid East & N Africa	Lower Mid	Less indebted
131	Mozambique	Sub-Saharan Africa	Low	Less indebted
132	Myanmar	East Asia & Pacific	Low	Severely indebted
133	Namibia	Sub-Saharan Africa	Lower Mid	Less indebted
134	Nepal	South Asia	Low	Less indebted
135	Netherlands	..	High: OECD	Debt not classified
136	Netherlands Antilles	..	High: nonOECD	Debt not classified

(*Cont.*)

World Bank list of economies (*Cont.*)

137	New Caledonia	..	High: nonOECD	Debt not classified
138	New Zealand	..	High: OECD	Debt not classified
139	Nicaragua	Latin America & Carib	Low	Severely indebted
140	Niger	Sub-Saharan Africa	Low	Severely indebted
141	Nigeria	Sub-Saharan Africa	Low	Severely indebted
142	Northern Mariana Islands	..	High: nonOECD	Debt not classified
143	Norway	..	High: OECD	Debt not classified
144	Oman	Mid East & N Africa	Upper Mid	Less indebted
145	Pakistan	South Asia	Low	Severely indebted
146	Palau	East Asia & Pacific	Upper Mid	Debt not classified
147	Panama	Latin America & Carib	Upper Mid	Severely indebted
148	Papua New Guinea	East Asia & Pacific	Low	Moderately indebted
149	Paraguay	Latin America & Carib	Lower Mid	Less indebted
150	Peru	Latin America & Carib	Lower Mid	Severely indebted
151	Philippines	East Asia & Pacific	Lower Mid	Moderately indebted
152	Poland	Europe & Cent Asia	Upper Mid	Less indebted
153	Portugal	..	High: OECD	Debt not classified
154	Puerto Rico	Latin America & Carib	Upper Mid	Debt not classified
155	Qatar	..	High: nonOECD	Debt not classified
156	Romania	Europe & Cent Asia	Lower Mid	Less indebted
157	Russian Federation	Europe & Cent Asia	Lower Mid	Moderately indebted
158	Rwanda	Sub-Saharan Africa	Low	Severely indebted
159	Samoa	East Asia & Pacific	Lower Mid	Moderately indebted
160	San Marino	..	High: nonOECD	Debt not classified
161	São Tomé and Principe	Sub-Saharan Africa	Low	Severely indebted
162	Saudi Arabia	Mid East & N Africa	Upper Mid	Less indebted
163	Senegal	Sub-Saharan Africa	Low	Moderately indebted
164	Seychelles	Sub-Saharan Africa	Upper Mid	Less indebted
165	Sierra Leone	Sub-Saharan Africa	Low	Severely indebted
166	Singapore	..	High: nonOECD	Debt not classified
167	Slovak Republic	Europe & Cent Asia	Upper Mid	Moderately indebted
168	Slovenia	..	High: nonOECD	Debt not classified
169	Solomon Islands	East Asia & Pacific	Low	Less indebted
170	Somalia	Sub-Saharan Africa	Low	Severely indebted
171	South Africa	Sub-Saharan Africa	Lower Mid	Less indebted
172	Spain	..	High: OECD	Debt not classified
173	Sri Lanka	South Asia	Lower Mid	Less indebted
174	St. Kitts and Nevis	Latin America & Carib	Upper Mid	Moderately indebted
175	St. Lucia	Latin America & Carib	Upper Mid	Less indebted
176	St. Vincent Grenadines	Latin America & Carib	Lower Mid	Moderately indebted
177	Sudan	Sub-Saharan Africa	Low	Severely indebted
178	Suriname	Latin America & Carib	Lower Mid	Less indebted
179	Swaziland	Sub-Saharan Africa	Lower Mid	Less indebted
180	Sweden	..	High: OECD	Debt not classified
181	Switzerland	..	High: OECD	Debt not classified
182	Syrian Arab Republic	Mid East & N Africa	Lower Mid	Severely indebted
183	Tajikistan	Europe & Cent Asia	Low	Severely indebted
184	Tanzania	Sub-Saharan Africa	Low	Moderately indebted
185	Thailand	East Asia & Pacific	Lower Mid	Moderately indebted
186	Timor-Leste	East Asia & Pacific	Low	Debt not classified
187	Togo	Sub-Saharan Africa	Low	Moderately indebted
188	Tonga	East Asia & Pacific	Lower Mid	Less indebted
189	Trinidad and Tobago	Latin America & Carib	Upper Mid	Less indebted

(*Cont.*)

World Bank list of economies (*Cont.*)

	Economy	Region	Income group	Indebtedness
190	Tunisia	Mid East & N Africa	Lower Mid	Moderately indebted
191	Turkey	Europe & Cent Asia	Lower Mid	Moderately indebted
192	Turkmenistan	Europe & Cent Asia	Lower Mid	Moderately indebted
193	Uganda	Sub-Saharan Africa	Low	Moderately indebted
194	Ukraine	Europe & Cent Asia	Low	Less indebted
195	United Arab Emirates	..	High: nonOECD	Debt not classified
196	United Kingdom	..	High: OECD	Debt not classified
197	United States	..	High: OECD	Debt not classified
198	Uruguay	Latin America & Carib	Upper Mid	Severely indebted
199	Uzbekistan	Europe & Cent Asia	Low	Moderately indebted
200	Vanuatu	East Asia & Pacific	Lower Mid	Less indebted
201	Venezuela, RB	Latin America & Carib	Upper Mid	Less indebted
202	Vietnam	East Asia & Pacific	Low	Less indebted
203	Virgin Islands (U.S.)	..	High: nonOECD	Debt not classified
204	West Bank and Gaza	Mid East & N Africa	Lower Mid	Debt not classified
205	Yemen, Rep.	Mid East & N Africa	Low	Less indebted
206	Yugoslavia, Fed. Rep.	Europe & Cent Asia	Lower Mid	Severely indebted
207	Zambia	Sub-Saharan Africa	Low	Severely indebted
208	Zimbabwe	Sub-Saharan Africa	Low	Moderately indebted

1	World	WLD
2	Low income	LIC
3	Middle income	MIC
4	Lower middle income	LMC
5	Upper middle income	UMC
6	Low & middle income	LMY
7	East Asia & Pacific	EAP
8	Europe & Central Asia	ECA
9	Latin America & Caribbean	LAC
10	Middle East & North Africa	MNA
11	South Asia	SAS
12	Sub-Saharan Africa	SSA
13	High income	HIC
14	European Monetary Union	EMU
15	High income: OECD	OEC
16	High income: nonOECD	NOC
17	Heavily indebted poor (HIPC)	HPC
18	Least developed countries:	LDC

Index

Index Compiled by Terry Halliday